California

A Bicentennial History

David Lavender

W. W. Norton & Company, Inc.
New York

American Association for State and Local History
Nashville

Library of Congress Cataloguing-in-Publication Data

Lavender, David Sievert, 1910–
  California.

  (States and the Nation)
  Bibliography: p.
  Includes index.
  1. California—History.   I. Title.   II. Series.
F861.L37   979.4   75–45217
ISBN 0–393–05578–7

Printed in the United States of America

2 3 4 5 6 7 8 9 0

Contents

Illustrations

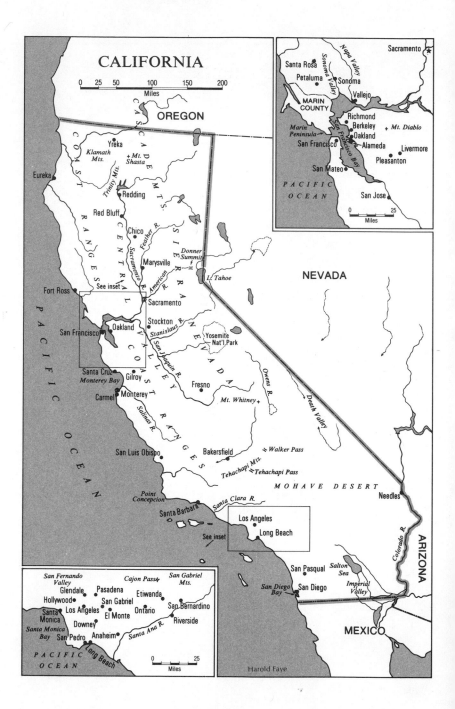

CALIFORNIA

0 25 50   100   150   200
Miles

OREGON

CASCADE

COAST

Klamath
Mts.

Yreka

+ Mt.
Shasta

Eureka

Trinity Mts.

Redding

CENTRAL

Red Bluff

Chico

RANGES

Feather R.

Marysville

Sacramento R.

American R.

Donner
Summit

SIERRA

L. Tahoe

NEVADA

Fort Ross

See inset

Sacramento

Stockton

Oakland

San Francisco

VALLEY

COAST

Stanislaus R.

San Joaquin R.

NEVADA

Yosemite
Nat'l Park

Santa Cruz

Monterey Bay

Gilroy

Carmel

Monterey

Salinas R.

RANGES

Fresno

Owens R.

Mt. Whitney +

Death Valley

San Luis Obispo

Bakersfield

Walker Pass

Tehachapi Mts.

Tehachapi Pass

MOHAVE   DESERT

Point
Concepcion

Needles

Santa Barbara

Santa Clara R.

See inset

Los Angeles

Long Beach

Colorado R.

San Pasqual

Salton
Sea

ARIZONA

San Diego
Bay

San Diego

Imperial
Valley

MEXICO

PACIFIC

OCEAN

Inset (top right)

Sacramento

Santa Rosa

Sonoma Valley

Napa Valley

Petaluma

Sonoma

Vallejo

MARIN
COUNTY

Richmond

Berkeley

+ Mt. Diablo

Marin
Peninsula

Oakland

San Francisco

Alameda

Livermore

San Francisco Bay

Pleasanton

San Mateo

PACIFIC
OCEAN

San Jose

0   25
Miles

Inset (bottom left)

San Fernando
Valley

Cajon Pass

San Gabriel
Mts.

Glendale

Pasadena

Hollywood

San Gabriel

Etiwanda

Santa
Monica

Los Angeles

El Monte

Ontario

San Bernardino

Santa Monica
Bay

Downey

Riverside

San Pedro

Anaheim

Santa Ana R.

Long Beach

PACIFIC
OCEAN

0   25
Miles

Harold Faye

Invitation to the Reader

IN 1807, former President John Adams argued that a complete history of the American Revolution could not be written until the history of change in each state was known, because the principles of the Revolution were as various as the states that went through it. Two hundred years after the Declaration of Independence, the American nation has spread over a continent and beyond. The states have grown in number from thirteen to fifty. And democratic principles have been interpreted differently in every one of them.

We therefore invite you to consider that the history of your state may have more to do with the bicentennial review of the American Revolution than does the story of Bunker Hill or Valley Forge. The Revolution has continued as Americans extended liberty and democracy over a vast territory. John Adams was right: the states are part of that story, and the story is incomplete without an account of their diversity.

The Declaration of Independence stressed life, liberty, and the pursuit of happiness; accordingly, it shattered the notion of holding new territories in the subordinate status of colonies. The Northwest Ordinance of 1787 set forth a procedure for new states to enter the Union on an equal footing with the old. The Federal Constitution shortly confirmed this novel means of building a nation out of equal states. The step-by-step process through which territories have achieved self-government and national representation is among the most important of the Founding Fathers' legacies.

The method of state-making reconciled the ancient conflict between liberty and empire, resulting in what Thomas Jefferson called an empire for liberty. The system has worked and remains unaltered, despite enormous changes that have taken place in the nation. The country's extent and variety now surpass anything the patriots of '76 could likely have imagined. The United States has changed from an agrarian republic into a highly industrial and urban democracy, from a fledgling nation into a major world power. As Oliver Wendell Holmes remarked in 1920, the creators of the nation could not have seen completely how it and its constitution and its states would develop. Any meaningful review in the bicentennial era must consider what the country has become, as well as what it was.

The new nation of equal states took as its motto *E Pluribus Unum*—"out of many, one." But just as many peoples have become Americans without complete loss of ethnic and cultural identities, so have the states retained differences of character. Some have been superficial, expressed in stereotyped images— big, boastful Texas, "sophisticated" New York, "hillbilly" Arkansas. Other differences have been more real, sometimes instructively, sometimes amusingly; democracy has embraced Huey Long's Louisiana, bilingual New Mexico, unicameral Nebraska, and a Texas that once taxed fortunetellers and spawned politicians called "Woodpecker Republicans" and "Skunk Democrats." Some differences have been profound, as when South Carolina secessionists led other states out of the Union in opposition to abolitionists in Massachusetts and Ohio. The result was a bitter Civil War.

The Revolution's first shots may have sounded in Lexington and Concord; but fights over what democracy should mean and who should have independence have erupted from Pennsylvania's Gettysburg to the "Bleeding Kansas" of John Brown, from the Alamo in Texas to the Indian battles at Montana's Little Bighorn. Utah Mormons have known the strain of isolation; Hawaiians at Pearl Harbor, the terror of attack; Georgians during Sherman's march, the sadness of defeat and devastation. Each state's experience differs instructively; each adds understanding to the whole.

The purpose of this series of books is to make that kind of understanding accessible, in a way that will last in value far beyond the bicentennial fireworks. The series offers a volume on every state, plus the District of Columbia—fifty-one, in all.

Each book contains, besides the text, a view of the state through eyes other than the author's—a "photographer's essay," in which a skilled photographer presents his own personal perceptions of the state's contemporary flavor.

We have asked authors not for comprehensive chronicles, nor for research monographs or new data for scholars. Bibliographies and footnotes are minimal. We have asked each author for a summing up—interpretive, sensitive, thoughtful, individual, even personal—of what seems significant about his or her state's history. What distinguishes it? What has mattered about it, to its own people and to the rest of the nation? What has it come to now?

To interpret the states in all their variety, we have sought a variety of backgrounds in authors themselves and have encouraged variety in the approaches they take. They have in common only these things: historical knowledge, writing skill, and strong personal feelings about a particular state. Each has wide latitude for the use of the short space. And if each succeeds, it will be by offering you, in your capacity as a *citizen* of a state *and* of a nation, stimulating insights to test against your own.

James Morton Smith
General Editor

California

1

Almost Eden

*T*HE first considerable gold discovery in California was made by a Mexican rancher, Francisco López, about noon on a warm March day in 1842. The site was thirty-five miles north of Los Angeles, in a small, shaggy canyon branching out of the Santa Clara River of the south.

The word of the find created a small rush. By the end of 1842 Mexican prospectors, many of them experienced workers from Sonora, had scratched up $10,000 worth of metal—this at a time when the United States mint at Philadelphia was paying $18 an ounce for gold. The next year the miners unearthed dust worth about $43,000.

Reports of the activity were forwarded to the seat of the government in Mexico City. As for the gold, some of it traveled from merchant to merchant until it reached the mint at Philadelphia. But nothing developed. The shallow placers were soon exhausted, and further search through the dry mountains bordering the Santa Clara Valley revealed no additional deposits.

The American experience, of course, was different, and it was the American reaction to that difference that gives the tale such significance as it has. In American hands, California was deemed to be a very special place.

Look at the record, the stampeders said. Spain and Mexico had been laying claim to various parts of North America for upward of three centuries. Citizens of those nations had occupied the coastal area between San Diego and San Francisco bays for seventy-nine years. Mexico was one of the premier mining countries of the world. Nevertheless, Mexicans had not found worthwhile gold deposits in California. But Americans had, in their opinion because Providence recognized that their religion, racial background, and personal virtues were superior to those of the "Californios," as the Mexican inhabitants of the Pacific province liked to be called.

The timing of the American gold strike was adduced as yet another example of Providence's favor. James Wilson Marshall made his famous discovery in the race of a sawmill he was building for John Sutter in the foothills of the Sierra Nevada at some point between January 19 and January 24, 1848—documentation is not firm. But whatever the date, it certainly was well before February 2, 1848, the day on which representatives of the United States and Mexico, quite unaware of what was happening in California, formally ended the war between their countries with the Treaty of Guadalupe Hidalgo.

Under the treaty's terms the defeated nation surrendered to its conquerors two-fifths of its territory, a total of 1,193,061 square miles comprising disputed Texas, California, and the rest of what is now the American Southwest—Nevada, Utah, Arizona, New Mexico, and part of Colorado. For this land the United States paid Mexico, partly as balm to its own conscience, $15 million and in addition assumed responsibility for $3,250,000 in claims that American citizens held against the Mexican government. Within a decade—that is, by the end of 1858—miners had unearthed from the goldfields of California alone thirty times that sum. Even counting the cost of the war, it was a good bargain for the Yankees. No wonder California seemed special.

Nor was that all. The discovery had taken place, as the rules of drama said it should, on the ultimate frontier. It was thus a fitting climax to the nation's achievement of continental wholeness—its Manifest Destiny. This feeling of distinction, of standing at the apex of continual progress, has never quite left the California group consciousness.

Another characteristic of the newcomers, bred into them in

part by their headlong rush for gold, was an impatient refusal to wait for the good things they wanted. Without marking time until Congress could establish the territory of California, which was the normal procedure in forming new governments, the voters, stirred to action by a suggestion made by President Zachary Taylor during his first annual address to Congress, set about creating legislative machinery that would express their regional wishes within the national framework. The first step was the election of forty-eight delegates who met in the old California capital of Monterey on September 3, 1849. There they spent the next six weeks arranging for the area's political future. From the beginning it was a foregone conclusion that the majority of the participants would vote to skip the territorial stage and announce to Congress that they intended to enter the Union as a full-fledged state. Although Texas, an independent republic, was admitted through annexation, an equally unique method, no other state ever was accepted as California was, on its own terms.

How big should the state be? The northern and southern boundaries presented no problem. The northern line followed the 42nd parallel, designated in 1819 by the Adams-Onís treaty as the division line between the Oregon country and Spanish California. The southern line followed demarcations set more recently under the Treaty of Guadalupe Hidalgo. But east! California as defined by the Mexicans had reached to the Rocky Mountains. Yet any attempt to maintain such pretensions would probably offend Congress, already wracked by debates over the extension of slavery into the newly acquired lands. Certainly it would offend the Mormons, who were already settling Utah and who had not been invited to attend the deliberations in Monterey.

In the end the state-makers compromised. They decreed that the eastern boundary should follow the 120th meridian southward from Oregon to the 39th parallel, a point that turned out to be in the middle of Lake Tahoe. At Tahoe, the line was to bend southeast, roughly parallel to the eastward-trending coast, and continue in that direction until it met the Colorado

River, which in those days was deemed to be navigable—and to an extent was. The boundary then followed the river south to the Mexican border.

Although sorely reduced in size from what the Mexicans had called Alta California, the new entity was hardly niggardly, being second only to Texas in area. (Alaska had not yet been purchased from Russia.) Moreover, as the new residents discovered when they looked beyond the goldfields, the bent rectangle possessed so unique a climate, such a variety of landforms, and so many valuable resources that those things too became part of the state's sense of specialness.

California's length along a medial line from north to south is 780 miles. An equivalent stretch on the Atlantic coast would extend from Cape Cod, Massachusetts, almost to Savannah, Georgia. To the contrasts in climate occasioned by the ten-degree spread in latitude are added those caused by altitude. This ranges from 282 feet below sea level in Death Valley to 14,494 feet above that level at the summit of Mt. Whitney, only 90 miles away—or, on a broader scale, from the rich, below-sea-level oases of sweltering Imperial Valley near the Mexican border to the perpetually ice-sheathed top of Mt. Shasta, 14,162 feet high, within clear sight of Oregon.

Precipitation is equally varied, ranging from more than 100 inches a year in the state's northwestern corner to a skimpy 2 inches in the southeast. And yet there is one constant: rain seldom falls anywhere in California between April and November, a climatic phenomenon that in North America is confined to the Pacific states. The storms that do strike are likely to be torrential. The amounts of water they dump on the state from year to year fluctuate widely. "Average annual precipitation" is a mathematical abstraction, not a probability. Yet always there is enough to produce the heart-lifting magic of California's two-season year—the explosion of green that with incredible rapidity ends the long months of tan dustiness.

Temperatures near the coast are more predictable than rainfall. They range from a rare frost in December, January, or February, to about ninety degrees in midsummer, except when occasional Santa Ana winds from the desert add another ten or fifteen degrees. Boosters like to describe the balmy, mountainous coast as Mediterranean in its feeling, though whether they mean Spain, Southern France, Italy, Greece, the Holy Land, or North Africa depends largely on the associations they carry with them. In any event, the coastal ambiance is exotic and unusual—dazzles of sunshine, low humidity, and the scenic splendor of rugged headlands plunging into an indigo sea.

Landforms contrast sharply. The Coast Range, heavily timbered in the north, matted with highly inflammable brush in the south, and rumpled into idyllic pleats by dozens of longitudinal valleys, lines a waterfront 1,264 miles long. Eastward is the magnificent uplift of the Sierra Nevada, rising slowly in the west but dropping with startling abruptness on the east. Between the Coast Range and the Sierra is the oval-shaped Central Valley, more than 400 miles long and, on the average, 50 miles wide. North of the valley is a jumble of mountains, where the Coast Range fans out to mingle with the sharp-peaked Trinities, the wild Klamaths, and the volcanic Cascades, the last-named of which spear down from Oregon to join the Sierra. South of the Central Valley is a series of east-west uplifts called the Transverse Ranges, which link the coastal mountains to the dwindling Sierra. Most prominent of the Transverse Ranges are the Tehachapi Mountains. Until Los Angeles spread its commercial net out far enough to engulf the lower reaches of the Central Valley, the term "south of the Tehachapis" was a synonym for Southern California.

Table-flat and deep-soiled, the vast Central Valley has no duplicate in North America. The Sierra Nevada Range to the east draws extravagant quantities of snow and rain from the storms of winter and sends the moisture roaring toward the flatlands through canyons from 2,000 to 5,000 feet deep. In the northern part of the valley, this runoff gathers in the Sacramento River; in the south, in the San Joaquin River. Hence the northern part of the great interior bowl is called the Sacramento Valley and the southern part the San Joaquin Valley.

Just before the south-flowing Sacramento and the north-flowing San Joaquin meet each other, they bend west. The area surrounding the confluence of their main channels is a maze of waterways some 1,200 square miles in extent known as the Delta. The Delta opens onto a narrow strait that leads into the northern arm of San Francisco Bay, one of the most visually exciting harbors in the world and the only significant water break in the Coast Range from one end of California to the other.

Beyond the valley and its encompassing mountains are other unique geographic provinces, all of them desiccated by the rain shadow thrown by the Cascades and the Sierra Nevada. In the northeast are tortured lava beds where in 1873 a handful of Modoc Indians killed seventy-five United States troopers before succumbing to a siege by superior forces. Nearly 400 miles south of the Modoc country is Death Valley, guarded by the stark mountains and shimmering *playas* (dry lake beds) of the Mojave Desert, their higher reaches giving thin nourishment to blade-leafed Joshua trees, which grow nowhere else. Still farther south is the strange Salton Sea, created during the early 1900s by a catastrophic overflow of the Colorado River. Southeast of that, between the Imperial Valley and the Colorado River, are miles of eye-searing sand dunes where some of the highest natural temperatures on earth have been recorded. It is hard to believe, when staring at those dunes and remembering the fog-wet redwoods that tower beside the surf of the northwest coast, that a single state can embrace such extremes.

Within those extremes is a cornucopia of natural resources. During the early days great runs of salmon thrashed up the Sacramento River, while the oceans yielded, and still yield, multimillion-dollar harvests of tuna and other fish. The giant redwoods and Douglas fir of the northwest corner and the soaring sugar pines of the Sierra make California the second lumber producer (behind Oregon) in the United States. Gold output has passed the billion-dollar mark. There is borax in Death Valley, extensive pasturage for cattle and sheep in the Sierra and other mountain ranges, and enough blossoms, both wild and domestic, to put California in the forefront of the nation's honey-producing states. The salt ponds of San Francisco Bay yield a million tons a year, one-third of all the sodium chloride obtained in the world by solar evaporation. But nature's outstanding money-maker—yielding revenues of some $3 billion a year now—is the deep alluvial soil of the interior valleys, warmed by nine months of hothouse temperatures. Once wheat—of which California was for years the nation's leading producer—was the dominant crop. Now there is fantastic diversity: rice, asparagus, sugar beets, hay, citrus, avocados, grapes, raisins, dates, walnuts, almonds—a harvest of almost two hundred different fruits and vegetables.

So many resources have emerged just when they were needed that a belief in luck has become ingrained in California folklore. When gold production began to dwindle during the 1860s, prospectors unearthed the fabulous silver mines of the Comstock Lode at what became Virginia City. Although Virginia City lay within Nevada, San Francisco entrepreneurs immediately spun wagon roads across the divide to lay hold of the discoveries, a grip that tightened when the route selected for the Central Pacific Railroad, the western half of the first transcontinental, happened to pass within a few miles of the humming mines.

For a time it seemed that California's lack of coal would stifle industrial development, but then such quantities of oil were discovered that for several years California led the nation in the production of petroleum. When shortages of readily available iron ore also militated against heavy industry, Californians made the most out of "light" industry—food processing, which has become a multibillion-dollar pursuit, petrochemicals, motion pictures, aircraft assembly, electronics, and the like. World War II, which faced as much toward Asia as toward Europe, and then the conflicts in Korea and Vietnam brought a booming prosperity to these industries and their affluent cousin, aerospace construction. Even the empty deserts became valuable as testing grounds for aircraft and weaponry of all kinds. Today, as energy shortages grow increasingly stringent, it may be that the huge steam-producing geothermal basins beneath the Imperial Valley will add one more element to the long tale of California's good fortune.

Topping all these resources, though a dollar value cannot be put on them, is the state's stunning variety of recreational settings. California has had a steady appeal to industrialists, who have quickly discovered that workers like the region's emphasis on informality and outdoor living. Tourism has kept pace, becoming a major enterprise. (Anyone who doesn't like the beach at Carmel or the cliffs in Yosemite can always go to Disneyland!) Throughout most of the year one can sail, ski, surf, camp, fish, scuba dive, ride on horses or trail bikes, play golf or tennis, hang-glide from the oceanside cliffs near San Diego, or just drive around looking at the sights in four national parks, one national seashore, several national forests, and a plethora of national monuments. That recreational magnet, plus a wide spectrum of jobs, has been so powerful that every two decades since the gold rush California's population has at least doubled.

Success like that feeds on itself. Land values have soared, so that millions of people have made at least a competence by reselling on a rising market the homes, store buildings, and vacant lots that they purchased on arriving or setting up housekeeping. With some reason, real-estate agents and savings-and-loan companies consider California a very special place indeed, though at times it seems that they are doing their best, with their thoughtless developments, to iron out the very distinctiveness on which they batten.

But to emphasize luck is to obscure the hard work, energy, and remarkable ingenuity that Californians have displayed while exploiting their state's tempting resources. Trees grow tall in the Sierra, but to harvest them lumbermen had to develop giant, canyon-spanning flumes through which the logs could be floated to market. The last fine dustings of gold could not be released from the hills until engineers had devised hydraulic jets capable of tearing down mountainsides. New methods of mine timbering developed on the Comstock by California inventors allowed shafts and stopes to be sunk to unprecedented depths. Lacking a good natural harbor, Los Angeles and Long Beach created an artificial one that within a few decades became one of the world's busiest ports. Though the state's climate is benign and the growing season long, those attributes could not be utilized in full until methods had been worked out for transporting enormous amounts of water across hundreds of miles of rugged terrain in order to counteract summer's annual drought. The same techniques were also adapted to slaking the thirst of growing urban and industrial areas.

Such innovations, along with others in the fields of banking, education, housing, and social welfare, were pushed to fruition in spite of California's persistent fear that, as far as the rest of the country was concerned, it stood half-forgotten on the far edge of American progress. Until the air age, isolation was always a key factor in the state's economic and psychological experience. Deserts and adverse sea winds prevented any easy flow of commerce and people between Mexico and Alta California. The Rocky Mountains, the deserts of the Great Basin, and the formidable peaks of the Sierra Nevada blocked the way from the settled portions of the United States.

Because of the gold rush, emigration to California broke with traditional patterns. The normal mode of settlement was for a frontier region to fill up and then overflow into contiguous regions. Gold, however, led to a jump of more than a thousand miles. For decades, those who followed the stampeders had to make a similar wrenching leap, or else go by sea around Cape Horn or via the Isthmus of Panama. Even after trains and automobiles had reduced the land journey to a matter of days instead of months, the trip across the sparsely settled interior of the West seemed like an adventure into strangeness. Californians meanwhile remained convinced that railroads and steamship lines added yet another obstacle to easy communication by conspiring to maintain freight rates at artificially high levels. A thorny chapter in the tale of the state's struggle for recognition deals with attempts to force rate adjustments from the monopolists.

Because of distance, Californians became even more self-reliant than were ordinary frontiersmen. They struggled with little outside help to impose order on a restless, individualistic, often greedy and corrupt flood of opportunists who had little interest in the state's future. They had to solve unusual problems of internal transportation, summer drought, and shortages of manufactured goods. They had to learn how to amass capital at home instead of letting it all flow eastward, from whence they would only borrow it back, and how to gear imports to demands in order to avoid continual, devastating sequences of glut and famine.

As the more violent dislocations stabilized, Californians became self-satisfied as well as self-reliant. In 1878, historian John S. Hittel wrote of the first generation, "No golden era of romance or chivalry, no heroic period of Greece or Rome provokes their envy, or, in their conception, outshines the brilliancy of the scenes in which they have been active." [1] Nearly a hundred years later, in 1963, the editors of the *Saturday Review* recognized the state's continuing brilliancy by entitling a special issue of that magazine, "California, the Nation within a Nation." Economically at least, the accolade was justified. By then California was the most populous state in America, with an output of goods and services exceeded in value by only five countries, the United States itself, the Soviet Union, West Germany, France, and Great Britain. (Three years later Japan joined the list.)

A very special place—almost an Eden. And yet California's very success has generated her greatest problems. The American belief that equality could be achieved by granting all citizens equal opportunity of access to material resources—an ideal that prompted the distribution of cheap and eventually free homestead claims, timber claims, and mining claims to all who asked—was corrupted in the West, and especially in California, to what Richard Hofstadter has called "the democracy of cupidity." [2] If you were smart enough or strong enough, you were more than equal: you were entitled to extra shares, for didn't the laws of social evolution, no less than those of biology, say that survival went to the fittest? Justified by that pseudoscience and by the tolerant laissez-faire theories of the mid-nineteenth century, competition between special-interest groups either became unbearably ferocious or else was replaced, wherever possible, by stifling monopolies in land, water, and trans-

---

1. Quoted in T. H. Watkins, *California: An Illustrated History* (Palo Alto, Calif.: American West Publishing Co., 1973), p. 77.

2. Richard Hofstadter, *The American Political Tradition* (New York: Vintage Books, 1948), p. viii.

portation. In either case, the weak and the unprepared were the victims.

In a context of affluence such attitudes bred reckless speculation. Californians grew convinced that a quick, profitable strike was a better road to fortune than hard work, that it was wiser to court the values to be derived from unearned increment than those added by toil and craftsmanship. Such a philosophy does not breed stable communities and helps account, observers believe, for the frequency with which many Californians move from place to place and job to job. It helps explain their high divorce rates, their alcoholism and suicides. Not irrelevant either is the fact that California has always offered fertile soil for odd religious sects, strange economic panaceas, weird burial practices, and hosts of utopian colonies ranging from congregations of socialistic freethinkers to communes of hippies.

Further troubles have sprung from the widespread use of expensive, highly sophisticated machines for bending nature to man's will. The land and those who labor on it have become less important than the capital that provides the machinery. There is a strong temptation to value whatever pays today and to ignore tomorrow. Labor's most desirable quality has been its cheapness, a fact that has inevitably led to the exploitation of ethnic minorities with low levels of expectation—American Indians in the early days of Southern California, Chinese, Japanese, Irish, Mexican, southern Europeans, blacks, and the "Okies and Arkies" of the depressed 1930s (regarded by some chauvinists as ethnic undesirables).

But if California's record of exploitation is long, so too is the state's record of protest. During the 1860s Bret Harte lost his job on a Northern California newspaper for decrying a massacre of inoffensive Indians at Humboldt Bay. Henry George worked out his single-tax theories as a reaction to land monopoly in California. Hiram Johnson's Progressives won office during the early part of this century by promising to kick the Southern Pacific out of politics. Cesar Chavez still seeks to bring dignity to agricultural workers. During the 1950s San Franciscans revolted successfully against an arrogant highway department that planned to bisect their city and its parks with freeways. As environmental scars and the pollution of air and water grew steadily worse, the Sierra Club, founded in 1892, stepped into the van of the nation's conservation movement.

Not all of these conflicts over what makes the good life have been peculiar to California, but, because California's advantages have been unusually numerous, her tensions, failures, and attempts at remedy have seemed particularly significant. Some commentators have gone so far as to call the state "a window on the future." If the metaphor is valid, then it is well to look as judiciously as possible through that window at some of the old futures that are now past, and especially at California's regional manifestations of the nation's unending dilemma: how to reconcile impassioned drives for full economic, social, and political freedom with the imperatives of social responsibility. That, essentially, is what this book will be about.

2

The Hispanic Legacy

STATISTICALLY, Hispanic California was a failure. In 1846, after three-quarters of a century as a province first of Spain and later of independent Mexico, the area's population, not counting native Indians, numbered fewer than 8,000, of whom 6,000 or more were women and children. Of the original settlers, most were sent to California against their will, either as soldiers or as exiled convicts. The few hundred civilians who now and then appeared in bedraggled bands were enticed to make the move by promises of government subsidies in cash, food, clothing, tools, and livestock. If those reluctant pioneers had not been prolific enough to overcome staggering rates of infant mortality, the population in 1845 would have been even lower than it was.

So static a population had no chance of maintaining its cultural identity against the explosive Anglo-Americans. The gold rush completed the conquest begun by force of arms in 1846. By 1850, 115,000 non-Indians had swarmed into California, inundating the tiny Hispanic capital of Monterey and the pueblos around San Francisco Bay. Thirty-five years later, the Southern California land booms finished erasing the last Hispanic ranchos and settlements in that area.

By the time the sweep was over, the only visible remnants of the original settlers were a few hundred place names and twenty-one mission buildings, some of them in ruins and all beloved by local romantics. Yet, if the physical imprint of the first colonists was slight, their impact on the imaginations of the peoples who followed them has been remarkable. Trying to discover why may reveal much about not only the Hispanic past but also the American present.

Spain did not want California. The coast was first visited, without creating the least excitement in government circles, during the winter of 1542–1543. The expedition consisted of two clumsy, undecked ships about sixty feet long by twenty of beam, constructed on the west coast of Mexico by ill-trained workmen using indifferent equipment transported to them by mule train from the Atlantic. The commander of the "fleet" was a capable Portuguese adventurer with the Hispanicized name of Juan Rodríguez Cabrillo. His second in command was a Levantine, Bartolomé Ferrelo. They and their mariners hoped to find lands redolent with spice, Indians as rich in gold as Montezuma's Aztecs had been, and, if luck held, the Strait of Anián, a saltwater passage that was supposed to lead around the top of North America.

On September 28, 1542, the explorers entered what we now call San Diego Bay. Cabrillo recognized its topographic advantages, but what good is a harbor without commerce? The Indians they encountered were unversed in agriculture and possessed nothing in the way of metal. The aborigines they met farther north were equally devoid of allurements. Moreover, navigation was difficult. After Cabrillo had died of injuries from a fall, Ferrelo pushed the inadequate ships against furious headwinds as far, perhaps, as the present boundary between Oregon and California. Giving up finally, the mariners scudded back south, reaching their point of departure after an arduous and, in the minds of Mexico's bureaucracy, a totally fruitless adventure.

The next people to see the California coast were those who manned the famed Manila galleons. The pattern of that lucrative commerce was worked out during 1564–1565. Ships laden with silver from the mines of Zacatecas and Nueva Vizcaya (now Chihuahua) sailed directly west from Acapulco to the Philippines, purchased silk, spice, chinaware, and other exotics from the traders there, and then zigzagged north to catch the westerlies of the northern hemisphere. Those winds bore the galleons across the Pacific to landfalls that came anywhere between Cape Mendocino and Baja (Lower) California. Half-starved on maggoty food and wracked with the raging itch of scurvy, the crews then drove southward as fast as possible to the profits awaiting at Acapulco.

To the difficulties of distance English freebooters added another threat. Sir Francis Drake raided treasure ships from South America in 1578, and the next year, after refurbishing his *Golden Hind* somewhere near San Francisco Bay (scholars still vociferously dispute the exact location), he sailed on around the world to London. Inspired by his success, Thomas Cavendish also entered the Pacific and in 1587, near the tip of Baja California, seized the seven-hundred-ton Manila galleon *Santa Ana*. Alarmed by these intrusions by a mortal enemy, Spanish authorities decided to develop a port of refuge somewhere along the California coast.

The search for a suitable spot eventually devolved on a former Manila trader, Sebastián Vizcaíno. His recommendation, after a harrowing journey in 1602, during which half his crew perished, was Monterey Bay, "well protected from all winds. There is much wood and water in it, and an immense number of great pine trees, smooth and straight, suitable for masts . . . good meadows for cattle, and fertile fields for growing crops." [1] He was exaggerating—actually the roadstead at Monterey is very exposed—for he hoped that, as a reward for finding a good harbor, he would be named commander of the next Manila galleon. It was a wasted falsehood. A new viceroy, intrigue for favoritism, and the desire of the galleon traders to reach Acapulco without delay led to the abandonment of the project. For another 166 years California remained unwanted and untouched.

1. Father Antonio Ascensión, diarist of Vizcaíno's expedition, translated and quoted in Henry R. Wagner, *Spanish Voyages to the Northwest Coast of America in the Sixteenth Century* (San Francisco: John Howell, 1929), p. 246.

Action came finally from renewed fear. The Seven Years' War in Europe ended in 1763 with the expulsion of France from North America and the advance of England to the Mississippi and north into Canada. Although Spain acquired France's claims to the vast reaches of the Louisiana Territory, that barrier could be outflanked if the English chose to drive through Canada to the Pacific and then south along the California coast toward the rich mines of northern Mexico. And if England did not make such a move—no one yet grasped how great the distances really were—then Russian fur hunters working along the newly discovered chain of Aleutian Islands toward Alaska might do so. Did not foresight dictate defensive measures?

The need coincided with the determination of Charles III of Spain to reform his country's corrupt and inefficient colonial empire. As his agent for revitalizing Mexico he appointed dynamic José de Gálvez. Partly with his own future glory in mind, Gálvez worked out, amidst a multitude of other duties, a plan for thrusting Spanish settlement at least as far north as the two sites that had appealed most strongly to Vizcaíno in 1602, San Diego and Monterey bays.

The basic element of Gálvez's plan was the mission, a device for colonizing that epitomizes the differences between the Spanish and English approaches to the New World. The English pioneers emigrated as families because they were seeking betterment of one kind or another. They relied mostly on their own efforts (black slaves in the South were an exception) to subdue the wilderness. Although a few among them hoped to convert the Indians to Protestant Christianity, the majority of the newcomers looked on the "savages" as tools of the devil opposed to the spread of the true Gospel. Such natives should either be removed by treaty from the land the whites desired or, if necessary, exterminated.

The Spanish, on the other hand, found the Indians worthy of cultivation. The red people not only had immortal souls whose saving would redound to the credit of the savior, but they also had bodies capable of performing useful labor. The last point was crucial. Settlers did not emigrate from Spain to Mexico as

readily as they did from the British Isles and northwestern
Europe to England's American colonies. In an effort to remedy
the deficiency, Spain adopted, as official government policy, a
program of using Catholic missions as a tool for transforming
uncivilized Indians into productive citizens.

The procedure went roughly like this. One or two missionaries, protected by a few soldiers, would build crude habita-
tions at some likely spot on the frontier and with food, music,
kindness, and religious pageantry induced neighborhood Indians
to settle nearby, where they could be tutored both in Christianity
and handicrafts. As soon as the students achieved self-sufficiency, a process that the law said was to be completed in ten
years, the mission was secularized. That is, the land it had been
using for raising crops and livestock, the animals, and the
equipment were divided among the new citizens. The mission
village became a pueblo (town) with its own *alcalde,* a kind of
mayor, while the mission itself was turned into an ordinary
parish church. It was fully expected that frontiersmen from the
outside, most of them *mestizos* (offspring of Spanish soldiers,
miners, and cowboys married to Indian women) would drift into
the new pueblo and help the fledgling citizens adapt to their new
life.

Actuality did not keep pace with theory. Ten years were not
enough for remaking a people. Besides, the missions, like most
bureaucracies, preferred self-perpetuation to self-destruction and
resisted secularization. But, even though integrated new towns
appeared very slowly, the missionaries and their wards did
prove remarkably successful at dotting parts of the frontier with
fine gardens and profitable herds of livestock. As far as this narrative is concerned, the two key areas, both occupied originally
by Jesuit missionaries, were Baja California and southern Arizona.

José de Gálvez, stirred into action by reports of Russian advances in the North Pacific, would have preferred using the missions in southern Arizona as springboards for the occupation of
Alta (Upper) California. Unhappily for that plan, rebellious Indians blocked the route, and the stations in Baja were the only

satisfactory substitute. A further complication was the almost si-multaneous expulsion of the Jesuits from Mexico and the trans-ference of their establishments in Baja California to a small con-tingent of Franciscans led by Fray Junípero Serra.

Would Serra be a satisfactory leader for the religious arm of the occupation of Alta California? He was fifty-five years old, only five feet two inches tall, frail, and devoid of all knowledge of either section of California. But he was also devout, intense, ambitious, and, in the words of Felipe de Neve, a California governor who later clashed with him, "of unspeakable artifice and cleverness." [2] Gálvez decided to draft him—with Serra's joyous acquiescence. Less enthusiastic, but equally loyal to his country, was Serra's secular counterpart, Gaspar de Portolá, forty-four, the newly appointed governor of Baja California.

The expedition was made up of four units. Two ships, the *San Carlos* and the *San Antonio*, were to carry soldiers, ar-tisans, and heavy equipment to a rendezvous at San Diego Bay. More soldiers—cavalrymen whose main weapons were lances and whose shields were made of bull hide—and hard-twisted roustabouts for handling several hundred head of pack mules and beef cattle were to march by land in two widely separated columns to the same destination. Among the roustabouts were eighty-six Christian Indians from the Baja missions. After they reached California, it would be the duty of those converts to help erect the first buildings, lure in the wild Indians of the north, and then assist in training them. Not a single woman or child accompanied the expedition.

Battered by the adverse winds that blow almost constantly southward along the California coast, the ships, particularly the *San Carlos,* had such dreadful journeys that they reached San Diego Bay with the majority of their crews and passengers im-mobilized by scurvy. Exhausting work and threats of Indian at-tack plagued the land parties to such an extent that two-thirds of the eighty-six red roustabouts either deserted or died from

2. Edwin A. Beilharz, *Felipe de Neve, First Governor of California* (San Francisco: California Historical Society, 1971), p. 154.

overexertion. Serra, who rode with the last column, suffered from an agonizing abscess on one of his legs—until a mule skinner finally cured him with salve used for treating the sore backs of the animals.

After setting up a rough camp at San Diego, where Serra stayed to comfort the dying and nurse the sick, Portolá continued northward four hundred miles to establish the capital of Alta California beside Monterey Bay. With him he took one hundred mules, thirty-five soldiers and officers, two priests, two servants, seven mule skinners, and fifteen Christian Indians, all of them so emaciated that he spoke of them as his "skeletons." It was an arduous trip made doubly taxing by their failure, caused by Vizcaíno's overblown description, to recognize Monterey Bay when they reached it. Laboring still farther northward, they discovered what Spanish mariners, standing well out from the rocky shores, had been missing for more than two hundred years—San Francisco Bay.

Realizing at last that they must have passed their goal, the men turned back to what they now identified as Monterey. A supply ship they had been expecting was not in evidence, however, and they feared they could not live off the country while waiting for it. Back they dragged to San Diego, so short of food during the last days of their journey that they subsisted on mule meat. They found the camp destitute. Portolá was about to order its abandonment, against Serra's impassioned protests, when a vessel laden with supplies appeared in the nick of time.

Their spirits lifted by this apparent miracle, the colonists erected a presidio (fort) and a temporary mission building of interlaced, mud-daubed sticks. Then part of the group, led by Portolá and Serra and paralleled by one of the ships, marched north again to repeat the work at Monterey. That done, the ship weighed anchor for Mexico. Portolá and a small escort headed in the same direction by land, leaving the occupation of all Alta California to four priests, two or three dozen soldiers, a reluctant artisan or two, and a handful of Christian Indians who discovered belatedly that they could neither understand nor get along well with the native inhabitants.

How many Indians lived within the bounds of California when the Spanish appeared is unknown. Estimates by competent authorities range from 133,000 to 350,000. Whatever the number, it was the densest concentration of native people north of Mexico. It was also a very isolated concentration, cut off from contact with other Indians by barriers of ocean, desert, and mountains. Hence the culture of the California Indians was in many ways unique.

Most importantly, no sense of tribal identity and very little formal political organization existed among any of the groups other than the Yumans, who lived along the lower Colorado River. Life revolved around small villages and the adjacent territory through which the inhabitants roamed in search of game and vegetable foods. These "tribelets," as one anthropologist has described them, spoke about 135 different dialects.[3] Although members of the different groups drifted back and forth on occasion to trade, hold festivals, and sometimes intermarry, they did not act in concert about anything. Thus they were never able to mount the sort of formidable opposition to outsiders that made the Indians of the eastern woodlands and the Great Plains such a terror at times to the white invaders of those regions.

Except for the Klamaths of the northwest coast, the California Indians had no sense of individual ownership. This simplicity, if that is the word for it, extended to their housekeeping arrangements. Because of California's benign climate, they did not need elaborate shelters and spent most of their time outdoors, clad in scanty garments or none at all. Cloaks of rabbit fur sufficed for warmth during the rainy season.

They harvested and stored seeds from a wide variety of grasses and flowers; they gathered plants, roots, small game, and shellfish. The tribelets who lived where acorns grew learned how to grind the meal with stone implements and leach out the tannic acid with hot water.

Because food was plentiful the California Indians enjoyed an

---

3. A. L. Kroeber, "The Nature of Land-Holding Groups in Aboriginal California," in *Aboriginal California: Three Studies in Culture History* (Berkeley: University of California Press, 1966), p. 99.

unusual amount of leisure. Much of this extra time was diverted into the performance of elaborate rituals and, says historian William Brandon, into "the creation of myths, or complex dance-cycles and song-cycles" whose content varied greatly from region to region.[4] Though they fought at times over the kidnapping of a woman or trespasses onto favorite acorn groves, they were not an aggressive people. Indeed, so nearly as can be told now, they were unusually happy. But they did not fit Spanish notions of what useful citizens should be, and so Junípero Serra and his fellow missionaries set about to remold their entire way of life.

By the end of 1772, less than three years after the landing at San Diego, there were five missions and two presidios in California.[5] About five hundred converts, mostly women and children, had accepted baptism.

The figures suggest more progress than had actually been achieved. The unwalled presidios that overlooked San Diego and Monterey bays consisted of a few earth-floored huts and primitive breastworks housing tiny iron cannon. The thatch-roofed missions and their fields of dry earth broken by plows made of forked sticks were no more prepossessing. Because suitable quarters for the converts were unavailable, most of them continued living in their home villages and showed little evidence of their new faith.

Dependent for the most part on supply ships that reached them only once a year, the settlements existed on the verge of starvation. The local Indians resented abuses endured by their women at the hands of the sex-starved soldiers. There were bloody clashes at San Diego and San Gabriel. Junípero Serra meanwhile wrangled continually with the civil governors of the province over the right to discipline the guards stationed at the

4. William Brandon, "The California Indian World," *The Indian Historian*, 2, no. 2 (1969): 6.

5. The missions were San Diego (1769); San Carlos Borroméo (1770), located first at Monterey and later moved a few miles south to Carmel; San Antonio de Padua in the Salinas Valley (1771); San Gabriel, nine miles east of present Los Angeles (1771); and San Luis Obispo (1772), forerunner of today's city of the same name.

missions and about his plans to extend his operations before he could claim success with what he had already begun.

In 1773, the Franciscan carried his problems to the viceroy at Mexico City, Antonio Bucareli, and returned triumphant. Supply lines were to be improved; the missionaries could order unsatisfactory guards back to the presidios without having to argue with the military about reasons; and several artisans were going to be sent to California to supervise the building of necessary structures while helping train the converts in useful crafts. Even more noteworthy was Bucareli's assurance that, insofar as was possible, the presidios would be manned by married soldiers who could bring their families with them. After the husbands' terms of enlistment had expired, the families would be encouraged to settle in villages beside the forts to provide a stable population with which the mission Indians could eventually integrate.

Although a few of the new military colonists marched north from Baja California, the main point of departure was to be southern Arizona, where the rebellious Indians had finally been pacified. The man in charge was a tough army captain named Juan Bautista de Anza. Anza's first step, in which he was aided by one of the great explorers of the Southwest, missionary Francisco Garcés, was to work out a suitable trail through the stark deserts of the interior and on over the mountains to the coast. Having accomplished this during the opening months of 1775, Anza returned to Mexico to recruit soldier colonists for the founding of a new presidio beside San Francisco Bay.

California! Just the sound of the word was chilling. Despite liberal inducements, Anza's recruiters could persuade only 40 married men to join the expedition. They brought with them, in addition to their wives, about 125 children. Three priests, several roustabouts for handling more than 1,000 head of horses, mules, and cattle, and a small escort that would return to Sonora with Anza after the journey had been completed brought the total number of marchers to roughly 240.

The party began its trip in October 1775, and spent fourteen weeks reaching Monterey. The travelers were cold most of the time, often thirsty during the early weeks and drenched by rain during the later stages. Eight babies were born during the migration; one mother died of childbirth. After a pause in Monterey, 193 of the new arrivals continued north to complete an adventure that in 1976 could be commemorated as another American bicentennial: the founding, on September 17, 1776, of the presidio of San Francisco on a windswept bench commanding a spectacular view of the still unnamed Golden Gate. Three weeks later, on the inland side of the peninsula, the mission of San Francisco de Asís was founded beside a small stream, Dolores Creek, that flowed into the southern arm of San Francisco Bay. In time the mission, too, came to be known as Dolores.

The first six missions and the fifteen others that followed at intervals through 1823 were located with an eye toward agricultural self-sufficiency. They stood in fertile valleys beside permanent streams where Indians were wont to congregate. It was different with the four presidios—San Diego, Monterey, San Francisco, and Santa Barbara, the last-named founded in 1782. Of necessity, they occupied exposed sites overlooking strategic anchorages. Primarily they were symbols of empire rather than its defenders. They could not possibly have turned back an attack by warships from any one of Spain's European enemies. That fact did not make them helpless, however. If a hostile shell should explode inside a California presidio, the riposte would come from Madrid. And so it was useful to maintain those poor adobe forts on their scenic but unfertile sites, where fogs were frequent and soils unrewarding.

Maintain how? The crops planted around the presidios by retired soldiers did not thrive. Cattle and horses had to be moved inland to sunny valleys and grazed on what were called the Ranches of the King. Supply ships were unsure and expensive, and as yet the missions were not producing crops in excess of their own needs.

Felipe de Neve, appointed governor in 1777, decided to solve the problem by founding agricultural pueblos in choice locations. Immediately, however, he ran into the same problem that had frustrated Anza's recruiters. In spite of a promise of subsidies, families were reluctant to leave the grim poverty of Sonora and Sinaloa for the uncertainties of California. Fourteen families made up of sixty-eight persons were all that Neve could scratch together for launching San José, California's first civil community, located near the southern tip of San Francisco Bay. The beginnings of the second community, Los Angeles, were even more meager. The pueblo was founded September 4, 1781, by eleven families numbering forty-four persons—a heterogeneous mix of Spaniards, Christian Indians, blacks, mulattoes, and mestizos.

Even these small beginnings were truncated by a disaster beside the Colorado River. Hoping to alleviate the harsh Arizona route to California, the government in 1780 placed on the western side of the river, approximately opposite the mouth of the Gila, a pair of conjoined presidios and missions. Located thirteen miles apart, the two establishments were designed to grow food and provide rest stops for California travelers.

California's most warlike Indians, the Yumans, resented the intrusion. They had been promised more gifts in exchange for the land occupied by the mission-presidios than they received; the soldiers molested their women; herdsmen let livestock wander into the Indians' corn and melon fields—the Yumans being the only California tribe (except for their neighbors, the Cahuillas) to practice agriculture. On the night of July 18, 1781, outrage flamed into an attack on both Spanish settlements. Every alien male there, including several California-bound emigrants, was massacred, while the women and children were taken captive. Although the latter were eventually ransomed, the overland trail stayed closed until well after Mexico achieved her independence.

Just how tenuous Spain's hold on California was during those years is illustrated by the miserable pueblo of Branciforte. Branciforte was part of the mother country's reaction to her humiliation by England at Nootka Sound on the west coast of Vancouver Island. Claiming suzerainty over that part of the North Pacific by virtue of the explorations of her naval men, Spanish marines seized ships belonging to certain English sea-otter hunters. Great Britain promptly mobilized. Frightened by the threat, Madrid backed down.

To shore up what remained of her coastal claims after the diplomatic defeat, the Spanish government ordered that California's growth be pushed. Five new missions were established during 1797–1798 (bringing the total to eighteen), and additional artisans were hurried northward to speed the transformation of the mission Indians into substantial citizens. Gestures were made toward reinforcing the presidios, and another agricultural presidio, Branciforte, was projected for the north shore of Monterey Bay.

When volunteers refused to go to Branciforte, the government was reduced to peopling the new town with a handful of wretched orphans and exiled convicts. In 1804, seven years after the pueblo's founding, its population had dwindled to thirty-one. Nor were San José and Los Angeles much more viable. The prices that the farmers received for their produce were set by the government at rates too low to stimulate ambition. According to the priests at the nearby missions, the *pobladores* hired Indians to sharecrop for them and then wasted their own time racing horses, gambling, dancing, and seducing Indian girls at neighboring *rancherías,* as Indian villages were called.

Fortunately for the Europeans living in California, the missions were at last taking root. When the nineteenth century opened, they housed 13,000 neophytes, as compared to 1,800 soldiers and civilians at the four presidios and three pueblos. Mission wheatfields, orchards, vineyards, and great herds of sheep and cattle flourished. The mission compounds began to take on the appearance associated with them today. Whitewashed stone church buildings roofed with soft red tiles and bordered by arched colonnades enclosed courtyards cooled by fountains. Indian artists decorated the interior walls with gay frescoes; Indian musicians played vigorously at church services and at such native celebrations as the priests allowed. In the workshops carefully regimented Indian craftsmen ground meal, tanned hides, turned out tiles, abode bricks, and blankets, made rough clothing and passable artifacts of hemp and leather.

This material success came when it was most needed. Throughout Mexico's war of independence, 1810–1821, very few supply ships reached the remote province. In order to obtain food, the presidios levied on the missions and paid with drafts issued against the Spanish treasury—drafts that were never honored.

In addition, the missions had to provide for their own people, who by 1820 numbered 20,000. Pressure on the converts to work harder and produce more increased steadily. A bloody revolt, soon crushed, that shook three missions near the Santa Barbara Channel in 1824 was blamed by the stunned padres on the extra labor occasioned by the demands of the military.

There were other problems. Throughout the mission period, 1769–1833, the religious establishments received through conversions and births an inflow of 82,100 Indians. According to the calculations of Professor S. F. Cook of the University of California, a normal number of deaths for this population during the sixty-four years concerned would have been 40,000. Actually 62,000 deaths occurred—as compared to 29,000 births.[6]

Epidemics flared in the crowded dormitories. As the years passed, infant mortality soared. In 1810, 50 percent of the children born at the missions perished. By 1820, the rate had reached a staggering 86 percent. To prevent such agonies, expectant mothers often resorted to abortion.

Unknown hundreds of men and women fled from the missions, to be ruthlessly pursued by the soldiers of the guard. While searching the rancherías for fugitives, the troopers often seized, for the sake of their records, Indians who had never been converted. Desperate for labor, the padres were not always careful to determine the true status of the cowed natives whom the military men tumbled roughly into the mission compounds.

When criticism reached the friars, they retorted that the charges were exaggerated. They pointed out that there were never more than three dozen or so of them in California at any one time, and no more than a hundred ragged guards for support. Could so few men keep 20,000 Indians in subjugation if the majority of the converts were truly unhappy?

Mexican liberals, flushed with the triumph of their successful

6. Carey McWilliams, *Southern California Country* (New York: Duell, Sloan and Pearce, 1946), p. 32, drawing on Sherbourne F. Cook, *"The Conflict Between the California Indians and White Civilization"* (Berkeley: University of California Press, 1943), pt. 1, *passim.*

revolution, were unconvinced. The California guards had guns, which were carefully kept from the Indians, and so a mere listing of numbers proved little. Moreover, the liberals did not want to be convinced. Anticlericalism had burned hot during the revolution, and the padres had not helped their situation by being loyal for the most part to Spain. Thus there was considerable animosity behind the liberals' righteous reminders, first, that even Spanish law had decreed that missions should be secularized with ten years of establishment and, second, that the Mexican constitution of 1824 had conferred full citizenship on all Christian Indians.

Economic opportunism lent heat to ideological arguments. As soon as Mexico achieved her independence, she opened California's ports to foreign traders. Soon Yankee and British ships were beating along the coast in search of beef tallow for making soap and candles and cowhides needed in the shoe factories of New England and Great Britain. By that time (the late 1820s) hundreds of thousands of mission cattle ranged across millions of acres of choice pasture land—land, the fathers declared, that was being held in trust for their neophytes.

Because this land was intended for the eventual benefit of the Indians, the missions managed for two-thirds of a century to hold private ranchers at bay. Between 1769 and 1834, California's governors issued only fifty-one land grants to private individuals. But as markets for hides expanded, the demand for rangeland skyrocketed. The easiest way to make it available was to secularize the missions: divide each establishment's equipment, livestock, and pasturage among the Indians—they wouldn't need more than half of it—and then open the rest of the area to private ranching.

The step was finally taken between 1834, when ten missions were placed under lay control, and 1836, when the last five were turned over to secular administration. In theory, the Indians were to settle in pueblos near the missions while the white administrators of the secularized property managed the undistributed part of the livestock and equipment for their benefit.

This radical program for redistributing California's wealth had little chance of working. The paternalistic priests had given

the Indians no training in either self-management or self-government. Few people had emigrated to California, and as a result
there was no stabilizing group to settle with the native people in
the new towns and help them adapt to new ways of living.
Worse, only a few of the lay administrators were fitted for their
jobs. The majority were incompetent. Others were venal, lining
their own pockets and those of their friends with property supposedly managed in trust for the Indians. Meanwhile, a succes-
sion of governors handed out land with increasing liberality to
private applicants. Close to 750 patents were issued between
1834 and the middle of 1846. Covering more than twelve million acres, those grants became, as we shall see, a prickly problem to the American occupants of the new state.

A few Indians did receive land and cattle. A few Indian
pueblos did take form. Most of the neophytes, however, were
cast adrift. Some clung around the decaying missions, shep-
herded by the handful of padres who chose to remain with them.
A few fled into the wilds. But those who had been born and
raised at the missions were, in general, afraid of the "uncivilized" tribelets, and so they hung around the pueblos, either
gambling away their property or being cheated out of it. Destitute, their only recourse then was to go to work at substandard
wages for the overnight ranches.

Supported by cheap labor, free land, and cattle that throve on
the undemanding ranges, the new rancheros developed a culture
that looked idyllic to the urbanized communities that eventually
replaced them. Each year, the Californios sold, as a group,
some 75,000 hides for an average of $2.00 each. Very little of
this income was taxed for the support of education, transportation, social work, or defense; it went, for the most part, into
luxuries. For the men, there were fancy suits emblazoned with
gold and silver braid, showy cowhide boots made in Boston, or-
nate saddles, and broad-brimmed beaver hats. For the women,
there were satin slippers, rustling petticoats, and *rebozos* of
Chinese silk that might cost $150 or more apiece. For house-
holds, there were spices, tea, cocoa, cutlery, tools, and elegant
table service.

Menial tasks fell to the Indians; even children had their personal servants. Yet living standards in the modern sense were abysmal. The majority of the people were illiterate. Few ranch houses had plank floors or window glass; none had running water. *El Camino Real,* the King's Highway, which followed Anza's route between southern Arizona and San Francisco, was little more than a track for horsemen. There were no public stagecoaches. The only public inns were occasional single-roomed, flea-infested *ramadas* where cooking was done in open fireplaces and one spread his own blanket on the floor in whatever corner was not pre-empted by the establishment's domestic animals.

To the Indians and poorer *mestizos* the elite could be arrogant. To each other they exhibited an innate dignity and courtesy that sprang in part from the fact that most of them were related either by blood or marriage. Life was family-centered and communal. According to legend, a dish filled with coins stood beside each ranch door so that travelers in need could help themselves. All classes loved music and dancing and spent much of their time riding from ranch to ranch to enjoy family celebrations and religious festivals. Superb horsemen, they relished wild races and the excitement of lassoing not just cattle but even grizzly bears. Pleasure rather than work, career, or public service was life's justification.

Many of the Americans who began arriving during the 1840s found so improvident an outlook incomprehensible. They regarded the Californios as benighted, wasteful, vain, undependable, and immoral. Yet some, like Richard Henry Dana, whose *Two Years Before the Mast* was the most widely read pre-Mexican War account of California, and Walter Colton, who became alcalde of Monterey in 1846, felt the tug of these sunny people even while clucking at their customs. If the migration from the east had proceeded as slowly as it began, an assimilation conceivably could have taken place that would have brought fundamental changes to the character of American California.

The greed of the gold rush ended that possibility. California was inundated by exploiters who accepted Spanish place names because they were convenient, borrowed Mexican mining customs and techniques because they were useful, and studied Mexican law because it helped them challenge the validity of the land grants. Otherwise, the conquerors brushed the Hispanic ways and people aside as irrelevant. By 1900, there were only 8,000 Mexican people in California, about the same number as when the American occupation took place half a century earlier.

And yet millions of Americans never quite forgot the presence of those Hispanic remnants. At first, the backward looks were compounded of syrupy romance and nostalgia. Mexican bandits, of whom there were several, were apotheosized as western Robin Hoods avenging the injustices inflicted on their people. The missions became, in novels like Helen Hunt Jackson's *Ramona*, pastoral heavens where kindly padres paced with serene wisdom among their devoted charges. Sensing the power of such legends, real-estate promoters hawked them as part of the Mediterranean charm that was available, for a price, beside the golden coast.

Yet there were others—among them George Wharton James, author of *In and Out of the Old Missions of California*, editor Charles Lummis of *Land of Sunshine* (a title soon changed to *Out West*), and the architects of Stanford University's tawny campus—who looked beyond the phony romance and saw in the Latin's enjoyment of life a meaning that the more sophisticated, ever-hurrying urbanites of the dawning twentieth century might take to heart. As Kevin Starr has suggested more recently in *Americans and the California Dream* (1973), the Spanish motifs in the two expositions, one at San Diego and the other in San Francisco, which celebrated the opening of the Panama Canal, also insisted architecturally that the state's Hispanic roots still had validity.

Certainly the past gives a sense of dignity and cohesion to modern chicanos, who are now the largest ethnic minority in the state. True, they are newcomers, drawn by the hope of good-paying jobs, but that fact does not lessen their awareness that this was once Mexican land and that its loss and the dispersal of the original Californios were accompanied by many outrages.

Woodrow Wilson once said—this was in 1912, when planning for both the San Diego and San Francisco expositions was underway: "A nation is not made of anything physical. It is made of its thoughts and purposes." The remark is worth recalling when we reflect not just on the mistakes made by the governments of Spain and Mexico, by the friars and rancheros in the remote province, but also on the ways in which their frontier society, so very different from our own, adapted to an isolated, beneficent, and fantastically beautiful environment.

3

The Adventurers

ANY tightly knit group possessed of a minimum of backing could defy California's Spanish and Mexican authorities with impunity. Native Californians revolted regularly against administrators who for one reason or another did not suit them. Foreign commercial adventurers repeatedly broke national and territorial laws without suffering more than temporary inconvenience—if that.

To local observers, both native and alien, this weakness in the legitimate government naturally suggested outside intervention. For years, however, the potential intruders—the United States, Great Britain, France, and, for a time, Russia—seemed unwilling to risk the international repercussions that would follow naked aggression. Meanwhile, a heterogeneous mix of opportunists from many lands went blithely on fishing for their own material gain in the troubled waters.

The first interlopers—their intrusion began about 1800—were American otter traders in search of pelts that could be exchanged in China for tea, silk, and other Oriental wares in demand in New York and New England. Although Spanish law forbade commerce with outsiders, the clothing, hardware, and costume jewelry offered the Californios by these maritime peddlers proved irresistible. Certain smugglers' coves—the mouth of Refugio Canyon west of Santa Barbara was a favorite—became places of rendezvous. Brash *contrabandistas* even sailed at times into harbors overlooked by the little cannon of the presidios, to trade on the beaches under cover of darkness.

The trouble with straightforward smuggling, from the smugglers' point of view, was the scanty number of skins available. Indians were the chief hunters, and those in California lacked suitable boats. The Chumash of the Santa Barbara Channel split planks out of driftwood, stitched the boards together with sinew, and waterproofed the cracks with tar from nearby oil seeps. Other groups fashioned rafts out of bundles of coarse reeds. In these shaky craft they ventured as far as the islands off the coast, but they could not overtake swimming otter. A surer method, but still not very productive, was to slip up on the animals with clubs, spears, nets, or even lassos as they slept on some rocky beach. Christian Indians generally turned in the pelts they acquired by such devices to the missions. Unconverted Indians either swapped them for baubles at the presidios or lost them gambling with soldiers and ranchers. Contacting these various sources for a relatively few pelts was laborious.

Hoping to speed the process, a New England ship captain named Joseph O'Cain proposed to Alexander Baranov, head of the Russian-American Fur Company of Alaska, that he, O'Cain, be loaned twenty Aleut Indian hunters. These and their *bidarkas,* highly maneuverable canoes built of sea-lion hides, he proposed to take to California aboard his vessel. Baranov agreed to accommodate him, in return for a share of the pelts. It was a successful experiment. During five months of hunting, the Aleuts illegally ran down nearly 1,800 otter. Soon other Americans were invading the coastal waters of both Alta and Baja California with still larger crews hired through the Russians at Sitka.

As soon as they were able, the Russians followed suit. Because of a shortage of oceangoing vessels in the North Pacific, they decided to base their Aleuts on the shores of California itself. The trespass, Baranov hoped, would bring an additional advantage. Crops were hard to grow at foggy Sitka, and, when supply ships failed to appear on time, the garrison faced starvation. Perhaps supplementary food could be raised in the south. Thus, with those two motives prompting them, the Russians built Fort Ross on a seaside meadow some eighty miles north of San Francisco Bay.

Spanish, and afterward Mexican, officials protested without ardor to all of this. Now and then an American smuggler was fired upon or even captured and jailed, as were two Russian interlopers who were caught near San Luis Obispo. One party of Aleuts was ambushed and massacred inside San Francisco Bay. Intermittent messages were sent to the commander at Fort Ross, ordering him to leave. He paid no heed, and so finally, early in the 1830s, the governor of California ordered the planting of small settlements and fortifications in the sunny valleys that drain into the northern reaches of San Francisco Bay. His hope was that these signs of occupation would act as buffers against both the Russians and the beaver trappers of the Hudson's Bay Company, who by then were sweeping arrogantly southward from the Columbia River into the Central Valley. But no serious move was ever made to dislodge Fort Ross.

The truth is that the Californios did not want the otter traders to leave. Illegal or not, they provided a source of both luxuries and essential supplies, especially during the revolutionary years when few ships arrived from Mexico. Consequently, the trade continued until California's otter were all but exterminated. The Russians then voluntarily gave up Fort Ross (1841) while British and American hide ships took over the smugglers' function of importing manufactured goods.

Because beaver trappers stripped resources from the territory without leaving anything of value in return, the authorities at first regarded them more sternly than otter hunters—but the mountain men were none the less active because of that.

The first to arrive, in November 1826, was a party led to the gates of San Gabriel Mission by that most famous of the buskskin-clad folk heroes of the early West, Jedediah Smith. Smith's search was twofold: for new beaver grounds and for the mythical San Buenaventura River, which, if it existed, might allow small ships to sail from the Pacific inland to the Rocky Mountains and thus reduce the costs of supplying trappers working in the interior. Jedediah was not candid about these motives, however. The reason the Americans had entered forbidden California, he told Governor Echeandía at San Diego, was their destitution. When they had stumbled into the villages of the Mohave Indians beside the Colorado River, a little north of today's town of Needles, their horses had been so exhausted that they could not return over the hard trails by which they had come. What the party requested was permission to buy fresh animals and supplies so that they could ride north through Mexican territory to the Columbia River. From that point they would be able to swing east to rejoin their associates in the Rockies.

Sensing the danger that might come to Mexican California if Americans thought there were no teeth in either the deserts or in Mexican law, Echeandía clapped Smith into jail and wrote his superiors in Mexico City for further instructions. Before a reply could come back, American ship captains who happened to be in the harbor at the time interceded on Smith's behalf. An indecisive man, Echeandía yielded to their entreaties and released the prisoner in exchange for Jedediah's promise to leave California immediately by the route he had followed on arriving.

Instead of obeying, the group veered into the Central Valley and spent the spring trapping beaver enough to yield 1,500 pounds of fur. When the time came for them to start toward the trappers' rendezvous scheduled for the summer of 1827 at Bear Lake on what is now the northern border of Utah, they found they could not take their pack stock through the snow of the High Sierra. Retreating to a pleasant site beside the Stanislaus River, they erected a stockade that eventually proved strong enough to bluff off a group of Echeandía's soldiers who had come looking for them.

While the bulk of the party waited at the stockade, Smith and two companions again tried to reach the rendezvous. After an epic struggle, first with snow and afterward with the grisly deserts of Nevada and western Utah, they succeeded. Picking up eighteen fresh hunters, Smith returned through sledgehammer heat to the Mohave villages beside the Colorado River. This time the Indians launched a surprise attack, killed ten of the men, and seized most of the horses and equipment. When the survivors reached the stockade at the Stanislaus, they truly were destitute. Of necessity, Jedediah visited the settlements in search of horses and food. Again he was jailed—and again released when four ship captains at Monterey signed a bond guaranteeing the trespassers' withdrawal from California. Thoroughly subdued, the party obeyed this time, only to die— most of them—during another surprise Indian attack beside the Umpqua River in Oregon.

Another land party, this one led by Sylvester Pattie and his son, James Ohio Pattie, suffered even more grievously at Echeandía's hands. Sylvester died in the San Diego jail; James was released only because his medical skills proved valuable during an epidemic of smallpox at the missions—or so he says in the mishmash of tall tales that were shaped for him by a ghost writer into a book called *The Personal Narrative of James O. Pattie, of Kentucky.*

Although news of these unhappy experiences filtered back to the fur brigades that during the late 1820s were probing every section of the American West, it did not act as a deterrent. New bands of hunters kept arriving. As early as 1832, they had worked out a trail between Santa Fe, New Mexico, and Mission San Gabriel that was followed not only by trappers but also by traders carrying silver coins and American cloth and hardware to swap for California horses, mules, and occasional sea-otter pelts. Another trail, followed regularly by the trapping brigades of the Hudson's Bay Company, came down from Fort Vancouver beside the Columbia River in the north. Soon the Mexican governors of California, who lacked manpower enough to police the long frontier, were not even pretending to oppose the activity.

Every season a handful of the invaders decided to leave their brigades and begin life anew in California. Some hunted sea otter for a living; a few tried ranching. Others turned their talents to targets of opportunity, acting as tinsmiths, carpenters, whiskey distillers, clerks in the new stores being opened in the principal towns by the hide traders, and as lumberjacks among the redwoods near Monterey. In these pursuits they were joined by sailors who had jumped ship or who, falling sick, were unceremoniously dumped on the beach by passing whalers and hide vessels.

Many of these newcomers eased their paths to security by becoming Mexican citizens and embracing the Roman Catholic faith. Fulfilling the two requirements allowed the traders at the pueblos to marry into prominent Californio families and own the buildings in which they established their stores and homes. Similarly, citizenship and Catholicism made would-be rancheros eligible to apply for one or more of the land grants being issued with increasing liberality by California's ever-changing list of governors.

By far the most notable of the dozen or more aliens who scrambled for these huge inland principalities was Johann Augustus Sutter. A fugitive from heavy debts and unhappy family life in Switzerland, Sutter had tried two unsuccessful trading trips on the Santa Fe Trail before emigrating to California by way of Oregon, Honolulu (where he hired some Kanaka laborers and picked up a Kanaka mistress), and Sitka, Alaska. To Governor Juan Bautista Alvarado this extraordinary dreamer said that if he were given the necessary land—he would of course become a loyal Mexican and Catholic—he would plant a colony of Swiss *émigrés* in such a way that they would act as a buffer against Russian advances out of Fort Ross, English trapping excursions from the north, and American trespassers from any direction.

Alvarado agreed. Sutter thereupon selected as the site for his proposed colony of New Helvetia the broad V formed by the junction of the Sacramento and American rivers. (The American had been so named because Jedediah Smith's American trappers had camped there during their penetration of the Central Valley, twelve years earlier.) Helped by his hired Kanakas, by a few drifters who attached themselves to him, and by foot-loose Indians trained originally at the missions, Sutter began building a stout adobe fortress surrounded by grain fields and pasture lands. In 1840, Alvarado granted him eleven square leagues of land—roughly 48,700 acres. A few years later, Sutter wheedled his way into two more grants of comparable size a little distance to the north.

In exchange for these principalities, Sutter did little. By 1841, a landmark year, conditions on the California frontier had changed radically. General Mariano Vallejo, commandante of the northern outposts, granted the English brigades from Fort Vancouver a license that permitted them to trap legally. A little later that same year the Russians left California; at once Sutter contracted to purchase their livestock, equipment, and the cannon at Fort Ross for $30,000, to be paid in wheat—a debt never liquidated. Thus Sutter was not called on in any way to checkmate those onetime interlopers.

Almost simultaneously, a new type of American began to appear—the avowed settler. During the summer of 1841, a small group that numbered among its members a married couple and their children rode south from Oregon. Another party that also included a woman and infant fought a way across the Sierra Nevada to the ranch of John Marsh near Mt. Diablo. Ironically, inasmuch as Marsh's letters extolling the wonders of California had been partly responsible for the trip, the newcomers soon quarreled with him and moved on to find succor beside the Sacramento River with Sutter and on the lands of yet another American rancher, George Yount, in the Napa Valley north of San Francisco Bay. That same year, 1841, a third group of Americans with Mexican wives traveled the caravan trail from New Mexico to Los Angeles. The three parties swelled California's foreign-born population to well over four hundred.

From then on, New Helvetia—Americans called it Sutter's Fort—shone like a beacon in the minds of pioneers from the United States. It was trail's end, the resting place where one replenished supplies and laid plans for the future. As for Swiss settlers, none appeared during those early years. Soon California's Mexican authorities were fearing that the fort, bristling with Russian cannon, was more likely to turn into a Trojan horse than a defender of their province's territorial integrity.

Meanwhile, the governors of California were suffering their own pangs of ambition and uncertainty. Part of the problem stemmed from clashing philosophies in Mexico. The "centralists" there advocated a strong government in Mexico City, with state governments reduced to mere administrative units. Their opponents, the "federalists," wished to curtail the powers of the central government while making the states all but autonomous in everything except matters of international concern. Because California was a territory, not a state, its affairs were administered by an appointed official who, by the nature of things, was a symbol of centralism.

The few Californios who concerned themselves with politics disliked the arrangement. They decried having both military and civil functions combined in the same autocrat, and they felt that their interests would be better served if the federalists held power in Mexico City.

In 1836, after having endured nine governors and acting governors in five years, two native-born Californios, young Juan Bautista Alvarado and his cousin, José Castro, fomented a revolution. To lend strength to their body of ill-armed, untrained followers, they recruited with promises of land grants about thirty English and American backwoodsmen led by Isaac Graham, a whiskey distiller and occasional lumberman.

Like most California uprisings of the time, the Alvarado-Castro coup produced a barrage of proclamations but few casualties. It nevertheless succeeded, thanks in part to its "foreign legion." Alvarado became provisional governor in charge of civil affairs, while his uncle, Mariano Vallejo, only two years his elder and not yet thirty, was named military commander. Sonorously, the victors proclaimed California free *unless* Mexico restored a federalist government. This qualified independence ended in 1838, when Alvarado accepted from the centralist regime an appointment as California's legitimate governor!

One reason for the easy-going opportunism was the fact that, despite a great deal of ideological bombast during times of stress, the real dynamo of politics in both California and Mexico was factionalism, not programs. Rivals for power were continually plotting against each other. Los Angeles, which by then was the most populous pueblo in the territory, kept trying to snatch from Monterey the capital and the customs house with its essential revenues.

Wearied of the turmoil, Alvarado in 1842 surrendered his governorship to yet another Mexican appointee, General Manuel Micheltorena. Although the new administrator gained the support of the foreign-born rancheros by his liberality with land grants, the three-hundred-man army of drafted convicts that he brought with him outraged the populace with their wanton behavior. In 1844, he was ousted by one more bloodless revolution. Pío Pico, a leader of the uprising and a native of Southern California, thereupon declared himself governor and Los Angeles the capital. Monterey, however, retained the customs house, and there José Castro, the new military commander, ruled as if ultimate power rested with him. By 1846, it was clear that Pico and Castro would soon be warring with each other for supremacy.

Throughout these troubled times, a parade of foreigners kept urging their governments to assert sovereignty over California. The populace would rejoice in the resultant stability, they argued, and the new mother country would be rewarded with a wealth of undeveloped resources. An official French observer, Eugène Duflot de Mofras, wrote Paris that in his opinion Sutter would assist a French takeover. The British minister to Mexico backed a scheme, proposed first in a widely read book by a British merchant, that Great Britain accept the province in lieu of $50 million owed to the English holders of worthless Mexican bonds. But the sharpest agitation came, as might be expected, from Americans.

It was a time of expansionist zeal gilded by the high-minded slogans of Manifest Destiny. If the United States acquired California, the busy American whaling fleet would obtain a valuable base in San Francisco Bay. By being able to draw freely on the resources of the California hinterland, the merchants trading with the Orient would quicken their business, while at the same time the new land would fill with sturdy American yeomen. And the Californios would receive, whether they wanted them or not, the blessings of American forms of religious and political liberty.

Besides, American supporters invariably concluded, if the United States did not occupy California, either France or England would. Actually, as diplomatic records later revealed, neither of those governments had any intention of stirring up a hornet's nest over California. At the time, however, no one in Monterey or Washington, D.C., knew that. Prompt action against European rivals was deemed necessary, and yet no excuse for armed intervention existed. Accordingly, American presidents beginning with Andrew Jackson sought to acquire at least the northern part of California, including San Francisco Bay, through purchase. The rationale was that the new territory would enter the Union as free land to offset the eventual admission of Texas as a slave state. Indeed, throughout this period, California was never anything more in most American eyes than a somewhat bedraggled tail hitched to the Texas kite.

The job was bungled by the Americans. Jackson's emissary had to be recalled because of his attempts to win his way by bribing Mexican officials. Although talks were resumed during the Tyler administration, they were frustrated by the impetuosity of the commodore of the United States squadron in the Pacific, Thomas ap Catesby Jones. Noting a British fleet sailing out of Callao, Peru, and convincing himself from garbled dispatches that war had broken out between the United States and Mexico, Jones decided that the English were on their way to take California. (Actually, they were bound for China.) Hoping to forestall the lion, the commodore dashed to Monterey and on October 19, 1842, "captured" the town without opposition. After Thomas Larkin, Monterey's leading merchant, soon to be United States consul to California, had convinced him that there was no war, Jones apologized and withdrew. Mexico took umbrage, however, and broke off negotiations about the purchase. Although Polk sought to revive them on his ascension to the presidency in 1845, tensions over the recent annexation of Texas had reached such a heat that the Mexican government refused to receive his messenger.

Despite their awareness of America's yearning for California, the financially strapped, internally divided administration in Mexico City made no effort to soothe dissatisfaction in the province or to dispatch military and naval help. Unanchored, California quite probably would have drifted into the American fold of her own free will if time had allowed. Many influential Californios admired the manner in which the Constitution of the United States had solved the inherent clash between federalism and centralism. Yankee brashness annoyed them, yet they were awed by Yankee energy and ingenuity. To leaders like Mariano Vallejo, amalgamation with such a people was by no means repugnant.

Polk himself tried to foster annexation as an alternative to purchase. His secretary of state, James Buchanan, instructed Consul Larkin to "arouse in their [the Californios'] bosoms that love of liberty and independence so natural to the American Continent," while reminding them that "if the People should desire to unite their destiny with ours, they would be received as brethren." [1] Promptly, Larkin set about corresponding with naturalized Mexicans whom he trusted, most of them American-born.

The strategy was wrecked, unintentionally, by overland immigrants in the interior. They, too, wanted annexation but were less patient about achieving it. Their plan, so far as the fuzzy proposals being voiced around Sutter's Fort can be called a plan, was to quicken the flow of settlers to the Coast and then, when numbers had made the foreign colony irresistible, to seize the province. This, the talkers reasoned, would present the United States with a *fait accompli*. If Mexico tried to retake California, Washington would have to come to the aid of her citizens.

In 1844, Lansford Hastings, a leader of the agitators, went east to recruit settlers and publish a guidebook purporting to show how easily emigrants could reach California by land. Unhappily for the scheme, he lined up only ten men, and the guidebook came out too late to be influential in 1845. Scouts sent by Sutter to the Oregon Trail to divert travelers southward fared better, but still the influx of '45 fell below expectations. In the meantime, the United States Congress voted to annex Texas.

Mexico City responded by threatening war and decreeing the expulsion from her territories of all aliens without valid passports, a definition that included most of California's overlanders. General Castro let the existence of the order of eviction be known to the people around Sutter's Fort, but made no effort to

1. Quoted in Walton Bean, *California: An Interpretive History*, revised edition (New York: McGraw-Hill Book Co., 1973), pp. 94–95.

enforce it. Probably he was being merciful rather than timid—winter was at hand and the aliens had no place to go—but his restraint did not allay their fears and consequent truculence.

Into this scene of uncertainty there came, on December 10, 1845, that most enigmatic catalyst of destiny, Capt. John Charles Frémont of the United States Corps of Topographical Engineers. It was Frémont's second visit to California. The first had come in February 1844, at the conclusion of a successful trail-scouting expedition into Oregon. Although his superiors had given him no authority to visit California, he had made a reckless, nearly fatal winter crossing of the Sierra Nevada to Sutter's Fort. His stated reason: he needed fresh horses. After talking at length with Sutter and several others about the California situation, he had picked up the animals he needed and departed for the east via the San Joaquin Valley and Walker Pass.

In Washington, where his wife helped him turn the official story of his adventures into one of the decade's most popular books, Frémont learned of the growing tensions between the United States and Mexico. Consequently, when he went West again, he took with him sixty-eight heavily armed soldiers, scientists, and Delaware Indian hunters, a force strong enough to deal with emergencies—or perhaps create them; there is no way of knowing what he had in mind.

Castro reluctantly granted the armed Americans permission to winter in the San Joaquin Valley. Instead of keeping his word, Frémont for reasons never satisfactorily explained led the group west to the vicinity of San José. Castro promptly mustered two hundred poorly equipped cavalrymen and ordered the trespassers out of California.

After defying the Mexicans for three days from a fortified mountaintop, Frémont decided against precipitating hostilities and withdrew into Oregon. There he was overtaken by a Marine Corps courier, Lt. Archibald Gillespie, who had crossed Mexico disguised as a traveling merchant. Exactly what messages Gillespie brought with him has never been revealed. War had not been declared when he left Washington, but evidently he convinced Frémont that it would be. Deciding to be on the scene, ready for glory when the inevitable occurred, the young officer turned back into California.

His reappearance excited the nervous aliens of Northern California into mounting what they considered a Texas-style revolution. First, a group of them seized a herd of horses that Castro was rounding up for an attack on Pío Pico—the raiders claimed that they thought the horses were to be used against them—and then, on June 14, 1846, thirty of them invaded the little pueblo of Sonoma. There they captured General Mariano Vallejo.

Vallejo was not on active duty, he had no troops in Sonoma, and he was an advocate of joining California to the United States. But as the only available symbol of Mexican authority, he was imprisoned with his brother and other leading residents of the area in barren cells at Sutter's Fort. Meanwhile, revolutionist William B. Ide, a former schoolteacher, composed a florid proclamation declaring California an independent republic. Because of a homemade flag decorated with a single star and a crudely drawn grizzly bear that was raised over the plaza at Sonoma on the day of the victory, the new "nation," whose sway extended over one small town, was known as the Bear Flag Republic. That banner, considerably refined and romanticized, is now the state flag of California.

Frémont promptly came riding to the aid of the Bear Flaggers, as no doubt they had anticipated, and helped them fend off Castro's counterattack. Although each side accused the other of atrocities, the weight of evidence lies against the revolutionaries. The crass episode fired the resentment of the Californios and scuttled Larkin's hopes of bringing about a peaceful separation of California from Mexico. Not that it mattered in the end. On May 13, 1846, the United States had finally declared war on Mexico. As soon as word reached American naval units on alert in the Pacific, they set out occupying, during July 1846, every port in California.

The occupation also scuttled the month-old Bear Flag Republic. Hoping to play a major role in what followed, Frémont enrolled his own exploring group, the Bear Flaggers, and various other exultant emigrants into what he called the California Battalion of Mounted Riflemen and led the ragtag column into Monterey. To keep the men from getting out of hand, Comdr. Robert Stockton mustered them into United States service.

The rest of the occupation probably would have been bloodless except for the repressive conduct of Archibald Gillespie, who was placed in charge of Los Angeles. The *pobladores* there grew so exasperated at his petty tyrannies that they chased him and his soldiers out of town. From Los Angeles the uprising spread throughout Southern California, culminating on December 6, 1846, near the Indian town of San Pasqual, in a successful predawn attack on Gen. Stephen Watts Kearny, who was marching 125 men overland from Santa Fe to San Diego. The victors at San Pasqual did not press their advantage, however. Superior forces closed in by land and sea, and on January 13, 1847, the Californio "army" capitulated. Except for some skirmishing in Baja California, the war in the West was over, although another year would pass before Mexico yielded and signed the peace treaty of Guadalupe Hidalgo.

It was an eventful time for California. In 1846, the territory for the first time attracted more immigrants than Oregon did. Its gain was costly, however. A group known as the Donner party, belated by poor advice and their own clumsiness, was trapped by snow in the Sierra. During the subsequent winter nearly half perished. Those who survived until their rescue in 1847 did so only by devouring the flesh of the dead.

The Mormon migration to new homes in the West added more population. For a time Brigham Young and other leaders of the persecuted church in Illinois considered Mexican California as a destination. Assuming that the decision had been made, 238 New York Mormons led by Sam Brannan sailed in a wretched ship around Cape Horn to San Francisco, where they landed on July 31, 1846, shortly after the American occupation. Later, in January 1847, the famed Mormon Battalion of Kearny's Army of the West arrived in San Diego after a rigorous march from Santa Fe.

Young, however, did not appear. He stopped with his followers near the Great Salt Lake and by messenger ordered the Mormons in California to stay there, earning and saving as much money as possible until the new community in Utah was able to absorb them. Obediently, the faithful scattered to work in lumber camps on the Marin Peninsula across the Golden Gate from San Francisco, around Sutter's Fort, and at the gristmill and the sawmill that Sutter was building in the foothills beside the South Fork of the American River. Although the majority eventually made their way to Utah, a sizable number, Brannan included, decided to stay on the Coast.

Another group that contributed to the population was a regiment of New York volunteers led by a Tammany hack, Col. John D. Stevenson. Californios heard familiar echoes in the maneuver: like Anza seventy years earlier, Stevenson conducted his recruiting among poor artisans and shipped them and their tools without charge to California with the understanding that on their discharge they would settle on the coast. Nor, to digress briefly, was that the only echo. Frémont and Kearny quarreled as bitterly over power as any Mexican governors ever had. In the end, Kearny clapped the rambunctious explorer under arrest and sent him east to court-martial in Washington. Californios smiled delightedly: which race was unstable politically?

At least the newcomers were energetic. They established newspapers in Monterey and San Francisco, created ferries, laid out townsites. San Francisco, which the Mexicans had called Yerba Buena, attracted them particularly. A hotel and wharves took shape; whaling ships appeared; real-estate values jumped.

Until notice of peace arrived, the army had to administer the government. In the main the officers acted wisely and humanely. Squatters on church lands were dispersed. Local affairs were turned over to alcaldes, who under Mexican law had the power to proclaim civic regulations (the new alcalde of Monterey forbade Sunday gambling, for instance), issue writs, hear disputes, which they generally tried to arbitrate, reach decisions, impose sentences, and see that they were carried out. Though the first alcaldes were appointed by the conquerors—about half were Americans because of the refusal of patriotic Californios to serve—elections soon followed, and several Mexicans were placed in office, especially in the south.

Most signs during that period pointed toward a peaceful transition that would end with the Californios holding places of re-spect and influence in the new society. But that was before Sam Brannan traveled to San Francisco from his new store at Sutter's Fort in the spring of 1848. According to legend, he strode through the streets of the growing town waving a vial of yellow metal and shouting "Gold! Gold! Gold in the American River!"

Order crumbled. The new territory plunged into a turmoil of individualistic greed and opportunism that shattered both the old Hispanic culture and the new society of the first American set-tlers. Looking back on the frenzy years later, Josiah Royce, a California-born professor of philosophy at Harvard University, declared sadly that the best one could say for the period was that it provided a terrible schooling in a fundamental social truth: true freedom cannot be attained unless the aspirations are ac-companied by a simultaneous commitment to the broader com-munity in which each person lives.

4

Treasure Hunt

OLD? Skeptically, yet with excitement, too, John Sutter searched for information in an encyclopedia he had at his fort. Following guidelines it laid down, he subjected to crude laboratory tests the yellow flakes that James Marshall had brought him from the unfinished mill building at Coloma beside the South Fork of the American River. The material held up.

Gold! With his disbelief completely evaporated, Sutter began to plan: how could he keep his affairs from being disrupted while engrossing as much of the metal as he could for himself and Marshall, a partner now by necessity?

First he rode to the mill to deal with the workers, most of them discharged members of the wartime Mormon Battalion. Urgently, he besought them to stay on the job until the lumber he needed started coming from the saws. As a bribe he gave the crew pocketknives so that they could spend their Sundays prying nuggets from cracks in rock surfaces from which the earth had been stripped. He also entreated secrecy, even though he must have sensed how hard it would be for the men to hold their tongues—and for him to hold his—when possessed of such news as this.

His next hope was to gain control of the area where the gold had been found. Two or three years earlier, he would have petitioned the Mexican governor of California for an addition to the land grants he already held. But American military men now ruled in Monterey, and, although no word of a peace treaty had yet reached California, it was safe to assume that future policies concerning the disposal of California's unclaimed lands would henceforth emanate from Washington.

Sutter decided to anticipate those policies by setting up a presumptive title. In exchange for $200 worth of trade goods, he prevailed on the local Indians to give Marshall and him a lease to a large block of land along the river. He then sent a messenger to Monterey with documents requesting that Gen. Richard B. Mason, the military governor, approve the transaction.

None of the precautions worked. Although the Mormons at the sawmill did stay on the job, they talked to teamsters who were hauling equipment to the site, and they showed the nuggets they had scratched up with their knives to fellow Mormons from a gristmill that Sutter was building farther down the river. Sutter himself boasted about his prospects in letters to business associates. His messenger to Monterey blurted out information at every stop along the road. The final blow was the governor's rejection of the lease on the grounds that American policy did not countenance private land treaties with Indians.

Sutter's and Marshall's response to the setbacks was to enter into a partnership with Isaac Humphrey, a miner from the goldfields of Georgia. The idea was for Humphrey to teach simple placer mining to Sutter's Indian workers and then skim the gold out of the area around the mill before it disappeared into the pockets of outsiders.

Unhappily for the new partnership, which soon dissolved, Humphrey began work in the least rewarding section of the neighborhood. Ironically, meanwhile, workers from the gristmill down the river discovered in a widening of the valley the first of California's fabulously rich diggings, Mormon Bar. Shortly thereafter, some of Sutter's widely scattered acquaintances in the Central Valley heard rumors of what was afoot and rode over to check. They noticed the streamside characteristics of the area and watched Humphrey's Indians wash flakes of gold from the gravel in pans, wooden bowls, and even tightly woven grass baskets. Rounding up Indian workers of their own, they sought out similar streams in other parts of the Sierra. Unlike Sutter and Marshall, who never found extensive deposits of gold, some of them unearthed fortunes. More importantly, they showed that the occurrence of the yellow metal was not limited to a small area, as the earlier strikes in Southern California had been, but extended far and wide throughout the foothills.

Rumors of the activity soon percolated back to San Francisco, softening the doubts that had greeted the first casual newspaper announcements of the discoveries. Thus the popular mind was receptive when Sam Brannan, hoping perhaps to start a rush that would benefit his new store at Sutter's Fort, walked along Montgomery Street on May 12, 1848, showing passersby a vial filled with nuggets from the American River. A madness seized the 850 residents of the little city. Within two weeks the *San Francisco Californian* had to suspend publication for want of readers and staff members. The whole country, the editor mourned in his last issue on May 29, "resounds with the sordid cry of gold, GOLD, GOLD! while the field is left half-plowed, the house half-built, and everything neglected but the manufacture of shovels and pickaxes."

On that same day, May 29, word of the frenzy reached Monterey. Shaken but dubious, the alcalde of the town, Walter Colton, on June 6 dispatched a scout to the American River to learn what was happening. On the 14th, the fellow was back from his four hundred-mile ride, to be greeted in the center of the main street by a sea of upturned faces. Colton's description of what followed is probably the most frequently quoted paragraph in California history.

> The blacksmith dropped his hammer, the carpenter his plane, the mason his trowel, the farmer his sickle, the baker his loaf, and the tapster his bottle. All were off for the mines, some on horses, some on carts, and some on crutches, and one went in a litter. An American woman, who had recently established a boarding-house here, pulled up stakes, and was off before her lodgers had even time to pay their bills. Debtors ran, of course. I have only a community of women left, and a gang of prisoners, with here and

there a soldier who will give his captain the slip at first chance. I don't blame the fellow a whit; seven dollars a month, while others are making two or three hundred a day! [1]

Coastal trading vessels carried word of the strikes north to the lumber mills and grainfields of Oregon, south to the cattle ranches around Los Angeles, then to Mexico, Peru, and Chile, and out to the great crossroads of the Pacific, Hawaii. Reaction was instantaneous. At least half of the male population of Oregon poured south, at first aboard overloaded lumber schooners and later with pack trains following the difficult trails past Mt. Shasta. Hawaiian adventurers sailed to the mainland with Kanaka workers, intending to mount the same sort of gang labor attack on the gold fields that white Californians were using with Indians. In Latin America and especially in the Mexican province of Sonora, *patrones* grubstaked whole families of experienced peons and sent them north.

California luck played straight into the hands of all these stampeders. Normally gold is difficult to mine. During the formation of the mountains eons ago, molten magma from the earth's interior deposited relatively small amounts of various minerals in veins in the rocks or in minute particles dusted throughout the stone itself. Mining this ore, as mineralized rock is called, crushing it to break the gold loose from its bonds, and separating the particles of metal from the waste calls for expensive mechanical, and, often enough, complex chemical, procedures.

Fortunately for man, nature in some places has done much of the work unaided. Streams have slowly eroded bits of gold from their rock fastenings and have tumbled them downward until they have settled with other debris in quiet eddies behind boulders or in bends in the river. These accumulations of sand, gravel, and metal, the last-named generally resting on or near bedrock, are called by the Spanish-derived term, "placer deposits."

1. Walter Colton, *Three Years in California* (New York: A. S. Barnes and Co., 1850), pp. 246–247.

   As mining historian Rodman Paul of the California Institute
of Technology has pointed out, the geologic history of California, with its repeated uplifts during which heavy mineralization
took place, followed by tiltings and subsequent erosions, was
such that "in 1848 the lower western slopes of the Sierra Nevada were one of the richest gold-placer regions in the
world." [2] The deposits were also extensive, dotting (if the Trinity Mountains near Oregon are included) nearly 35,000 square
miles of rugged land. Moreover, many of the accumulations
were easy to exploit. They were shallow. They occurred at relatively low elevations, where water draining from the high
country was plentiful and where the temperatures of the rainless
summers made outdoor living not only tolerable but often pleasant. The work itself, though laborious, was not complex. As a
result the firstcomers, most of whom were wholly ignorant of
mining technology, were able to solve their problems with the
exercise of nothing more than ordinary common sense.
   For a few months mankind's ageless dream of the touch of
Midas came true. Not everyone succeeded. But some scooped
up gold by the pound. The mountain Indians participated not
only as hired hands but as workers on their own account. James
Clyman, a former trapper and emigrant guide, wrote to a friend
on Christmas Day, 1848, "There are at this time not less than
2,000 white men and more than double that number of Indians
washing gold at the rate of two ounces per day." [3] M. T.
McClellen, an emigrant from Missouri who went straight to the
mines on reaching California in the fall of 1848, did even better
than that. "My little girls," he wrote a friend, "can make from
5 to 25 dollars per day washing gold in pans . . . My average
income this winter will be about 150 dollars per day," [4]—this
at a time when clerks in the East earned, on the average, $30 a
month.
   Such returns, the same men warned, were offset by skyrock-

   2. Rodman W. Paul, *Mining Frontiers of the Far West, 1848–1880* (New York:
Holt, Rinehart and Winston, 1963), pp. 17–19.
   3. Charles L. Camp, editor, *James Clyman: Frontiersman* (Portland, Ore.: Cham-
poeg Press, 1960), p. 239.
   4. Camp, *Clyman*, pp. 295–296.

eting costs—though in view of today's inflation they no longer seem so drastic. Flour, wrote James Clyman in his Christmas letter, "sells at $1 per pound—dried beef and bacon $2 per lb." Shirts went at $30 each, McClellen informed his correspondent, and "serappies" at $100. Even these quotations were deceptive because the gold dust used in the barter, most of it mingled with impurities, was valued at $8.00 per ounce. In terms of coin, which was very scarce in the back country, dust at first was worth still less—from $1 to $3 an ounce. Rancher William Garner of Monterey took about $1,800 worth of silver pieces to the mountains in the summer of 1848 and returned seven weeks later with thirty-six pounds of gold that he resold for approximately $9,000. Indians were particularly susceptible to temptation. In the early days of the stampede they would trade a cupful of gold, which meant nothing to them, for an equivalent quantity of raisins or sugar.

The first reports of this extraordinary "revolution," as prospector McClellen called it, reached the eastern United States in August. In mid-October, Archibald Gillespie, the marine lieutenant who had played a notable though hardly exemplary part in the American conquest of California, wrote from New York to Abel Stearns in Los Angeles, "The public in general are mad about California, & the late news respecting . . . El placer has made many adventurers look towards that region." [5]

Official pronouncements fueled the excitement. During the summer General Mason and other officers, including William Tecumseh Sherman, explored the goldfields, wrote reports, and sent the papers along with samples of gold, by special courier to Washington. On December 5, 1848, President Polk told Congress, "The accounts of the abundance of gold in that territory are of such an extraordinary character as would scarcely command belief were they not corroborated by the authentic reports of officers in the public service." [6]

Much of the country was ready for the kind of excitement the president's words released—as if he had pulled the trigger of a

5. John A. Hawgood, editor, *First and Last Consul, Thomas Oliver Larkin . . . A Selection of Letters* (San Marino, Calif.: Huntington Library, 1962), p. 100.
6. U.S. Congress, House, *Executive Documents*, 30th Cong., 2nd sess., 1848, 1: 14.

shotgun already loaded. The first disruptions of industrialism were bringing to a primarily agricultural nation a malaise only partially diagnosed by the sufferers. On top of that was the restlessness engendered by the war with Mexico. California might soothe some of the pangs. Most importantly, the adventure seemed feasible; a decade before, it would not have. The American whaling fleet and the Boston hide-trading ships had made sea lanes to the Pacific familiar, at least by reputation, to most New Englanders. Government mail service to the West Coast by way of the Isthmus of Panama was about to begin. Frémont's reports, the publicity accorded the missionary treks to Oregon, the Mormon migration to Utah, and the successful march of hundreds of soldiers across the continent to California had removed the terrors of the unknown from the land trip.

An easy, exciting journey—and at its end, so the president himself had implied, a world of easy gold. Why not go?

Philosophers like Henry Thoreau offered emphatic reasons. The stampeders, he railed, wanted to live by luck, contributing nothing to society. The rush "makes God to be a moneyed gentleman who scatters a handful of pennies in order to see mankind scramble for them." [7]

The few stampeders who heard such sentiments scoffed at them. Nothing of value to society in their ambitions? True, there were absconders, wife deserters, gamblers, fugitives, and con men aplenty among the migrants. But the bulk of the travelers regarded their adventure as a unique opportunity to accumulate enough money so that they could return home and realize dreams that until then they had hardly dared mention. The yearning was in their very songs:

> Oh, Sally, dearest Sally!
> Oh, Sally, for your sake,
> I'll go to Californy
> An' try to raise a stake. [8]

7. Quoted by J. S. Holliday, "The California Gold Rush Reconsidered," in *Probing the American West: Papers from the Santa Fe Conference* (Santa Fe: Museum of New Mexico Press, 1962), p. 37.

8. From "Joe Bowers from Pike," in *The Gold Rush Song Book*, compiled by Eleanora Black and Sidney Robertson (San Francisco: Colt Press, 1940).

Or, as Melvin Paden wrote his wife, "Jane, i left you and them boys for no other reason than this . . . to come here to procure a little property by the swet of my brow so that we could have a place of our own that i mite not be a dog for other people any longer." [9]

Not only Americans felt the tug. Hopefuls poured out of nearly every country on the globe, and they too planned to return home. Such attitudes made the rush to California a very different kind of folk movement from the one that had already become an ingrained part of the American experience. Earlier emigrants had crossed the Atlantic, had breached the Alleghenies, had forded the Mississippi, and had made the long leap to Oregon primarily for the sake of finding new homes. In 1849 there were many of that kind, too, drawn westward by the ending of the war and the acquisition of promising new agricultural lands beside the Pacific. The vast majority, however, were avowed transients.

Women and children stayed home, waiting for the return of suddenly wealthy husbands, fathers, and lovers. Thus the federal census takers of 1850 discovered to their surprise that more than half of all Californians were males in their twenties, an age when the desire for female companionship is at its peak. Yet only one Californian in thirty was a woman in the same age bracket. In the mining camps the percentage was even lower, females in some regions comprising only 1 percent of the population.

Other statistics from the census of 1850 are equally revealing. The illiteracy rate for adults in the nation as a whole was 10.35 percent; in California, 2.86 percent. Such a comparison suggests in turn that the average Forty-Niner was more prosperous than the average American, a conclusion buttressed by simple logic: the only ones who could make the trip were those who could afford to buy passage and equipment out of their savings, the sale of property, or loans from friends and relatives.

Geography had much to do with the choice of routes. New Englanders and Europeans tended to travel around Cape Horn

9. Quoted in George W. Groh, *Gold Fever* (New York: William Morrow and Co., 1966), p. 232.

by ship, a method that in 1849 allowed them several months' advantage over wayfarers journeying by land. Affluent New Yorkers, Philadelphians, and people from the lower Mississippi Valley accounted for the majority of those choosing the expensive but (they hoped) quick way across Panama. Stampeders traveling by land from Texas and Arkansas sought to match the early start of the seafarers by following the snow-free Gila River trail through southern Arizona or alternate routes across Mexico.

Most land travelers waited until the grass on the plains began to green in April and then turned their mule- or ox-drawn wagons along the established trail up the Platte and Sweetwater rivers to the South Pass crossing of the Continental Divide. From there the wagons either pushed on across southern Idaho or else detoured to the Mormons' brand-new Salt Lake City in order to obtain fresh animals and provisions. After following the sluggish Humboldt River through Nevada, they found that they could surmount the Sierra by any of three routes, all hard: Peter Lassen's trail into northern California, roundabout but lower in elevation than the others; the Truckee River crossing north of Lake Tahoe, a region still regarded with dread because of the Donner tragedy; and the new Carson River route south of Tahoe. To avoid snow, late travelers swung south from Salt Lake City into the deserts of Southern California, scene of the intense suffering that in 1849 brought Death Valley its name.

Many of the travelers, both by sea and land, sought to increase their material and spiritual resources by banding together into companies. Some groups adopted fancy uniforms, loaded themselves with armament, and chartered ships or bought community wagons. Nearly all composed lengthy constitutions detailing methods of governance. Formal organizations of this sort were not innovative; Santa Fe traders, fur companies, and Oregon immigrants had pioneered similar systems years earlier. The constitutions, moreover, proved not to be very adhesive; disgruntled members frequently seceded at will along the way. Nor were the companies enduring; nearly all disintegrated when their original purpose, reaching California, had been accomplished. Still the efforts did give tens of thousands of Americans an immediate, intense introduction to the virtues and pit-falls of grass-roots democracy.

It is not possible to do more than guess at the numbers of people who traveled the different routes. Upward of 700 ships, carrying perhaps 40,000 people drawn from all parts of the globe, put into San Francisco Bay in 1849. Another 15,000 persons may have crossed Mexico or the Southwest by a variety of routes. The storied California Trail, the route that springs automatically to mind with the words "Gold Rush," reputedly saw the passage of at least 6,200 wagons and 1,500 horsemen. Estimates about the number of persons traveling in and with those wagons range all the way from 22,500 to 45,000.

Whatever the grand total on all the routes, and in my opinion 80,000 for the year 1849 is a conservative figure, the adventurers were unusually articulate. In addition to keeping a record number of diaries, they wrote endless letters either to their hometown newspapers or to friends and relatives who showed the letters to reporters. Since there was hardly a family in the settled parts of the country that did not have at least a cousin or close acquaintance making the long trip, the widespread communications were followed with fascination by stay-at-homes. The result, even after tales of discouragement began to appear, was a worldwide gilding of the name California with a patina of romance that it has never lost.

But discouraging notes sounded early. All of the routes proved more difficult than anticipated. Cape Horn travelers were alternately nauseated and bored stiff in a medley of coal ships, whalers, coastal traders, and even river ferries that had been hastily and clumsily converted to passenger use. Many of the wallowing, overcrowded vessels took from six to eight months to make the journey. The passengers endured tropical heat at the equator, icy gales at the Horn, and deadly calms in the Pacific. Food for the most part was wretched. Scurvy was the common physical ailment; lassitude the common psychological enemy, fought with varying degrees of success with improvised theatrical productions, musicales, debates, readings, and Sunday preachings.

By comparison, a sea voyage to the Isthmus of Panama was a

lark, but there another nightmare began. Native boatmen charged extravagant rates for poling itinerants up the insect-infested Chagres River in cramped bongos. The mule trail down the Pacific slope was often a morass of steaming mud fetid with the stench of dead animals. Baggage was mishandled and often lost. Yet worse than those experiences during the first half of 1849 was the suspenseful wait at Panama City for the few ships that called at the shallow harbor. Each appearance brought forth desperate struggles for the limited space aboard. For those who lost, nothing remained but to settle back for another wait in Panama's jammed hotels or in the unsanitary shanty towns that sprang up outside the crumbling city walls.

Except for outbreaks of cholera, which afflicted several of the wagon trains toiling up the Platte Valley, the land trail was pleasant at first. Unusually heavy rains assured plentiful supplies of grass for the livestock at the crowded campgrounds. The only real ordeal was facing up to the fact that most of the wagons were overloaded and that many objects packed aboard with infinite anticipation would have to be jettisoned.

Animals stampeded occasionally; Indians pilfered. The bottlenecks at the river ferries caused tedious waits. But major problems were reserved for late summer, when the desert heat increased and grass grew short. Overworked animals began to die then, and some hard-used equipment fell apart. The travelers improvised hastily, cutting wagons down to carts or making wooden packsaddles to fit on the backs of their remaining mules and oxen. Ahead loomed the Sierra, a dismaying sight, where every delay would increase the possibility of being caught by snow.

Although the season was late when the majority of the land travelers reached California, they at least ended their journey in the heart of the mining country. Argonauts who arrived by ship had to work their way through black clouds of mosquitos in the delta where the rivers of the Central Valley enter San Francisco Bay. Having gained the valley, they had to fan out across its hot plains, hunting in bewilderment for some mining camp where their dreams could be realized. There they joined the land travelers and set about learning the techniques of their new trade.

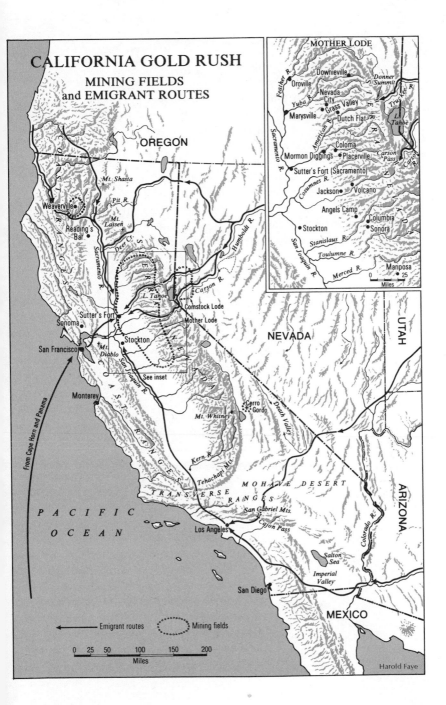

CALIFORNIA GOLD RUSH
MINING FIELDS
and EMIGRANT ROUTES

OREGON

Mt. Shasta

Weaverville

Reading's Bar

Pit R.

Mt. Lassen

Deer Cr.

Sacramento R.

L. Tahoe

Carson R.

Comstock Lode

Mother Lode

See inset

Sutter's Fort

Sonoma

Stockton

San Francisco

Mt. Diablo

San Joaquin R.

Monterey

Humboldt R.

NEVADA

UTAH

Cerro Gordo

Death Valley

Mt. Whitney

Kern R.

Tehachapi Mts.

MOHAVE DESERT

TRANSVERSE RANGES

San Gabriel Mts.

Cajon Pass

Los Angeles

Colorado R.

ARIZONA

Salton Sea

Imperial Valley

San Diego

MEXICO

PACIFIC OCEAN

From Cape Horn and Panama

← Emigrant routes   ⬭ Mining fields

0 25 50   100   150   200
Miles

Harold Faye

MOTHER LODE

Feather R.

Oroville

Downieville

Donner Summit

Nevada City

Yuba R.

Grass Valley

Truckee R.

Marysville

Dutch Flat

L. Tahoe

Sacramento R.

Coloma

Mormon Diggings

Placerville

Carson Pass

Sutter's Fort (Sacramento)

Carson R.

Cosumnes R.

Jackson

Volcano

Angels Camp

Stockton

Columbia

Sonora

Stanislaus R.

San Joaquin R.

Toulumne R.

Merced R.

Mariposa

0   25
Miles

Pocketknives and gold-washing pans seldom sufficed as tools any longer. By the second half of 1849 (by then the rush had been on for more than a year), the richest bars near the streams had been found and plundered. The need now was for mass treatment, so that small amounts of gold could be profitably sifted out of large quantities of earth.

All of the devices that were employed—cradles, long toms, and eventually sluice boxes hundreds of feet in length—depended on using a rush of water to break up the earth that was shoveled into the upper end of the contraption. While the material was being diffused, it was also washing downward across bits of shaggy carpet or transverse barriers called riffles. These created eddies in which the heaviest particles of gold were trapped. (Lighter material was lost, but everyone was in too big a hurry to care very much.) The captured gold was retrieved, along with some dross, during the weekly cleanups.

Here again California luck came into play. Mercury, or quicksilver as most miners called it, has the ability to absorb gold in the form of amalgam. Placed in the bits of carpet or behind the riffles, mercury increased gold recovery almost immeasurably. Once the principal source of mercury had been Europe, but in 1845 one of the superlative quicksilver mines of the world, New Almadén, had been discovered a few miles south of San José. Unguessable millions of dollars were saved by that simple coincidence.

Opening up deposits of gold-bearing earth that could be shoveled into the sluice boxes was another problem. Some treasure troves, it was discovered, lay underneath rushing rivers. Others were high on dry slopes where ancient streams had once run. Much was covered by scores of feet of overburden or held fast in the veins of quartz that seamed the hills.

Attacking these deposits called for co-operation. Since laborers were almost impossible to hire, men formed working partnerships to exploit and share their discoveries. Materials were purchased with credit provided, in the main, by mining-camp merchants. Using the simplest of tools, the partners built log dams that turned rivers from their courses, constructed stilt-legged flumes for carrying water to remote hillsides and dry gullies, and dug long tunnels through risky ground toward bed-rock that might—or might not—be the resting place of reward-ing amounts of metal. By 1852, they were devising crude mills for grinding quartz that could then be washed in the customary way over riffles in their sluice boxes. Shortly thereafter, they in-vented hydraulic hoses whose powerful jets were capable of demolishing whole hillsides.

The devastation connected with all this was appalling. Forests were stripped away for lumber or destroyed by carelessly set fires. Erosion scarred the hillsides; salmon could no longer live in the silted streams. The oyster fisheries of San Francisco Bay were destroyed by accumulations of muck washed from the hills, and more than a century later the fish of the same bay showed traces of mercury that had escaped from the sluice boxes in the Sierra foothills.

The ugliness reached into the ramshackle camps with their un-tended streets and primitive sanitation. After all, improving matters would have taken time from digging. And so the young men who stayed in the hills endured conditions they would not have tolerated at home. The wet work they did twelve hours a day was arduous in the extreme. The food that they prepared for themselves was tasteless and expensive. Facilities to care for the sick and injured were either crude or nonexistent. Relaxation was limited to reading tattered books, listening to acquaintances who had musical instruments, joining contrived literary socie-ties, or paying outrageous prices to see rare performances put on by traveling theatrical companies. Because the restraints of fam-ily and neighborhood custom did not exist, many youths inevita-bly turned to gambling and, less frequently, to explosive out-bursts of heavy drinking.

It was not the kind of life that had lured the stampeders West. Many gave up in despair and went home, often without having lifted a shovelful of earth. Others, lacking passage money East, turned to the trades they had followed at home—farming, clerk-ing, services, or working as mechanics in the industrial plants taking shape around San Francisco Bay. Some became outlaws or wandering indigents. Many kept fitfully roaming the moun-tains in hope of finding a truly great strike; these were the men who, chasing every will-o'-the-wisp into other regions of the West, helped produce the rushes that brought still more American states into being. Finally, of course, there were the untold thousands who did go back to their families with the stakes they had sought.

The momentum engendered by the frenzy of 1849 kept more thousands flowing westward in 1850. In 1851, however, there was a sharp drop. The slowdown resulted in part from the tales of hardship that by then had spread throughout the East, and in part from diversions to the Northwest occasioned by the famed Donation Land Law that Congress had passed for Oregon's benefit. As the inflow of people dwindled, San Francisco's overheated economy stagnated, and gloom filled the distribution towns of Stockton, Sacramento, and Marysville. Then, amazingly, the trend reversed. More people came by ship and wagon to California during 1852 than in any of the preceding years.

Why? A partial explanation is suggested by the increase in the numbers of women and children who made the trip in 1852. Though they were still a minority, their presence indicated that attitudes were shifting back to normal. Homeseekers and not just restless prospectors were on their way West again.

In the crowds were stampeders who had gone home in disgust only to find that the East had suddenly become too tame for them. Others were Forty-Niners who had glimpsed the future in California's new farms and growing towns, and had hurried back for their families. The majority, however, were ordinary "movers" of the kind who had filled Kentucky after the Revolution and then the trans-Mississippi states of Missouri and Iowa. Encouraged by California's sudden rise to statehood, they had decided that perhaps there was more to the region than the dubious attractions of gold. Now they were headed West to share in the building of yet another commonwealth. It was a familiar American trend reasserting itself after the explosive aberration of the treasure hunt that Henry Thoreau had denounced with such scorn.

5

The Unauthorized State

WHEN Brig. Gen. Bennet Riley reached Monterey in April 1849 to assume his duties as California's seventh military governor in three years, he found himself confronting near anarchy. The war with Mexico had formally ended fourteen months before, on February 2, 1848. California itself had been at peace even longer. The American merchants who had followed the armed forces to the West Coast naturally expected that they could soon have their businesses rolling ahead under the aegis of a familiar government. Congress, however, at loggerheads over the issue of extending slavery into the newly won lands, had not created a civilian administration for any part of the Southwest.

Only the military had authority. As a matter of expediency, it still exerised its jurisdiction through Mexican institutions that had prevailed at the time of the occupation—an "inefficient, mongrel" arrangement, one of the area's first newspapers railed.[1] As opposition grew, Americans in the principal towns began arguing that, inasmuch as the military had no right to supervise them in times of peace, they should take matters into their own hands and form their own government.

In a sense the miners in the foothills were already doing just that. Whenever a group of them found tempting promises of

1. *The California Star* (San Francisco), January 22, 1848.

gold, they acted as spontaneously as other Americans moving into empty lands had been acting since the Mayflower Compact of 1620. They met together to decide on rules of conduct adapted to their particular situation.

They had to be eclectic. No national precedent existed to furnish them with models, for the United States had never yet had occasion to promulgate laws concerning the acquisition of title to public lands valuable for precious minerals. So the stampeders drew from whatever sources were available—from their own experiences with local government, from the example of Mexican miners whom they met, and from the talk of migrants familiar with the Cherokee goldfields of Georgia, the lead mines of Wisconsin, the tin deposits of Cornwall, the silver regions of Germany.

These fragments produced a series of codes whose skeletons were almost identical. No group attempted to extend its ordinances beyond its own small "district," which was generally circumscribed by self-evident geographical features. None attempted to establish full title to the ground its members mined. For one thing, the lawmakers realized that, technically at least, they were trespassers on the public domain and hence could not perfect title. For another, unqualified ownership would have made them subject to taxes on real estate. Few wanted permanent possession, anyway. They simply hoped to strip from the land whatever mineral it contained and then abaondon it, no matter how ruined it was, without having it encumber them further.

The area over which an individual could assert these bald usufructuary privileges was determined by the apparent richness of the district. In the early days claims were sometimes as small as ten feet square. Later, as yields diminished, size was increased to as much as 100 by 300 feet. The discoverer of a district was sometimes allowed to appropriate two claims; otherwise the limit was one. Once a usufructuary right had been established, it could be sold, and partners were allowed to combine their holdings for the sake of volume operations. Wherever water existed, all were allowed access to it. In the codes mention was seldom made of the timber that belonged to the United

States. When the miners needed wood, they simply went into the nearby forests and helped themselves.

If a claimant failed to work his allotted rectangle for more than a stated number of days, it fell open for refiling by someone else. A claim holder could hire labor if he was able to find anyone willing to work for wages (there were not many applicants in the early days), but he could not use Negro slaves or gangs of Indians and Kanakas, as some of the most successful miners of '48 had done. The Latin American system of *patrones* and *peons* was also outlawed, except for some instances in the southern hills, where Mexican miners were the first to become established.

A recorder, sometimes called an alcalde out of deference to the military jurisdiction then prevailing, was elected by popular balloting to note in the camp's record book the filing of each claim and any subsequent transfers. When arbitrating disputes about possession, the recorder could collect evidence, summon a jury if need be, and render decisions. Often he handled criminal as well as civil cases. If the charges were particularly serious, the entire camp might meet to listen to the evidence. Sentences were executed immediately. There was no right of appeal.

Punishments were "cruel and unusual," partly because such normal disciplinary institutions as jails did not exist and partly because the code-makers hoped that harsh penalties might act as deterrents to crime. Persons convicted of robbery or assault were whipped, branded, or subjected to mayhem—having all or part of an ear cut off—before being banished from the camp. Murderers were publicly hanged from improvised gallows.

Often—too often, in fact—the mining-camp codes have been offered as examples of the instinctive upwellings of democracy characteristic of America. It is true that the rules guaranteed that all legitimate claimants were to have equal access to mineralized ground. It is also true that uneducated rustics and factory hands mingled freely under the umbrella of the codes with doctors, lawyers, and college professors. But it is not true that all potential claimants were regarded as being equally legitimate.

After Chinese immigrants had become numerous during the

early 1850s, many codes ruled that claims could not be taken up by or sold to Asiatics. Later, however, after dwindling returns from the ground had discouraged American claimants, the rules were ignored and the usufructuary rights were passed on at high prices to the more patient Orientals. The Indians, many of whom had mined successfully in 1848, were thrust aside. But they struck back, of course, and soon a long series of clashes, always fatal in the end to the Indians, was underway. Latin Americans were also bullied out of some of the camps, and, after the state legislature had come into being, it made Mexicans and Chinese the actual, though unnamed, targets of a special tax on foreign miners. The situation of free blacks was more ambivalent. They were barred from certain camps but accepted in others, where some of them profited. Like the Indians and Chinese, however, they were forbidden by statute to give testimony in cases involving whites, which meant that all three groups could be mauled, practically with impunity, by the dominant race.

Although the mining-camp codes contained few safeguards for the accused, trials in the main were orderly—until racial animosities grew heated. Then the dangers inherent in a lack of directives concerning rules of evidence, unprejudicial settings, and processes of appeal became manifest. One notorious example was the multiple whipping and lynching at Hangtown, later Placerville, of five French and Chileans who could scarcely speak English and were denied the assistance of interpreters. Another was the frenzied public execution at Downieville of a Mexican woman charged with stabbing an American who, it seems evident, had accosted her with insults and violence.

There were other defects in the codes. Their phrasing was often inexact. Records were sloppily kept and sometimes lost, circumstances that invited costly litigation whenever exceptionally rich strikes were made. The patchwork of laws did meet the primitive needs of the times, however, and hence they evinced remarkable staying power. Eventually, some five hundred mining-camp codes were adopted in California. In 1851, the state legislature elevated them to the status of common law by ruling that "in actions respecting Mining Claims, proof shall be admitted of the customs, usages, or regulations established and in force at the bar, or diggings, embracing such claims; and such customs, usages, or regulations . . . shall govern the decision of the action." [2] The California Supreme Court upheld the statute, and from California the sanctified codes spread throughout the West.

They were, of course, no substitute for broader forms of government. They dealt with only one occupation, and their details varied from district to district. Because no uniform machinery of law enforcement existed, criminals could move about almost at will. The practice of brutally punishing a culprit and then running him out of the camp simply meant that some other district had to absorb an embittered and often vengeful lawbreaker.

No governmental agency could be called on to provide roads and bridges in the mountains or navigational aids on the rivers. The rapidly growing seacoast cities and valley towns had not received (and under military rule could not receive) the kind of American charters that would empower them to found and maintain sewer and street-paving facilities, fire departments, courts, public schools, health departments, or hospitals. Above all, nothing definite had been done about the vexing problem of the huge Spanish and Mexican land grants that were depriving would-be American agriculturalists of farms and building lots they felt should be theirs by right of conquest.

Beset by agitation concerning all these matters and painfully aware that he did not have enough dependable troops in the area to control even minor disorders, General Riley decided to let California's restless inhabitants set up whatever kind of government they wanted. Whether he acted with the unofficial approval of Washington is uncertain. The situation along the Potomac was even more explosive than in California. Proslavery and antislavery states were evenly divided, fifteen to fifteen. If California should be admitted to the Union, as President Zachary Taylor had recommended in his first annual message to congress, the balance would be destroyed. Inevitably, the South would object. Taylor nevertheless was reported to believe that,

2. Quoted in Paul, *Mining Frontiers*, p. 169.

if California moved quickly and vigorously, she could be admitted as a free state before the impasse became total. To that end he sent a personal representative, Thomas Butler King, by ship to the West Coast to sound out local sentiment. If King discovered it to be favorable to statehood, he was to push for speedy action.

Possibly Riley had received forewarnings. In any event, he knew that if he did not act the people would force his hand. Accordingly, on June 3, 1849, seven weeks after arriving in California, he issued a proclamation calling for the election of forty-eight delegates to assemble in Monterey on September 1 to draw up a constitutuion. The next day, June 4, Taylor's emissary, Thomas King, landed in San Francisco and, presumably to the governor's relief, nodded approval of what had been done.

The delegates met on schedule. The eleven ranchers who came from Southern California were strongly opposed to statehood, for they feared, with reason, that funds for running a state government would be raised primarily through taxes on real estate and not on the mines. By contrast, if a territorial government were established, Washington would provide most of the funds until such time as shifts in the economy provided California with the kind of broad, equitable tax base that a state needed. Wasted breath. The more numerous delegates from burgeoning San Francisco and the golden foothills overwhelmingly voted the Southerners down. California was to skip the normal territorial stage and become an instant state.

In drawing up the organic laws for the new entity, the delegates leaned heavily on the constitution of Iowa, specially printed for their use by member William Gwin, and that of New York, which had been extensively revised only three years before. Slavery was outlawed, as much because the delegates disliked the idea of free men working beside Negroes as from principle. A few of the statemakers even discussed the possibility of barring all blacks, free or slave, from the area, a step already taken in the Oregon Territory.

Another constitutional clause forbade the forming of banking corporations lest they issue paper money, a fiscal tool whose mishandling had caused great suffering throughout the Midwest during the depression of the late 1830s. Married women were granted the right to hold property in their own names, a rare guarantee in the world of 1849. Pious declarations were made concerning education, and electoral procedures were laid down. The draft was completed on October 13, 1849. As the delegates were affixing their signatures, the guns of the Monterey presidio fired thirty-one salutes in honor of America's thirty-first state—a decided presumption, since there could be no state until the voters of California and the Congress of the United States had both legitimatized the actions of the forty-eight delegates.

The voters acted first, on November 13. They also cast ballots that same day for candidates who would take office if the constitution carried: state officials, members of the legislature, and two congressmen. Partly because rain was drenching much of the area at the time and partly because many miners had no intention of staying in California and hence lacked interest, the voting was light. It was decisive, however. The constitution was approved 12,061 for and 811 against.

The new legislature met in San Jose in December 1849. One of its first acts was to elect two United States senators, William M. Gwin and John Charles Frémont. They and the congressmen went straightway to Washington with no assurance that they would be received. Back in San Jose, the lawmakers passed a divorce statute that was unusually liberal for the times, issued municipal charters to several towns, established a court system, and invited all interested hamlets to bid on becoming the capital city of the new state. After considerable shifting hither and yon, the legislators settled on Sacramento.

News of California's stand on slavery intensified the fury in Congress. Fearful of a national catastrophe, Henry Clay proposed and Daniel Webster and Stephen A. Douglas supported what became known as the Compromise of 1850. Under its terms, New Mexico and Utah were organized as territories with the right to determine the question of slavery for themselves. The slave trade was abolished in the District of Columbia, a stringent fugitive slave law was adopted, and, of utmost importance to the West Coast, California was admitted as a free state. President Millard Fillmore, Taylor's "dim and forgotten" suc-

cessor,[3] signed the bill on September 9, 1850, a date still celebrated as a legal holiday in California. The news reached San
Francisco on October 13, touching off uproarious celebrations.
Statehood was now as official as the written word could make
it, but, as the rowdy population soon discovered, much more
than the forms of law were needed before the new entity could
claim to be a viable member of a professedly democratic nation.

3. Allan Nevins and Henry Steele Commager, *A Short History of the United States,*
5th edition (New York: Alfred A. Knopf, 1966), p. 231.

6

Difficulties with Democracy

$\mathcal{C}$ALIFORNIA'S superabundance of gold and golden opportunities inevitably meant that dreams of human equality became welded to hopes for economic betterment. Hundreds of ordinary people found quick riches not by mining but by
responding to the most humble of desires. One famous tale tells
of a woman in the mining country who earned $18,000 in one
year by baking pies in an iron skillet over open campfires. In
1851, George Briggs planted watermelons on twenty-five acres
of Sacramento Valley land, sold the fruit for $17,000, and used
the money to establish an orchard that within six years was net-
ting him $35,000 annually. Young Alexander Todd, tired of
mining, told his neighbors that he would go to San Francisco,
search out whatever mail was waiting for them in the overloaded post office, and bring it back in exchange for one ounce
of gold per letter. The adventure proved so successful that Todd
left mining entirely to build a pioneering express company—
gold to the city, packages back—that for a little while grossed
$1,000 a day.

Ranch owners who once had sold their lightweight, mul-
ticolored, longhorned Mexican cattle for hides, horns, and tallow alone discovered that the animals were worth eight to ten
times more if delivered to butcher shops in the mountains. After
the rains had started the grass growing in the fall, vaqueros from
the southern part of the state pushed herds of a thousand head or

so each across the rugged Tehachapi Mountains and on through the San Joaquin Valley to the mines. Bandits and Indians harassed them, but those who got through rode home with canvas sacks stuffed with gold slugs. With these they embarked on reckless spending sprees. If they overextended themselves buying silks and satins for their wives, gold spurs and silver-mounted saddles for themselves, no matter. Their acres were unlimited, or so it seemed, and they could always borrow more money from local merchants at interest rates of 5 percent a month.

Gold slugs were the outcome of an early-day shortage of coins. Gold dust was an inadequate substitute for hard money. Inconvenience, small losses, and occasional fraudulent additions of brass filings accompanied the weighings that were part of every transaction. To overcome the difficulties, merchants and bankers paid premiums for whatever would circulate easily; American dollars, Mexican pesos, English sovereigns, French francs, Prussian florins, and Indian rupees—a bewildering mélange whose values shifted so rapidly that only experts could keep abreast of the quotations. Yet the growth of California's population was such that even this money supply was not enough.

To relieve the strain, private mints took to manufacturing circular, rectangular, and octagonal $20 and $50 gold slugs. The fabricators' profit came from the supposedly slight difference between the value of the gold actually contained in the slug and the value that was stamped on it under the supervision of an assayer appointed by the United States government. Since assaying and coining companies were often identical, the differences in value were at times greater than appeared. Rumors of such sleight of hand, never really proved, surrounded the profits that young David Broderick, fresh from New York City, earned in a private mint that he operated with a partner named Frederick Kohler. By reinvesting his profits in San Francisco real estate, Broderick swiftly reaped a fortune that he used for creating a Tammany-style political machine. Half a dozen years later, the organization lifted him into the United States Senate.

Profits as flamboyant as the ones that have been listed, plus multitudes of others, depended on an abnormal imbalance between supply and demand. Quick readjustments were inevitable. In 1854, the United States government established a branch mint in San Francisco, and by 1856 it had minted enough legal coins to drive substitutes off the streets. Scores of pie bakers and boardinghouse keepers moved into the mining towns; hundreds of farmers began growing fruit in the foothills.

Livestock operators from as far away as Texas and Missouri trailed great herds of cattle and sheep across thousands of miles of desert and mountains, and developed ranches from which to challenge the Californios. In spite of heavy consumption of meat throughout the 1850s, California by 1860 contained three million cattle and one million sheep, many times more than had grazed there during the heydey of the rancheros. As a result prices soon tumbled, a sharp discomfort to the more improvident Californios when their debts began falling due.

Fortune hunters in California were even less inclined than their counterparts in more settled regions to accept such disappointments. Wherever circumstances allowed, they tried to restore profits by creating artificial shortages. The obvious method, long since pioneered in the East, was either to buy out competitors or crush them with superior resources. Then, it was hoped, prices could be lifted back to their former levels.

Were such practices undemocratic? Except perhaps for those who were crushed, not many people thought so at the time. Current economic theory decreed that the government had no right trying to bring equality to the marketplace. Fiscal democracy, it was argued, flourished best when free men were allowed to work out their destinies in their own ways.

Work they did, with extraordinary vim. Again the express business is illustrative. Such swarms of private letter and package carriers followed Alexander Todd into the trade that prices plummeted from an ounce of dust per letter ($16 on the average) to 25 cents. Among the newcomers was a powerful express firm, Adams and Company, whose headquarters were in the East. Tired of struggling with hordes of rivals for shrinking returns, Todd sold his business to Adams.

After becoming one of California's principal handlers of

gold, Adams and Company drifted into the banking business, as did another rival from the East—Wells, Fargo and Company. (Banks as places of deposit were legal under the state constitution if they were not incorporated and if they did not issue certificates that could pass as money.) But in 1855 a sharp business depression caused Adams and Company to fail. Stepping swiftly into the vacuum, Wells, Fargo placed agents in nearly every hamlet in the state. During the next five years the company transported nearly $60 million in gold out of the mountains. Here was glamor indeed! Yet surprisingly there was almost no competition. The few independent expressmen who remained in the state were mostly small operators who served feeder routes too insignificant for the giant to bother with.

This thrust toward momopoly was of course nationwide. California's distinction lay in the speed with which combinations were effected and in the uniqueness of some of the struggles.

A prime example was James Birch, age twenty-one when he began hauling passengers between Sacramento and Mormon Bar in a springless frame wagon pulled by four ill-tempered horses. Four years later, Birch and a partner, Frank Stevens, controlled through their million-dollar California Stage Company, more than 80 percent of the coach travel in the central and northern parts of the state. Their swaying Concord vehicles, pulled by trained horses imported at costs of $2,000 or more per span, provided service along 1,500 miles of road—"the most extensive and complete line of stages," the company's advertisements boasted, "in THE WORLD." [1] Overwhelmed by such magnificence, the public scarcely noticed that other operators were for the most part relegated to unprofitable regions in the back country.

Another classic case of the thrust toward monopoly was the California Steam Navigation Company. Here geography was the determining factor. Every pound of freight and every passenger traveling toward the mines by sea had to pass through the Golden Gate. At San Francisco goods and people were trans-

---

1. John W. Caughey, *California: A Remarkable State's Life History,* revised edition (Englewood Cliffs, N.J.: Prentice-Hall, 1970), p. 294.

ferred to river boats. On these they traversed the northern part of the bay and then turned south into the San Joaquin River or north up the Sacramento.

San Francisco, it is worth noting, also had a monopoly of its own. Although promoters sought to locate other bayside towns closer to the interior, they never succeeded, largely because the lean clipper ships that sped merchandise around Cape Horn could not maneuver satisfactorily where the town's would-be rivals were located. Thus all transhipments to river boats and small coastal steamers took place in San Francisco. As the dominant wholesaling mart for the Pacific Coast, the city's ambitious merchants managed for several decades to control the entire region's economic, and to a large extent its political life.

At first there were not enough boats to meet the demands of river traffic. Pilots who could navigate the bay and the delta asked as much as $500 for supervising a single trip—a miserable expedition that in the early days might stretch to a week if the original little sailing vessels lay becalmed amidst the mosquito-infested swamps that bordered the sluggish streams. Paddelwheel steamers that cut travel time while providing lavish comfort for passengers were welcomed ecstatically. The stateliest, the *Senator,* is said to have netted $600,000 during her first year of operation.

Again competitors swarmed in. They slashed rates fiercely, and, because parts and labor were costly, they neglected maintenance. Meantime, with the excited acquiescence of the passengers, the steamer captains challenged rivals to headlong races that all too often ended in fatal boiler explosions. Bled white by the extravagant warfare, the owners of the principal boats formed an amalgamation in 1854 called the California Steam Navigation Company. By using its superior resources to drop rates while creating dazzling "palace boats" its rivals could not match, the CSN, as it was called, soon had commerce on the bay and rivers almost entirely in its grasp.

Monopoly did bring gains. Dangerous racing ended, schedules became more dependable, and shippers found that dealing with a single well-organized firm was preferable to being continually beset by hordes of salesmen representing patched-up craft of uncertain reputation. But there were also disadvantages. As soon as monopoly seemed secure, the company dispensed with its "frills" and boosted rates back toward early-day levels. These high charges in turn created new competition.

The company met the challenges ruthlessly. On April 5, 1864, to give a single example, a certain George Washington Kidd launched a rival boat, the *Washoe*. During the next six months the *Washoe* was "accidentally" rammed twice by the CSN ship *Yosemite*. When state inspectors absolved the monopoly of blame, cynics found an explanation in the firm's powerful lobby at Sacramento. Until the Central Pacific Railroad absorbed it, the California Steam Navigation Company was far and away the state's dominant business corporation, its grip fortified by a unique geographical situation that prevented potential rivals from outflanking it anywhere along the coast.

Odd circumstances sometimes created opportunities for one-shot monopolistic speculations. A particularly odious practice, made possible by alternating gluts and shortages of merchandise, was that of "market cornering." Because certain articles commanded extraordinary prices, Eastern wholesalers frequently rushed materials around Cape Horn in the mere hope that if luck broke right they might make a killing. Wholesalers in California, who should have been wiser, often gave way, when ordering new stock, to the same sort of uncalculating optimism. To complicate the problem, ships sometimes arrived just as heavy rains made roads into the mountains impassable.

At such times immovable heaps of merchandise piled up on the docks. Warehouses were in short supply, partly because of the fires that periodically swept the wooden towns during their infancy. Of necessity, whole cargoes had to be auctioned off at sacrificial prices, or, at times, simply abandoned. An oft-repeated bit of San Francisco folklore tells of muddy streets being paved with discarded sacks of flour from Chile, crates of tobacco from Virginia, and cookstoves from New England.

This improvident casting away of imports naturally created shortages. When demand began to pick up again, canny merchants surveyed the stocks that were on hand, made shrewd guesses about what was likely to arrive, and then tried to corner the market, even rowing in cockleshells into the mouth of the harbor to intercept incoming vessels and buy up any part of their cargoes that might interfere with the speculation. The most notorious instance was the flour monopoly of 1852 that skyrocketed the price of bread almost beyond reach and brought distress to thousands of consumers.

Although complaints were vociferous, government made no effort to intervene. The practice of market cornering continued with so little restraint (often bringing bankruptcy to speculators who miscalculated) that, as late as April 1856, the *San Francisco Chronicle* grumbled with inverse pride, "There is probably no other city in the world where this kind of gambling is carried on to a greater extent." [2] With some reason, a visiting British journalist wrote in 1861 of being struck by the fact "that almost every man is dressed in handsome black clothing, and there is a superficial appearance of Picadilly about the whole population. . . . [But] on examining these extra well dressed people you will remark a certain wildness about the eyes, showing that life is at high pressure. . . ." [3] An unusual percentage of San Franciscans, he added, were prematurely gray.

Grievous though such contrived shortages were, none created as much discontent as did the unavailability of land. During the three centuries preceding the gold rush, Americans, either as colonials or as citizens of an independent nation, had insisted on their right to push ever westward into the public domain, obtain a plot of ground, and on it create, as they could not have done in Europe, farms for themselves and their families.

One obstacle to acquiring land had been the greed of speculators—individuals or companies that bought up large blocks of land from the government as rapidly as it was surveyed (unsurveyed lands were not for sale) and then subdivided it for redistribution at high profit to themselves. That form of monopoly had been attacked in 1841, less than a decade before the gold

2. Quoted in Roger W. Lotchin, *San Francisco, 1846–1856* (New York: Oxford University Press, 1974), p. 75.

3. John Haskell Kemble, editor, "Andrew Wilson's 'Jottings' on Civil War California," *California Historical Society Quarterly* 32 (1953): 219.

rush, when Congress passed a pre-emption bill that allowed settlers to go onto unsurveyed lands, break out farms, and then, when surveying had been completed, buy 160 acres on easy terms for a modest $200.[4] In other words, wealthy speculators could no longer dominate the market simply by being first in line when large areas of surveyed land were opened for sale.

American would-be settlers in California were outraged, therefore, to discover that more than 12 million acres of the best agricultural land in the new state were owned—or at least claimed—by a mere 813 Mexican grantees. As far as the Americans could see, this land was inefficiently utilized by relatively small numbers of scrawny cattle, a program that struck them as both unwise and undemocratic.

The Californios did not understand the American attitude. Livestock was what the grant holders valued; land was simply the area where the animals grazed. Because land was abundant and demands for it light, the routines of acquisition had been treated lightly. True, the Mexican government had laid down rules about mapping and filing applications for a grant, surveying its boundaries, and occupying and improving the land. The seat of government, however, was far away. No one bothered to oversee requirements. So why fret about details?

As the probability increased that California would be occupied by some foreign power, carelessness slipped toward fraud. Why not let Mexican citizens acquire as much land for their livestock as was possible before the invaders arrived? The last two Mexican governors, Manuel Micheltorena and Pio Pico, handed out great blocks of pasturage with only the merest insistence on technicalities. Pico, indeed, had made grants even after the American landing at Monterey on July 7, 1846, antedating the papers just in case the conquerors asserted that United States possession began on that date—which they did.

Anticipating that many grants would be invalidated because

4. The Homestead Act, which allowed settlers to gain title to 160 acres of government land simply by "improving" it over a period of years, did not come into effect until 1862.

of "fraud" and resentful at being denied homesites by recent enemies of their country, thousands of California's new citizens defiantly squatted on the ground they wanted. To them, their action was nothing more than a pre-empting of their fair share of the public domain. Yet many of them, shiftless and belligerent by nature, made no effort to improve the sites they occupied lest they eventually be evicted as trespassers.

Conflicts were inevitable. Under the terms of the Treaty of Guadalupe Hidalgo, the United States was bound to respect all legitimate land titles in the areas ceded by Mexico. In California, where fighting had ended a year prior to the signing of the treaty, American immigrants were already encraoching on Mexican grants, and swift action was needed to resolve the tensions. March 1851 was at hand, however, before Congress, following precedents set as early as 1785, sent land commissioners west to review all grant titles.

The law under which the commission operated presumed titles to be invalid until each claimant proved otherwise. Every grantee accordingly had to gather together witnesses and documents (if the latter had not been lost), journey to wherever the commission was sitting (generally San Francisco), and there be subjected to legal procedures that to the Californios were unfamiliar and incomprehensible.

The loser of the first hearing, whether the government or the claimant, could appeal the decision to the district courts and, eventually, to the Supreme Court of the United States. The government's attorneys were particularly persistent. They appealed 417 decisions favoring the grantees—but won only 5 reversals. By contrast, the claimants appealed 132 adverse rulings and gained 98 reversals. The victories were often Pyrrhic, however. The long procedures piled such high legal costs on top of debts already incurred through extravagance at a time of sinking cattle prices that the owners had to barter away most of their salvaged property in order to retain a part. Thus the bulk of the grant lands ended in American hands regardless of court decisions— and in the hands of speculators, in the main, and not those of ordinary settlers. Not until truck and fruit farmers began paying high prices for land adaptable to intensive cultivation were some of the huge holdings subdivided into familiar American patterns.

Meanwhile, the uncertain state of titles tempted various entrepreneurs to manipulate grant boundaries in an effort to gain control of valuable resorces. One notorious case involved Las Mariposas on the east side of the San Joaquin Valley. The original title was illegal, for its claimant, Juan Alvarado, had met none of the conditions laid down by the Mexican government. Nevertheless, Alvarado in 1847 sold his claim to John Charles Frémont. The land commission ruled against Frémont, but the Supreme Court, influenced by the Pathfinder's reputation and powerful relatives, reversed the decision. Frémont thereupon realigned the grant boundaries in order to include three sections where gold had been discovered. During the riots that followed, several miners were killed or hurt.

Even more odorous were the battles over California's two great quicksilver mines, New Almadén and New Idria. The former, discovered by Mexicans in 1845, had soon passed into the hands of a British company but was wrenched from them by San Francisco capitalists on the basis of an adverse landgrant title of questionable validity—a hurt soothed by a payment of $1.75 million to the British for the improvements they had made on the property.

Soon New Almadén was producing more than half of the world's supply of mercury. In order to maintain prices, the company, whose principal stockholders also controlled the agency that distributed the mine's product throughout the globe, forced three or four small producers in Northern California to join them in a cartel designed to limit the amount of mercury placed on the market. The one chink in this proposed monopoly was the New Idria mine, located in the bleak Panoche Grande hills on the western side of the San Joaquin Valley.

Title to New Idria was claimed through another dubious land grant by a rascally San Francisco grocer named William McGarrahan. The New Almadén people sought to oust McGarrahan as they had the British. They set up an adverse claim through an overlapping grant. In this instance their case was sounder than

McGarrahan's, but the means they used to press it were unabashedly brazen. Government land records were destroyed, documents were forged, congressmen were bribed. Grant's secretary of the interior, Jacob Cox, resigned in protest over what was going on. Even the president was tarred because of unfortunate comments he made. "The wreck of his fame," the *Nation* editorialized, "is a national misfortune." [5] None of this bothered the owners of New Almadén. By twisting the supposedly impartial agencies of democracy to their will, they gained what they wanted.

The uproar over titles extended into the settlements. The town of Sacramento, for instance, was built on part of a grant awarded originally to John Sutter. Even before the gold rush, much of the proposed townsite had passed into the hands of speculators who raised prices beyond the point that homeseekers were willing to pay. Insisting that Sutter's title was not valid under the laws of military conquest, the angry immigrants sought to pre-empt the vacant lots they wanted by squatting on them. In August 1850, a posse set about evicting them. In the clashes that followed, several were killed, including Sacramento's sheriff. Many were injured. The mayor eventually lost his arm because of an infected bullet wound.

The situation in San Francisco was equally confused. Contending that the town, unlike San Jose and Los Angeles, had never been a legally constituted pueblo and that ground in the area was therefore open to pre-emption, squatters invaded every vacant lot that was not occupied by at least a heap of lumber or a pile of bricks. Legitimate property owners were so worried that, when their buildings burned down during one of the city's numerous fires, they fenced off the hot ashes to keep squatters at bay.

Swindlers compounded the uncertainties with spurious claims. The most calloused was José Limantour, a French trader who had been in California since the early 1840s. By means of cleverly forged documents, Limantour persuaded the United

<hr>

5. Claude G. Bowers, *The Tragic Era* (Cambridge, Mass.: Houghton Mifflin Co., 1929), p. 328.

States land commission that he owned most of the city of San Francisco. He was collecting quitclaim payments from occupants of "his" ground when he was exposed by the detective work of Edwin M. Stanton, later secretary of war in Lincoln's cabinet.

These widespread land-grant problems were symptoms of deep ills. Greed, or at least the hope of bigger and quicker returns than were available at home, had propelled most of California's treasure hunters to the far edge of the continent. Although thousands of them shifted in disillusionment from mining to other pursuits, they did not abandon the attitudes they had brought with them. They still wanted to make money in a hurry and were willing to take major risks in order to do it. "Everything," wrote banker William Tecumseh Sherman in one letter home, "is chance, everything is gambling." [6]

The majority of these chance-taking businessmen were not dishonest. They were energetic, ingenious, hard-working, and generous. Their responses to charity drives aimed at helping the victims of catastrophe were legendary. But, lacking interest in residing permanently in California, they shirked the responsibilities of citizenship. Men who should have been community leaders were unwilling to leave their businesses long enough to form citizens' action groups or attend serious political meetings. They evaded taxes and avoided jury duty.

Government became a tool for profit. Unable to exert more than meager influence on the national scene, California's ambitious politicians feuded fiercely with each other for the sake of patronage and the sense of power it brought. Municipal officers found fees for services so lucrative that they poured thousands of dollars into the coffers of local machines in the hope of retaining their jobs as sheriffs, police judges, recorders, assessors, and district attorneys. Candidates for elective posts sought to pile up winning margins by stuffing the ballot boxes, bullying voters through what was known as shoulder-striking (pushing and shoving at the polling places), and running complaisant fol-

6. Dwight L. Clarke, *William Tecumseh Sherman: Gold Rush Banker* (San Francisco: California Historical Society, 1969), p. 305.

lowers through the polls as many times as the nodding watchers allowed.

Civic corruption, unsafe streets, and inefficient administration were so rank in San Francisco that the city's normally negligent residents three times (1849, 1851, 1856) formed committees of vigilance designed to restore health to the community. But how well did they succeed?

Obviously, the self-annointed group of 1849 accomplished little, for a sterner follow-up was deemed necessary in 1851. The need to control arson was said to be one reason for calling the 1851 group into being. Certainly the problem was serious. Beginning on Christmas Eve 1849, and continuing sporadically until May 1851, a series of wind-whipped blazes leveled large sections of the wooden city. At least some of the fires were set to facilitate looting and, so it was said, to keep the populace cowed under the rule of the criminal class. The committee of 1851 attacked that class with vigor. It tried eighty-nine people, hanged four (one for a minor robbery), publicly whipped another, banished twenty-eight, turned fifteen over to the police for routine processing, and acquitted forty-one. They conducted their hearings decorously and self-righteously, but in secret and with scant respect for the due processes of the law. Only a lucky accident kept them from hanging two innocent men whom they had arraigned for murder on the strength of one witness's mistaken identification.

Arson? The vigilantes did not apprehend a single firebug. Apparently, they didn't even frighten any. According to historian Roger W. Lotchin, of the 253 fires reported in the San Francisco newspapers between 1851 and 1856, nearly a third were deliberately set.[7] The fact that the post-1851 blazes were less destructive than earlier ones was occasioned not by improved civic alertness but by the erection of better buildings, the provision of adequate water supplies, and the creation of volunteer fire departments.

Meanwhile, municipal affairs went from bad to worse. After the city hall had been demolished by a fire, it was replaced in a

7. Lotchin, *San Francisco,* pp. 176–177.

scandalous deal by an inferior theater building that had to be remodeled and shored up at exorbitant cost. Favored contractors, given franchises to build plank roads along the main thoroughfares, charged outrageous tolls for their use. High assessments were levied for other street improvements. General tax levies soared to such an extent that a refusal to pay them became a badge of prestige. At the same time priceless waterfront property was allowed to slide into the hands of conniving bidders at ridiculously low prices.

The embezzlements of "Honest Harry" Meiggs brought resentment to a head. Meiggs was a city alderman and a real estate promoter who brought himself to the edge of bankruptcy trying to develop property he owned at North Beach. He staved off ruin by forging $800,000 worth of city warrants and then fleeing in a chartered ship.

The investigations that followed revealed a municipal administration sunk in corruption, negligence, and ineptitude, its officers linked by intertwining ties to unsavory contractors and notorious gamblers.

At last the voters began to stir. The city charter was revised in such a way as to allow desirable administrative reforms. A refunding commission began struggling with the problem of how to deal with more than a million dollars' worth of fraudulent warrants (Meiggs had not been alone in his work). The state legislature passed a consolidation act that joined the city and county of San Francisco and facilitated the paring away of overlapping functions. Action groups rallied to the defense of the imperiled waterfront.

These efforts at reform took place in an atmosphere of great tension. The frenetic city, expecting the gold rush to continue unabated for years, had overbuilt badly during 1853 and 1854. Returns from the mines dwindled, however, and by the end of 1854 a depression gripped the city. In February 1855, runs developed on the banks. Nine of sixteen failed, as did several insurance companies and other businesses. By 1856, San Francisco was in the trough of a slump that would last throughout the rest of the decade.

Battening on the disgruntlement and fear was a fanatic who called himself James King of William. A onetime banker, King had lost his job and most of his property when his employer, Adams and Company, collapsed during the bank panic of February 1855. Switching to journalism, he launched a crusading newspaper, the *Daily Evening Bulletin*. In it he vented his bitterness on evil (as he saw it) in every form. Although he covered the field—peculating bankers, shyster lawyers, fat-cat contractors, and so on—he aimed his most vituperative barbs at duelists, gamblers, prostitutes, and the minions of David Broderick's political machine, most of them Irish.

His strident voice played skillfully on the prejudices of the times. Anti-Catholic, anti-Irish sentiment was virulent; in September 1855, the California branch of the nativist American or Know-Nothing party had captured most of the state's elective offices. San Francisco's Protestant churches almost unanimously praised King's denunciations of Irish politicians. Even more intense support came from the city's growing numbers of family women, who were trying to tame the masculine city and drive open prostitution at least from the better sections of town.

Outrage crystallized on November 17, 1855, when gambler Charles Cora ended a long feud with U.S. Marshal William Richardson by shooting the lawman down in a quarrel that embraced Cora's mistress, Arabella Ryan, operator of some of the city's plushest bordellos. Richardson had been spoiling for a fight (his wife, it seems, urged him on because Arabella had dared speak to her one night in a theater), and Cora pleaded self-defense in justification. Ignoring the point, King pretried the case with inflammatory rhetoric in the columns of his widely read *Bulletin*. When a divided jury failed to convict the gambler, the offended editor cried in loud black type on January 17, 1856, "Rejoice, ye thieves and harlots! . . . The money of the gambler and prostitute has succeeded and Cora has another respite!"

During the lull that preceded Cora's new trial, King shifted his attention to James Casey, an Irish politician (and publisher of a rival newspaper) who had been elected supervisor of the Twelfth Ward by means of what was called the Double Improved Back-Action Ballot Box, guaranteed to make stuffing almost foolproof. Annoyed at King's attentions, Casey challenged him in the middle of the street on the evening of May 14, 1856, and, when King appeared to reach for a gun, wounded him mortally.

Seething with indignation, the city formed yet another committee of vigilance. This was not mere mob action. The leaders had learned organization in 1851. With merchant William Tell Coleman again heading the drive, military organizers enrolled and began drilling thousands of recruits while a financial committee drummed contributions from willing businessmen and bankers. Newspaper opposition was stifled by threats of lost advertising revenues.

Within four days the committee was strong enough to move. About 10 A.M. Sunday morning, May 18, some 2,500 smartly disciplined men marched against the jail, where both Cora and Casey were being held. Unable to resist, the sheriff surrendered the pair. The executive committee of the vigilantes, acting as both judge and jury, found the two men guilty. Though the trial had been secret, the hanging, held on May 22 at the very time King's funeral procession was wending its way toward the cemetery, was public and attended by an enormous throng.

Instead of disbanding, as opponents of the group had hoped, the executive committee fortified itself in a store building and went about its self-delegated work of cleansing the city. Its cohorts raided the state armories for weapons, conducted searches without warrants, and defied a writ of habeas corpus issued by the state supreme court for the release of a certain prisoner. Bedeviled by such floutings of authority, California's wavering governor, twenty-eight-year-old J. Neely Johnson of the Know-Knothing party, on June 3 placed San Francisco under martial law and directed William T. Sherman, commanding general of the state militia, to restore order.

Only a handful of men responded to Sherman's call, and he failed to get arms for them from the federal arsenal at Benicia. Perhaps he did not try very hard. Most of his business associates supported the vigilantes and brought such pressure to bear on him, he admitted privately, that "I cannot act with that decision that would otherwise suit me." [8]

8. Clarke, *Sherman*, p. 226.

A more aggressive opponent of the vigilantes was David S. Terry, a strapping six-footer whom the Know-Nothings had elected to the supreme court at the same time they had elected Johnson. During a scuffle with vigilante police, Terry stabbed a man named Hopkins. The vigilantes promptly jailed the justice, but the nature of their prize troubled them. If Terry's victim died, the committee would be obliged to try their prisoner for murder—yet what would the reaction be if they convicted outside the due processes of the law not small-fry ne'er-do-wells like Cora and Casey, but a member of the supreme court?

The issue did not have to be faced. Hopkins rallied, and after seven weeks of detention Terry was released. The committee then reasserted its fortitude by executing two common murderers. Shortly thereafter, on August 18, 1856, it held a grand review of 6,000 parading members. At the conclusion of the ceremony, the organization was declared disbanded—with this proviso: the members would keep their rifles, most of them purloined from state armories, until after the November elections, just in case the venal old machine tried its tricks at the polls. Governor Johnson responded by refusing to end martial law, ineffective though it was, while state weapons remained in private hands. With General Sherman acting as negotiator, the surrender of the weapons was finally effected, and at last the insurrection was over.

What had been accomplished? The vigilantes had hanged four men, equaling the record of 1851. One frightened prisoner had committed suicide in his cell. Thirty undesirables had been banished from the city. Scores more, it was alleged, had fled in terror.

More importantly, the committee brought into being what it called the People's party. This coalition did not try to supplant normal groups. Rather, its members were urged to support at the polls those aspirants for office, whatever their party labels, who gained the endorsement of a twenty-one-man caucus drawn from the People's party. The impact of the endorsements was considerable. By hitching themselves to the coattails of the caucus, California's new Republican party, founded in Sacramento in March 1856, scored its first local triumphs. The endorsers also had their rewards. By keeping out of office the politicians they had been bullying all summer, most of them Irish functionaries of Broderick's machine, the leaders of the vigilantes quite possibly avoided harsh reprisals.

For some years the anomalous People's party dominated San Francisco politics. The men elected with their backing cut taxes drastically and supported reform movements already launched under the revised charter and the Consolidation Act. Declared one vigilante many years afterward, "We gave to San Francisco new life, new hope, and a happiness she had not known from the moment restless hordes began to settle in her midst." [9]

Sherman's view was different. Shortly after the parade of August 18, he wrote a friend that robberies and murders were continuing as usual.[10] The statement did not spring solely from his antipathy toward the vigilantes, for, on October 22, 1856, the *Alta California* reported, "Offenders against law and the public weal are scarcely less numerous or successful than of old." One out of every four fires continued to be set by unapprehended arsonists.

By contrast, it is worth noting how the problems of the harbor, one of the most magnificent in the world, were handled during approximately the same time. The turbulent story, redolent again with corruption, began with a mistake in judgment made by Gen. Stephen Watts Kearny when he was military governor of California.

Under Mexican law the alcalde of a pueblo had the right to sell lots anywhere within the town limits and place the proceeds in the pueblo treasury. Assuming that the privilege extended to "water lots," Kearny authorized the alcalde of San Francisco to auction off a strip of sometimes submerged tidelands along the San Francisco waterfront and use the revenue for the benefit of the town. The purchasers of the lots immediately filled in their acquisitions and sold the reclaimed land at handsome profits to contractors in search of flat ground on which to build. On the

9. Edward P. Flint, "My Recollections of Vigilante Days," *Sunset, The Pacific Monthly* 32 (1914): 1227.

10. Clarke, *Sherman*, p. 234.

basis of that precedent, the chronically bankrupt city again and again auctioned off more submerged water lots to speculators who promised to provide commercial and harbor facilities for the people.

As fast as the lots passed into private hands, generally at prices kept low by rigged bidding, the land was filled with sandy soil produced by the leveling of the nearby hills. These encroaching fills steadily pushed the city's wharf companies outward toward deep water where the state held jurisdiction over the bay and its floor.

In effect, every wharf was an extension of a street. Soon each was treated as a street, lined with shops and resounding with the clatter of drays and brawling longshoremen. Unsupervised by either the city or the state, these bridgelike streets were wretchedly maintained. Such gaping holes appeared in the sidewalks that unwary pedestrians often fell through and drowned—fatalities totaled fifty-seven during the first half of the 1850s, according to the *San Francisco Chronicle* of January 9, 1856.

Another problem was the loose sand that had been used for filling in the cove. It continually oozed outward with the tides, creating navigational hazards and requiring expensive replacement. Finally, in 1856, the year of the vigilante cleanup, a group of wharf owners and speculators led by Judge Levi Parsons—ever afterward he was called Bulkhead Parsons—offered to build a retaining wall around the entire harbor if the corporation they formed received a fifty-year franchise granting it the exclusive right to build all new warehouses and docks in San Francisco's harbor and collect tolls for their use. In return for the privilege the corporation would remit 10 percent of its net profits to the state, *after* it had already skimmed off the first 10 percent.

Objections from San Francisco's municipal government—but not from the vigilantes, for some of the proponents of the scheme were also vigilantes—slowed but did not halt the project. A bill granting the necessary franchises was pushed through the legislature by a narrow margin in March 1860. It was vetoed by Gov. John Downey. When Downey visited San Francisco shortly thereafter, he was marched behind brass bands to a frenzied reception, where he was eulogized by the president of the San Francisco Chamber of Commerce as the slayer of "one of the most odious and oppressive monopolies ever attempted to be foisted upon the commerce of any country in any age." [11]

The struggle was not over, however. San Francisco wanted to control the port through its own city government. Merchants in the interior, as fearful of a public as of a private monopoly, protested. The upshot, after fierce tugs of war in the legislature, was one of the compromises that seem necessary where governmental jurisdictions are divided. Control of the port was placed in the hands of a three-man board of harbor commissioners. Though all were ultimately responsible to the state, one commissioner was elected by the voters at large, one by the voters of San Francisco alone, and one by the legislature at Sacramento.

The struggle had been long, disorderly, and not free from taint. But duly elected representatives of the people had at last reached a permanent solution without violating anyone's civil rights or demeaning a whole city's people with the public spectacle of extralegal executions. The vigilantes, to be sure, had attacked their problems with dignity and a show of moral exaltation that impressed many observers. Perhaps, however, the visible righteousness arose from the participants' subconscious feeling that they were wiping away, through the punishment of scapegoats, their own errors of greed, moral laxness, and political indifference. [12] Absolved, they could then return to their money-making routines with a smug assurance that their duty had been done—done more quickly and with less effort than democratic procedures normally demanded. In a golden land such speed seemed important. But it seldom solved anything for very long.

11. Margarette L. Voget, "The Waterfront of San Francisco" (Ph.D. diss., University of California, 1943), p. 14.

12. This thesis is advanced in Bean, *California,* pp. 136–138.

7

Links with the Union

WELL aware of the rewards that awaited speed and safety in transcontinental transportation, various entrepreneurs wrought prodigies in moving traffic between gold-rush California and the East Coast. In 1851, the clipper ship *Flying Cloud,* loaded with heavy freight and looking truly like a cloud under her enormous spread of canvas, covered the 13,610 nautical miles (15,670 "land" miles) between New York and San Francisco in a trifle less than ninety days. Two years later, the *Northern Light,* traveling from west to east, made the run in seventy-six days. The captain of the *Northern Light* was so overjoyed by his accomplishment that he wanted the figures engraved on his tombstone. But for San Francisco wholesalers anxious about expediting their next shipment to the mines, it was not fast enough.

The Pacific Mail Steamship Company, fortified by an annual $900,000 subsidy from the United States Post Office Department, waxed rich by loading passengers, mail, light merchandise, and (on the eastern journey) gold bullion onto steamers bound for the Isthmus of Panama. There a railroad, completed in January 1855 at a cost of $7.5 million, carried the traffic through forty-eight miles of fetid jungle to the opposite coast. With luck, the trip to or from New York could be completed in three weeks or so. To a man ordering groceries, waiting for mail from home, or taking a trip East to woo a hesitant sweetheart, that was not good enough.

93

Danger was another factor. Epidemics originating in New York or New Orleans sometimes ravaged the overcrowded cabins of the paddle-wheel steamers. In the mid-1850s, cholera was particularly dreaded; in September 1855, 113 persons out of 650 aboard one ship died of the disease, and 104 of the bodies were buried at sea—that is, tossed overboard. (The remaining 9 deaths occurred after the ship landed at San Francisco.) Other ships ran aground or caught fire. In 1853, the *Independence* burned off Baja California with a loss of 125 of 300 passengers. Four years later, the sinking of the *Central America* in the Atlantic took 400 persons and $2 million in gold to the bottom of the sea. In a single year, Cornelius Vanderbilt, who was trying to develop a route by way of Nicaragua, lost five vessels to the supposedly gentle Pacific.

Monopoly, too, turned out to be costly. The Pacific Mail Steamship Company bought off Vanderbilt's competition by paying him $60,000 a month over a period of several years. Obviously, the tribute came not from Pacific Mail but from its patrons.

Visionaries insisted that railroad technology was far enough advanced to make such problems obsolete. Stirred by their enthusiasm, Congress in 1853 sent army surveyors westward to determine the most practical route across the western half of the nation. In California, promoters incorporated short lines designed to reach from San Francisco south to the farming country around San Jose and from Sacramento eastward into the mineralized foothills of the Sierra Nevada. Although immediate goals were limited, each company dreamed of eventually growing enough to become the Pacific terminus of whatever road the government authorized.

The trouble arose over the announcement of choices. Although the army's topographical engineers declared at the end of their surveys that five routes were feasible, the secretary of war, Jefferson Davis, gave his approval to the southernmost. His stated reason: a road in that area would be the cheapest to build and the easiest to maintain during winter.

Northerners rejected the recommendation. They wanted the proposed line to tie their factories, not Southern cotton plantations, to California's hungry markets and to shipping lanes aimed toward the Orient. To these economic goals they added moral principles: no national railroad should be placed where it might further the expansion of slavery.

The South, eager for Western alliances that would help offset the growing political power of the North, refused to let the prize slip from its grasp. The tug of war that resulted paralyzed congressional action.

The isolated West kept hoping, however. As the presidential election of 1856 approached, each of the three major parties—the badly divided Democrats, the rising Republicans, and the fading Know-Nothings—nailed into their platforms planks advocating in general terms the building of a transcontinental railroad. California's most persistent lobbyist for the scheme, Theodore Dehone Judah, locating engineer for the recently completed, twenty-two-mile-long Sacramento Valley Railroad, hurried East to lend such weight as he had. In Sacramento the official organ of the state's infant Republican party, the *California Daily Times,* tried to show where it thought emphasis should lie by stating on August 28, 1856, "We are in favor of Frémont [their party's presidential nominee] and the Pacific Railroad. We have nothing to do with abolition—nothing to do with slavery; we are willing to have it stay where it is."

The strategy proved unrealistic. Slavery could not be waved aside, even in California, although the nearest cotton plantation was more than a thousand miles away. Besides, Frémont had alienated Western voters by his handling of Las Mariposas (see above, page 82) and by his lusterless record as one of the state's first two United States senators. Although he ran a strong second to the Democrats' James Buchanan in the nation as a whole, he was soundly trounced at home not just by Buchanan but also by the colorless Know-Nothing candidate, Millard Fillmore. The railroad, no matter how practical it might be, it was going to have to wait for the settlement of the sectional battle.

Sensing this, impatient Californians had already begun exploring alternatives. In 1854, businessmen collected 75,000 signatures to a petition that asked the federal government to build a military road approximately along the Platte River-Humboldt

River route followed by the majority of covered-wagon immigrants. As its part in the project, the legislature authorized
enough bonds to finance a graded, all-weather connecting road
across the Sierra at Johnson Pass south of Lake Tahoe.

Alas for the plans. Although the federal road was approved, it
amounted to little more than a scratch and ended, unbelievably,
a hundred miles north of the state's "connecting" link. Moreover, the national highway was ignored by the government that
built it. When Postmaster General Aaron Brown of Tennessee in
1857 awarded John Butterfield, one of the founders of American
Express, a $600,000 annual subsidy for carrying mail twice a
week from both St. Louis and Memphis to San Francisco, he
specified that the contractor's stagecoaches travel by way of
Fort Smith, Arkansas, El Paso, Texas, Tucson, Arizona, and
Los Angeles.

The 2,800-mile journey was about 800 miles longer than the
Platte Valley route. Much of it lay through harsh deserts and
was open to harassment by Apache Indians. Thus, when Brown
declared that he had chosen the southern route so that horse-
drawn vehicles could avoid insuperable winter difficulties farther north, few Northerners believed him. The *Chicago Tribune*
called the contract "one of the greatest swindles ever perpe-
trated upon the country by the slave-holders." [1] Residents of
Northern California agreed acidulously. Mail and passengers,
they pointed out, could reach New York faster and with less
shaking about if they traveled by way of Panama. So scandalous
a subsidy must be the result of Southern scheming.

It is worth noting parenthetically that some Californians
were becoming as paranoid in their suspicions of the South
as were some Northern abolitionists. Many residents of the
Santa Barbara-Los Angeles-San Diego area, for instance,
wanted to break away from the mining counties and form their
own territory. Economics, not slavery, was their motive. The
base of their livelihood was livestock and related pursuits. They

1. Quoted in LeRoy Hafen, *The Overland Mail, 1849–1869* (Cleveland: Arthur H.
Clark Co., 1926), p. 92.

shared few common interests with the commercial, industrial, gold-mining residents of the north. The state government gave them scant help in fending off Indians and outlaws. They were the victims of a discriminatory tax system that excluded most mining claims from levies while blanketing all other forms of real property. The six so-called cow counties of the south had one-twentieth of the population of the twelve mining counties of the north, but paid twice as much in property taxes. (The figures do not include such major cities as San Francisco, Stockton, and Sacramento.) Yet when the southerners first sought separation from the north in 1852, the move was denounced in San Francisco as a proslavery plot.

Eventually, in 1859, the state legislature did pass a bill that would split the state in two. At that the misgivings shifted to Congress. A Southern scheme!—the nation's lawmakers refused to consider the measure. Thus, because of the slavery issue, there has never been a separate Southern California. What difference this has made to the history of the West Coast is one of those imponderables about which historians with a speculative cast of mind can ruminate endlessly.

Skillfull organization and gigantic effort enabled John Butterfield to ready his 2,800-mile "oxbow route," as it was called in derision, within the twelve months allowed him by the Post Office Department. His drivers confounded critics by frequently shaving forty-eight hours or more from the twenty-five-day schedule the government had stipulated for the run. Even so, the route was lightly patronized by travelers. ("You talk of hell?" groaned one passenger on alighting in San Francisco. "I've just been there for three weeks!") [2] Such discontent gave competitors hope that they could wrest the mail subsidy from Butterfield by proving the advantages of the central route.

The most aggressive of the contenders was the freighting firm of Russell, Majors, and Waddell. Driven close to bankruptcy by reverses suffered while freighting for the army during the "Utah

2. David Lavender, *The Big Divide* (Garden City, N.Y.: Doubleday and Company, 1948), p. 51.

war'' of 1857 and afterward in Colorado during the opening years of that territory's gold rush, the company partners decided on a bold move to regain their footing. They reorganized their firm as the Central Overland California and Pike's Peak Express Company and then, hoping to win a mail subsidy for the new company, set about advertising it by means of one of the most famous publicity gimmicks in American history, the Pony Express.

Eighty carefully selected young riders handling a total of five hundred horses set about speeding mail on regular schedules across the nearly two thousand miles between St. Joseph, Missouri, and Sacramento, California, in an elapsed time of ten days. The extraordinary performance bequeathed to the nation an indelible saga of derring-do, but economically it collapsed because of a fatal coincidence.

The Pony Express began operations in April 1860. Three months later, Congress authorized the construction of a telegraph line from the Missouri frontier to California. There was delay at first because four different California companies (one of which had recently strung wires across the Sierra to the vicinity of the new silver mines of Nevada) clamored for the right to build the western end of the system. Finally, Jeptha Wade of Western Union, contractors for the eastern part of the line, pulled the antagonists together as the Overland Telegraph Company. Pole-setting then began at Carson City, Nevada, in July 1861. After that the pace was headlong. On October 24, 1861, the converging wires met at Salt Lake City, and the Pony Express was dead, the creator not of victory but of still more debts for its promoters.

Still another irony attended the demise of the advertising stunt. In November 1860, Abraham Lincoln was elected president of the United States. In February 1861, delegates from the states that seceded as a consequence of his victory met in Montgomery, Alabama, to form what they hoped would be a separate nation.

Aware of the vulnerability of the southern mail route to Confederate attack and eager to maintain ties with gold-rich California and silver-rich Nevada, Lincoln's postmaster general decided to shift the mail subsidy to some company operating on the central route. There the firm that had tried so hard to win the plum was no longer capable of handling it. William H. Russell, one of the principal partners of the Central Overland California and Pike's Peak Express had just been jailed for embezzlement, and the company was demoralized. Accordingly, the mail subsidy, boosted now to $1 million annually, was awarded once again to John Butterfield, with the proviso that he abandon the facilities he had established four years before and rebuild his line farther north.

The shift was made under the shadow of a giant question mark: how long would his stagecoaches be able to continue rolling? The departure of Southern congressmen from Washington had removed sectional opposition to a transcontinental railroad. Simultaneously, the authorization of that railroad became, for the North, a matter of political expediency.

To Republican strategists in Washington, California's loyalties seemed as ambiguous as those of any of the border states along the old Mason-Dixon line. The gold rush had mixed together a volatile population from all sections of the United States. The reactions of those heterogeneous people, and of the foreign miners associated with them, to the coming struggle might have real bearing on the ultimate destination of the precious metals being mined in the West. Accordingly, Lincoln's administration was eager to curry the favor of the Californians. One means was to reward past loyalties, such as they were (Lincoln had carried the state with only 35 percent of the popular vote during the three-way race of 1860),[3] and hold out an earnest of more benefits to come by authorizing the railroad the Westerners wanted. That is to say, a physical bond was to be used for strengthening moral commitments.

The authorization of the railroad did not necessarily mean that it would be completed. San Francisco's ocean-shipping interests might well prefer that it not be finished. Pessimists contemplating the chill heights of the Sierra Nevada declared that it could not be. Skeptical observers of California's chaotic political and

3. The figures: Lincoln, 38,699 votes; Douglas, 37,957; Breckinridge, 33,969.

economic scene doubted that the project could command the
united effort that success demanded. And so it might be that
stagecoaches would continue as the principal means of overland
communication for years to come. Certainly, John Butterfield
had no sound way of gauging what he faced.

Adding still more confusion to the issue of loyalty in California was a struggle for political power between implacable
foes—red-whiskered David Broderick of New York and tall,
courtly William Gwin of Mississippi. Both were Democrats.
Both had migrated to California with the express purpose of
being elected to the United States Senate.

They reached San Francisco at almost the same time in June
1849. Gwin, fifteen years the elder and well connected in high
Democratic circles in the South, got off to a head start. He
played a leading role in the constitutional convention that was
held in Monterey and later was chosen by the first legislature,
along with Frémont, to be one of California's first senators.
Thanks to the federal patronage he gained as a result of his victory, he quickly made the proslavery wing of the Democratic
party, called the Chivalry Wing, a leading force in California
politics.

Although Broderick rose more slowly, he built solidly. Ab-
stemious, hardworking, and hardened early in his career by the
Tammany tactics of the Democrats in New York, he created a
machine that by 1857 was able to seize control of the California
legislature. From that eminence he not only named himself as
the next senator but also forced Gwin, as the price for being returned to Washington, to grant him the right to fill all federal offices in California. President Buchanan refused to accept the
bargain, however, and continued to name Gwin supporters to
office in the West.

To Broderick, this seemed like a blatant double-cross. Returning to California, he poured personal abuse on his foes during the state elections of 1859. Taking offense, one of Gwin's
friends, David S. Terry, former justice of the supreme court,

replied in kind. The upshot was a duel with pistols between a United States senator and one of California's most highly placed jurists.

The meeting took place near the ocean south of San Francisco at dawn on September 13, 1859. Some eighty spectators watched Broderick's shot go astray, and then at the next instant saw Terry's bullet plow into his opponent's chest.

The statewide revulsion that followed sorely wounded Gwin's followers. During the presidential campaign of 1860, enough of Broderick's friends voted with the Republicans to give Lincoln his razor-thin victory in California. That victory in turn helped prepare the way for an alliance of Republicans and Union Democrats that in 1863, and for several years thereafter, dominated California politics.

This uneasy political alliance in what was then a normally Democratic state mirrored some of the mixed reactions with which California greeted the onset of war. Many people, perhaps a majority, went on about their business as if they felt the conflict was too remote to be of real concern. This indifference led some Southern sympathizers to propose that the entire Pacific Coast and the Southwest break away from both antagonists in the East and form an independent Pacific Republic. Behind the suggestion, which never made much headway, lay the hope that if the West seceded, then the North would be deprived of active help from California's gold producers.

Other Southerners were less restrained. Uniting in secret societies with such names as the Knights of the Golden Circle and the Committee of Thirty, they drew up wild plans for sudden coups. At first they looked for leadership to General Albert Sidney Johnston of Texas, commander of the Military Department of the Pacific. If Johnston had heeded the schemers and had rallied a guerrilla army to seize the federal installations under his command, the impact might have been profound. Instead, he scrupulously avoided any betrayal of his trust. Although he resigned his office, he stayed on the job until relieved by a Union replacement. He then rode east to join Robert E. Lee's gathering forces. Deprived of his support, Southern sympathizers were reduced to spiriting volunteers for the Confederate army out of the state past Union guards and making one harebrained attempt to outfit a privateer for raiding ships carrying California gold—an effort that aborted when the would-be pirates were captured while their ship was still in San Francisco Bay.

Earnest Northerners sought to counteract both indifference and Southern plotting by whipping up pro-Union sentiment through carefully orchestrated parades and rallies on each Fourth of July and after each Union victory. In several cities patriots who felt they could not leave their own affairs long enough to enlist in the army solaced themselves by drilling in the evenings with home guards modeled after the vigilantes of 1856. Private groups arrogated to themselves the right to sift through the credentials of suspect residents. After the Reverend William Anderson Scott, Southern-born minister of San Francisco's Calvary Presbyterian Church, undertook to ask God's blessing on both Abraham Lincoln and Jefferson Davis, one such cadre hanged the preacher in effigy on the porch of his own church, after which his trustees forced him from the pulpit—and then, as a parting gift, presented him with an $8,000 silver tea service. Out in the small towns of the Central Valley, mobs resorted to their own form of pressure tactics by smashing the presses of the handful of newspapers that espoused the Confederate cause.

Nearly 16,000 men, approximately 4 percent of California's total population, enlisted in the Union army. One column marched through the heat-seared deserts of the Southwest into New Mexico to help repeal invaders from Texas, but arrived after the Southerners had already been driven back by volunteers from Colorado. Another column was sent into Utah to keep an eye on two groups whose loyalty was doubted in Washington, the Mormons and the Shoshoni and Northern Paiute Indians. Members of this column distinguished themselves by making several mineral strikes in Utah and by slaughtering, near Franklin, Idaho, some 400 Shoshoni men, women, and children in one of the most horrifying Indian "battles" of the West.

Alarms closer to home now and then reminded busy Californians that a war really was on. The sharpest came in 1863, when Confederate privateers sailed into the North Pacific and began attacking California-based whaling ships on the assumption that whale oil, widely used in those days for illumination, was vital to the Northern war effort. Suddenly, San Francisco seemed naked and exposed to its inhabitants. "A bombardment of an hour," quavered the *Alta California* on March 17, "would set the town . . . on fire in fifty places. If a high wind—not at all improbable in summer—should be added, there is no power that we possess that would be sufficient to save San Francisco from destruction."

A series of frantic telegrams induced the navy to send a dismantled ironclad monitor, the *Camanche,* around the Horn in the sailing ship *Aquila.* Unhappily, a gale sank the *Aquila* shortly after she had docked at her destination. The *Camanche* was not retrieved from the bottom of the bay and fitted for service until the war was nearly over. Except for expense, the delay did not matter, however. No Confederate warships appeared. No sound of a gun fired in combat was heard anywhere along the West Coast.

Deprived of direct contact with the war, many Californians participated vicariously. Stirred to enthusiasm by the impassioned oratory of minister Thomas Starr King, they contributed $1.23 million to the Union's Sanitary Commission, a Civil War counterpart of today's Red Cross. This was 25 percent of all the money collected for the agency in the two dozen states and territories loyal to the Union. Generosity was only part of the donors' motives, however. They were also washing away feelings of guilt about the factors of distance and self-interest that kept them from enlisting—a mood akin to the one that prompted an elderly banker, Ralph Fretz (who, incidentally, was a native of New Orleans) to bequeath $20,000 to the Union in his will. The gift, he explained, was partial compensation for his inability to help defend with arms "the best government man ever had." [4] People who felt that way naturally gravitated toward a party formed by amalgamating Republicans with Union Democrats.

4. *Daily Alta California* (San Francisco), June 20, 1867.

To what extent Congress's authorization of a Pacific Railroad helped strengthen pro-Union sentiment, as it was supposed to do, is impossible to say. The news that the necessary bill had passed did touch off torchlight parades of rejoicing in both San Francisco and Sacramento. But it also sent shock waves through San Francisco's commercial community. Most of the Bay City's leading capitalists were deeply involved in ocean and river freighting, stagecoaching, and related activities. They had no desire to have their businesses undercut by a railroad or have their city's pre-eminence as a wholesaling mart challenged by a rail terminus at Sacramento. Accordingly, they attacked the new enterprise with a vehemence that for a time caused its builders almost as much trouble as did the awesome terrain of the Sierra Nevada.

The first to feel the animosity was Theodore Judah, the West's self-appointed lobbyist for the bill. Believing in the summer of 1860 that passage was nearer than was actually the case, he had hurried to California from Washington to locate a feasible route across the mountains north of Lake Tahoe and then to form a company capable of offering itself to Congress as the logical builder of the road. Aided by residents of mining towns that would benefit from the railroad, he soon found a suitable route, but, when he approached San Francisco with his maps and plans, he was rebuffed.

Furious, he shifted his efforts to Sacramento. There he won the support of a handful of merchants. Chief among them were Mark Hopkins and Collis P. Huntington, partners in a prosperous hardware store; Charles Crocker, proprietor of a dry-goods emporium; and Leland Stanford, a wholesale grocer who was also the Republican candidate for the governorship of California.

They were not rich men, but they did not have to be. Although California laws set forth strict provisions about the amount of stock needed to incorporate railroad companies (the total varied according to the number of miles involved), no more than 10 percent of the face value of the certificates had to be paid for in cash at the time of subscription. Thus the Big Four, as Judah's principal backers eventually were called, were able to gain control of a presently worthless but potentially lucrative firm, the Central Pacific Railroad, for an outlay of only $1,500 each.

The company formed, Judah ran a survey of his hastily chosen route. It climbed 7,000 feet from Sacramento to a crossing of the Sierra at what was called Donner Summit. Building the steep grades, tunnels, cuts, fills, and trestles along the 140-mile stretch to the Nevada border would cost, he estimated, $13 million, a staggering sum just to begin the road. But there were rich temptations as well. A new mining mania was shaking California. Thousands of miners and their suppliers were streaming toward the great silver strikes of the Comstock Lode, located in the desert mountains of Nevada, just east of the Sierra's precipitous foothills. As soon as the railroad had crossed the Sierra, it could thrive on that traffic alone. In fact, it would be possible to draw revenue from the mines even before the rails reached Nevada. Construction of the railbed would necessitate a wagon road for hauling supplies. This road could be turned into a toll highway. Extended to Virginia City in the heart of the Comstock area, it would pull traffic away from the rough, difficult Johnson Pass road south of Lake Tahoe and add funds to the company coffers while the rails were being laid.

As soon as Congress acted, other funds benefiting the railroad could be expected from the state, especially if Leland Stanford, the new president of the Central Pacific, became governor of California. In the face of all that, $13 million did not look hopeless, even to middle-class storekeepers.

For a time events went as planned. On September 4, 1861, Stanford was elected governor. The next spring Congress passed the long-delayed railroad bill, and President Lincoln signed it into law. Its terms looked generous. In return for building the road, two companies, the Union Pacific in the East and the Central Pacific in the West, were to be given alternate sections of land lying within a ribbon seamed down the middle by the new rails—a total of 6,400 acres for each linear mile of track constructed. Two years later the width of the ribbon was broadened to forty miles, in effect doubling the gratuity.

Until settlers began moving west, the land would have little value. As an added inducement, therefore, the government agreed to lend each company from $16,000 to $48,000 per mile of track laid, depending on the nature of the terrain the builders faced. The loans were made in the form of 6 percent, thirty-year bonds that the companies received in installments after completing specified amounts of construction. The borrowers could then finance the next stretch of track by selling the bonds in the open market for whatever they would bring. As security for the loan, the government initially held a first mortgage on rolling stock and completed track. In 1864, this was reduced to a second mortgage so that the companies could raise additional money by issuing first-mortgage bonds of their own.

As soon as Congress had acted, the Central Pacific, openly supported by Governor Stanford, began pressing for state and county aid in California. In order to raise money for immediate needs (no United States bonds would be available until a specified amount of track had been laid), the Central Pacific also sought to sell its stock to the general public.

At that point trouble began. Adverse whispering campaigns in San Francisco were so effective that the company representative there was able to sell only 14 shares of $100 par-value stock! Sacramentans subscribed to about 8,000 shares, but, since only 10 percent of the nominal value had to be paid in cash at the time of subscription, this produced only $80,000, hardly enough to build the first bridge over the American River.

As fast as bonds to aid the company were approved by the state legislature or by the electors in the counties through which the rails would pass, their legality was challenged in the courts. In time the company worked out compromises that brought it part of what had been authorized, but the delays were costly. Moreover, Huntington, who was delegated to market all bonds in the East, had to sell them at severe discounts and then take his money in depreciated greenbacks. Greenbacks could not be used in California, however, for the state stubbornly refused to accept paper as legal tender. At times the greenbacks had to be turned back into gold at rates of as little as 33 cents on the dollar. At one point federal bonds with a face value of $1.25 million produced in California only $400,000 worth of supplies. As for goods bought in the East, they had to be shipped around the Horn at dismaying cost.

It was partly to offset these problems that the Central Pacific established its own construction company, known eventually as the Contract and Finance Corporation. This company charged the railroad top prices for its work and accepted, as an outside company would not have done, Central Pacific stock as part of its pay. Soon the Big Four controlled, through the Contract and Finance Corporation, some 90 percent of all the Central Pacific's paper, a potential bonanza of breathless proportions if ever the railroad was completed.

During these manipulations Theodore Judah was thrust farther and farther away from the center of what had begun as his dream. Bitterly, he left for New York, hoping to obtain enough backing to regain control of the company. In Panama he contracted yellow fever, from which he died—an ultimate irony, since the very railroad he hoped to complete would end that threat to travel.

By the time the Civil War was over, the rails had reached only fifty miles into the mountains. But they were also 2,000 feet up, and momentum was growing. When the fifteen tunnels that had to be chipped through the cliffs proved to be bottlenecks, Charles Crocker, who headed the construction company, put rails and dismantled locomotives onto fleets of sleds and hauled them during winter across the summit into Nevada, where he began building a new segment of track far in advance of the main line. Soon he had 10,000 workers, most of them imported from China by Oriental labor contractors in San Francisco, strung out through the mountains and deserts.

Seeing the handwriting on the wall, John Butterfield sold his stage line to Wells Fargo. Shortly thereafter, the same organization bought out Ben Holladay, who had taken over the remnants of the Central Overland California and Pike's Peak Express. Wells Fargo then reorganized its new network of lines in such a way that they would act as feeders for the railroad, not as competitors. For, by then, the question was not whether the railroad would be finished but how far it could thrust, for the sake of increased land grants and subsidies, before meeting the Union Pacific.

The junction came on May 9, 1869, at Promontory, Utah.

Telegraphic news that the golden spike had been driven touched off gala celebrations among speculators contemplating the boom that would come when thousands of new residents poured in over the iron highway. During the excitement few people remembered the rhetorical questions that an obscure journalist named Henry George had asked the preceding October in an article in San Francisco's *Overland Monthly.*

"We want great cities, large factories, and mines worked cheaply, in this California of ours!" George had written. And then he turned the coin to look at the other side.

> Would we esteem ourselves gainers if New York, ruled and robbed by thieves, loafers, and brothel-keepers; nursing a race of savages fiercer and meaner than any who ever shrieked a war-whoop on the plains; could be set down on our bay tomorrow? Would we be gainers, if the cotton-mills of Massachusetts with their thousands of little children who, the official papers tell us, are being literally worked to death, could be transported to the banks of the American [River at Sacramento]?

Certainly, there would be more luxury and culture after the railroad came. But, George predicted, the coming of industrialism would also bring more squalor and misery. There would be less personal independence, less open-handedness, less of that breadth of thought and feeling and freedom that gave California "its peculiar charm." And would the commonwealth, he wondered, be able to resist the political effects of the concentration of great wealth in the hands of the few? Specifically, he named the Central Pacific as the dragon he feared most.

Few heeded. After two decades of isolation California had at last become welded to the Union. Prior events—even the unauthorized constitution of 1849 and the emotional outpouring of money into the North's Sanitary Commission—had in a sense been symbolic only, and the people had grappled with their destiny as if it had been a thing apart from the concerns of the rest of the nation. Now they had been returned to the mainstream of progress. What kind of perversion was it that focused on the nation's ills rather than on its accomplishments—accomplishments that California would at last be able to duplicate within its own favored borders?

8

In Pursuit of the
Fading Dream

T was appropriate that, of the four creators of the Central Pacific Railroad, Charles Crocker was the one to dramatize, in terms any American of 1869 could grasp, what the accomplishment meant. His three associates had migrated to California by sea. Crocker had traveled from the Missouri River by land, a trip that had taken four months plus a few days. Nineteen years later, he ordered a special car hitched to a sequence of trains that were granted fast clearance all the way to New York. The journey took four days plus a few hours. With him, Crocker carried not flour, rice, jerky, and dried beans, as on his first trip, but crates of California strawberries, cherries, oranges, and roses kept fresh by ice imported from the glaciers of Alaska.

The journalists who interviewed him were awed. Here was the California dream made visible in fruits that had reached perfection in the West weeks before similar produce, minus the oranges, would ripen in either New York or New England. And where but in California would thousands of tons of ice be imported each year from natural refrigerators near the Arctic Circle?

Then there was Crocker himself. Hearty and grossly overweight, he did not seem exceptional. Neither did his partners, all of whom had started their California careers as shopkeepers. Yet somehow the *ambiance* of the Far Coast had exalted them enough so that they had been able to meet the extraordinary challenges of the country's last frontier. Weren't upward climbs like that what America had always been about?

The symbolism of the train trip can be overstated, of course. In one sense Crocker had simply been crowing like any rooster. In another sense the crossing had been a promotional stunt calculated to increase train travel by stimulating desire. In 1869, those motives were already a California staple. As early as 1854, other braggarts had stripped the first 116 feet of bark from a redwood tree and had sent the monstrous peel in segments to P. T. Barnum, who had reassembled the shell and had exhibited it with spectacular success in New York. The message was clear: Come West and see for yourself how big we are.

In time such stunts bred satirical counterfables: "Did you know there's a ten-story building in California without a staircase or elevator in it?" "Really! How do people get to the top?" "Climate, boy, climate."

Californians laughed, too—with this difference. Even when the mockery cut deepest, a sizable majority never lost their faith that California *was* exceptional. Consider John S. Hittell. An educated and capable man, Hittell edited San Francisco's respected *Daily Alta California*. As a sideline, he poured out over the years a series of books that described in detail both the advantages and drawbacks of his chosen state and its inhabitants.

In one of those books, published in 1873, he undertook to define the typical Californian. Now, by 1873, Hittell knew perfectly well that no single image could blanket the state's unamalgamated mix of Americans from the North and from the South; there were Irish, English, French, Germans, Australians, Chileans, Mexicans, Chinese, and the few thousand crushed Indians still alive. But when he came to deal with an ideal type, incompatibilities disappeared. Californians were "a race marked by large size, healthy bodies, industrious habits, and clear complexions." Democratic, too. "The sandshoveler and the millionaire may change places tomorrow," and they acted accordingly, neither cringing nor strutting. Or, to quote again from the state's first major historian, Hubert Howe Bancroft, the West Coast was the inevitable place for "a final display of what man can do at his best . . . surrounded by conditions such as have never before fallen to the lot of man to enjoy." [1]

Such hyperbole was not the product of blindness. Both Hittell and Bancroft were capable of seeing and excoriating the wrong-doings of their fellows. It was Bancroft who described California's treatment of its Indians as "one of the last human hunts of civilization, and the basest and most brutal of them all." [2] Even so, he could rhapsodize about man at his best. Californians had already accomplished so much during their short stay on the coast that the future was bound to be bright.

Items: from 1860 to 1870, the population of the United States as a whole rose 26 percent; California's increased by 47 percent. During the next ten years, 1870–1880, America's rate of growth remained constant, 26 percent. California's climbed still higher, to 54.3 percent, so that by 1880 the state, not yet thirty years old, could boast of 865,000 residents.

Item: San Francisco's population jumped from 57,000 in 1860 to 234,000 in 1880—more people than lived in Washington and Oregon combined. The city's influence over the surrounding region, wrote that shrewdest of English observers, Lord Bryce, was "more powerful . . . than is any Eastern city over its neighborhood." [3] The neighborhood, moreover, was enormous. California's web of commerce reached from the ice fields and seal fisheries of Alaska to the tea plantations of the Orient. San Francisco money financed much of Portland and for a time bolstered the control that the Oregon Steam Navigation Company exerted over the interior of the Pacific Northwest. San Francisco coastal steamers fed Arizona by way of Mexican en-

1. John S. Hittell, *A History of San Francisco and Incidentally of the State of California* (San Francisco: A. L. Bancroft and Co., 1878), pp. 448–455 *passim.* Hubert Howe Bancroft, *Literary Industries* (San Francisco: Bancroft Co., 1890), pp. 4–5.

2. Quoted in Charles Wollenberg, "Ethnic Experiences in California," *California Historical Quarterly* 50 (1971): 224.

3. James Bryce, *The American Commonwealth*, 2 vols. (1891; revised edition, Chicago: Charles H. Siegel and Co., 1910), 2: 388.

trepôts on the coast of the Gulf of California. The new railroad hoped to make Utah as much an appendage of the city's trading marts as Nevada already was.

For relaxation, San Francisco socialites watched some of the nation's finest theatrical stars perform in the 2,900-seat California Theater. Art institutes flourished. But the great visual proof that the city had left its crude beginnings was the Palace Hotel, designed by William Ralston of the Bank of California to be one of the grandest hostelries in the world. It filled a full block. Its seven stories and eight-hundred high-ceilinged rooms were grouped around a huge central court roofed with opaque glass and floored with marble, across which carriages decorously rolled to deposit each day's guests amidst a forest of potted palms. Clustered within easy walking distance were fine shops, restaurants, and other amenities which, in Hittell's words, provided the people of the western third of America with "compensation for the toils and privations of frontier life." [4]

Although the gathering in and redistribution of goods and money were San Francisco's chief preoccupation, manufacturing also flourished. During the Civil War a shortage of ships and skyrocketing insurance costs had forced self-reliance. The suppliers of shoes, schooners, dry docks, cigars, sugar, wagons, blasting powder, and the like had stepped up the pace of their output. Because the North was deprived of cotton by the conflict, crash demands arose for wool to make uniforms and army blankets. Responding eagerly, California ranchers within a decade doubled the number of sheep they raised. Because they improved breeds at the same time, the wool clip jumped from 5.5 million pounds in 1862 to 22 million pounds a decade later. Woolen mills for processing part of this outpouring quickly appeared, and when the war was over they shifted, with relatively few casualties, from military to domestic markets.

Even more important was the fabrication of iron. Agriculturists needed plows; construction workers, shovels and picks. The operators of sawmills, mines, and river steamers demanded boilers; hydraulic miners and the managers of city water works

4. Hittell, *History of San Francisco*, p. 443.

and sewage systems needed endless miles of pipe. Although the Central Pacific Railroad imported its locomotives and rails from the East, the smaller lines radiating outward from San Francisco Bay called on the city's foundries for the bulk of their needs. Lumber mills throve, first along the northern coast, where giant redwoods grew close to tide line, and later, as the Central Pacific inched eastward, among the ponderosa and sugar pines of the Sierra Nevada.

Capital was either imported from New York and London or produced at home from a resource most frontier communities could not match—precious minerals. Having exhausted the shallow placers that brought the first rush of people west, Californians began sinking deep shafts into the quartz veins of the foothills. Where conditions were right, they also disintegrated entire hillsides by means of water hurled under high pressure from giant hydraulic nozzles. Both operations were expensive—hydraulic mining demanded complex systems of reservoirs, ditches, and canyon-spanning flumes—but because of them the long decline in gold production was checked. From 1865 to 1883, when the courts and the legislature curtailed hydraulic mining because of its destructiveness, output held at an average of about $17.5 million a year.

Added to that yield was the erratic outpouring of gold and silver from Nevada, a lush bonanza that San Francisco entrepreneurs quickly siphoned into their own coffers. Chief of the trans-Sierra producers was the fabled Comstock Lode of Virginia City. The giant fissure was two and a half miles long, scores of feet wide, and almost infinite in depth. The huge gash was not uniformly rich, however. Much of its ore was of such low grade that mining it did not pay. What counted were big blocks of rich gold and silver compounds scattered like plums throughout the otherwise worthless rock in the vein.

Because no one could tell where these plums might be encountered, mining companies kept assessing their stockholders to keep driving on. Sometimes they were rewarded; more often they were not. An account of the annual returns of the lode as a whole indicates how unpredictable results were. In 1864, the Comstock yielded $16 million; in 1869, $7 million. In 1876, the figure peaked at $38 million; five years later, it was down to $1.4 million.

Titanic legal battles were triggered by real or alleged trespasses by one company on another's ground. Financial wars raged for the control of milling facilities and supplies of water and timber. When upswings seemed in the offing (and appearances were sometimes contrived by mine superintendents and their cronies), trading in shares on the San Francisco Stock Exchange grew frantic. Such a situation, which diverted an estimated $400 million in capital from more stable enterprises, was by no means healthy. And yet Nevada's gold and silver, added to California's own output, had much to do with keeping the state's economy at fever heat for long, if intermittent, periods—and much to do also with the persistence of the image America held of California as a land of unfailing promise.

Agricultural developments lengthened the list of impressive statistics. Miners and swiftly growing urban centers provided ready markets for food. Convenient waterways along the lower reaches of the Sacramento and San Joaquin valleys provided easy transportation routes. A hothouse climate did the rest. Wherever land was available for intensive farming around Sacramento city or Stockton or in the smaller valleys that open into San Francisco Bay, fruits and vegetables appeared—as one newspaper said, like "spontaneous productions." [5] Another market was provided by turning enormous quantities of grapes into wine and brandy, both in the San Francisco area and in the gravelly soils of the Los Angeles Basin.

Far outstripping intensive farming was the stampede into wheat growing. Wheat is a staple crop on most frontiers. Initial investments are relatively low, and the crop can be harvested and shipped within a year. To men whose land titles stemmed from Mexican grants of questionable validity, these advantages were paramount, for they could avoid expensive improvements and still utilize their land while awaiting court decisions.

5. *Sacramento Transcript*, November 1, 1850, quoted by Rodman Paul, "The Beginning of Agriculture: Innovation *vs.* Continuity," in George H. Knoles, editor, *Essays and Assays: California History Reappraised* (Los Angeles: California Historical Society and the Ward Ritchie Press, 1973), p. 30.

Still more significant were the advantages of geography and climate. Though the deep alluvial soils of the coastal valleys and especially of the huge Central Valley appeared dead and brown at the end of the rainless summers, they were actually bursting with life-giving minerals. They were flat. They contained few rocks and almost no trees. As soon as the first rains of fall had softened the cracked earth, plowing was simplicity itself, and growth, which needed no stimulation (until after the minerals in the soil had been depleted) was phenomenal.

The grain sprouted in the spring, ripened as the rains dwindled, and was harvested with no worries about weather. It could stand uncovered in the fields until shipping was arranged. The fierce sun even improved the kernels, turning them so flinty that they could be transported long distances without deterioration.

The result was "one of the most extraordinary of all agrarian episodes." [6] In 1860, the state's wheat farmers produced six million bushels. Drought and a shortage of shipping retarded development during the Civil War—yet the drought turned out to be an aid because it removed hundreds of thousands of cattle from the parched ranges. With the return of peace and normal rainfall, plowmen swarmed across the empty lands. Their output in 1870 topped twenty-two million bushels. And there was this bonus. Industrialists had to import most of the coal and iron used in their burgeoning gas works and foundries. Until the wheat stampede gathered headway, the ships bringing in those materials had to sail away from San Francisco under ballast. Afterward they carried payloads of grain to huge wheat markets at Liverpool, England, a development that reduced freight rates on all three commodities.

The leaders who pushed development in manufacturing, mining, shipping, and agriculture acted with an audacity and ingenuity that continually impressed visitors. "London and New York and Boston," wrote newspaper editor Samuel Bowles of Springfield, Massachusetts, "can furnish men of more philosophies and theories, . . . but here in San Francisco are the men of acuter intuitions and more daring natures; who cannot tell

6. Paul, "Beginning of Agriculture," p. 32.

you why they do so and so, but who will do it with a force that commands success." [7]

Hydraulic mining, whose techniques soon spread throughout the world, was a California innovation. So was the system of square-set timbering that Philip Deidesheimer devised for withstanding the exceptional widths of the Comstock vein. Another California engineer, A. S. Hallidie, invented a special flat cable for lifting mine hoists from great depth and later adapted it to hauling cable cars up and down San Francisco's abrupt hillsides, a bit of ingenuity that appreciably increased the amount of city land available for building. Lumbermen produced special machines for handling massive redwood logs; shipbuilders devised special schooners for worming in and out of the coastal indentations where mills were located, and special scows for hauling hay and barley across San Francisco Bay to the tens of thousands of horses that kept the city mobile.

Wheat farmers, eager to speed the preparation of the earth in the fall, bolted several plowshares onto a single beam and so produced the "gang plow," which they worked in echelons. Novelist Frank Norris, who watched them operating near the town of Hollister and then for literary purposes transferred the scene to the San Joaquin Valley, left a vivid description in his novel *The Octopus*.

> The plows, thirty-five in number, each drawn by its team of ten [horses], stretched in an interminable line. . . . Each of those plows held five shears, so that when the entire company was in motion, one hundred and seventy-five furrows were made at the same instant. . . . A prolonged movement rippled from team to team, disengaging in its passage a multitude of sounds—the click of buckles, the creak of straining leather, the subdued clash of machinery, the cracking whips, the deep breathing of nearly four hundred horses, the abrupt commands and cries of the drivers, and, last of all, the soothing murmur of the thick brown earth turning steadily from the multitude of advancing shears. [8]

7. Samuel Bowles, *Our New West* (Hartford, Conn.: Hartford Publishing Co., 1969), p. 340.

8. Frank Norris, *The Octopus* (New York: Doubleday and Co., 1901), pp. 127–128.

Not all innovations were mechanical. In order to avoid competing with Midwestern wheat in the commodity pits of Chicago and New York, California brokers turned to Liverpool, England. This involved developing a complex chartering system capable of bringing the right number of ocean freighters—hundreds of them, the exact count varying with the volume of each year's harvest—into San Francisco Bay at the time their services were needed. Chief architect of this maritime chess game was Isaac Friedlander, a towering three-hundred-pound immigrant from South Carolina.

Other experiments dealt with quality of product. In the early 1860s, determined to improve the grapes bequeathed to California by the missions, a Hungarian-born nobleman, Count Agoston Haraszthy, journeyed with his grown son to France. There they selected 100,000 or more cuttings from choice vines, packed them carefully with their own hands, and brought them back to Haraszthy's Buena Vista Ranch in the Sonoma Valley north of San Francisco Bay. From Buena Vista the improved stock spread throughout the state, the beginning of California's fame as a producer of fine varietal wines.

During the early 1870s, Luther and Eliza Tibbets, working in Riverside with three Brazilian navel-orange trees sent them by the United States Department of Agriculture, transformed the sour, thick-skinned fruit introduced by the Franciscan missionaries into a new crop of winter gold for Californians. Shortly afterward, New Englander Richard Hall Gilman helped provide a balancing crop of summer gold by planting the first commercial grove of valencia oranges in what is now Orange County—four hundred trees that he kept alive by carrying well water to them in buckets. Hard on the heels of these untrained experimenters came famed botanist Luther Burbank, who in 1875 at Santa Rosa, north of San Francisco, began fifty years of scientifically controlled horticultural work to improve known varieties of fruit and vegetables and introduce new ones.

Not every experiment succeeded. Hoping to turn California into a great silk-producing state, the legislature in 1864 offered bounties to farmers who planted mulberry trees and produced viable silkworm cocoons. The pursuit turned into a speculative

118 CALIFORNIA

frenzy. Not only did the legislature thereupon cancel its payments, but what is more, the silkworms adapted poorly to the forced environment, and the industry perished. A few years later, William Ralston of the Bank of California reputedly lost a million dollars trying to develop a suitable process for curing the harsh-tasting tobacco that speculative farmers had planted near Gilroy. The incipient oil boom of the 1860s collapsed when scientific sleuths discovered that the clean-burning kerosene supposedly refined from local petroleum had actually come from Pennsylvania. Yet even these failures were important in that they indicated the willingness of producers to experiment and of financiers to support whatever bore promise of profit.

Growing industries, fabulous mines, endless forests, bonanza agriculture, sophisticated networks of finance and commerce; inventiveness, boldness, energy—a Hittell or a Bancroft could indeed find reason to proclaim that here were "conditions such as have never before fallen to the lot of man to enjoy." And yet this same decade of the 1870s seethed with discontent. Bankruptcies multiplied. Class struggles and racial animosities wrenched the social fabric. The California dream seemed in danger of dying—a paradox of plenty, the Jekyll-Hyde twinship that Henry George caught in the title of the world-famous book he wrote in San Francisco during those frustrating years— *Progress and Poverty.*

That mordant book, and dozens more before and after it, was based on a recurrent dissatisfaction—the failure of California to meet the expectations it had raised. Eden should not betray. When it did, men and women who had been propelled West by disappointments already incurred in St. Louis, Birmingham, Munich, Cardiff, Sidney, Valparaiso, or wherever were doubly incensed and, "ready," wrote Lord Bryce in *The American Commonwealth,* "to try instant, even if perilous, remedies." [9]

Chief generator of the short-lived hopes that followed the Civil War was the Central Pacific Railroad. Factory owners, wholesalers, and farmers thought that by means of its rails and connecting wagon roads they would be able to market their

9. Bryce, *American Commonwealth,* 2: 385.

CALIFORNIA

A photographer's essay by Joe Munroe

Photos in Sequence

goods as far away as the goldfields of southern Idaho and western Montana. They anticipated that enough eastern workers would ride its passenger cars west to bring down the high costs of skilled labor. Meanwhile, real-estate promoters, lumbermen, and construction workers envisioned themselves growing rich from selling homes to the newcomers. Land prices doubled, then tripled. New buildings arose in established towns; imaginary ones were planned for towns still unchartered.

To help guarantee that the influx would roll as scheduled, leading businessmen formed, under the leadership of insurance executive Caspar T. Hopkins, an Immigrant Union devoted to spreading the tale of California's advantages. The propaganda found receptive audiences. Soft spots that would spread until they precipitated the grim depression of the mid-1870s were already appearing in the American economy. Men and women whose livelihoods were threatened looked westward with hopes diametrically opposed to the aims of those who were enticing them. Workers envisioned high pay. Farmers pictured cheap land, either homesteads that they could file on under the land laws of 1862 or family-sized plots offered at reasonable prices by the railroad from grants that had been awarded it as an aid to construction. So great were the yearnings that during the three years of 1873–1875 more outsiders entered California than had appeared during any other period since the gold rush.

Those clashing expectations were not the only ones. While California manufacturers were looking beyond the state's borders in anticipation of new markets, Eastern industrialists were studying California. Even before the rails had been linked at Promontory, drummers from the Atlantic states were sweeping into the golden land "by scores and hundreds, soliciting everything from a pair of shoe strings to a well stocked variety store, . . . even accosting private individuals at the mines, on the farms, in the work shops, and on the street." [10] Clearly, both groups could not succeed.

The railroad, too, was counting on a rosy future. American traffic would be only part of it. Silk, tea, and other exotic wares

10. *San Francisco Evening Bulletin,* August 6, 1870.

bound from the Orient to Europe would pour into San Francisco Bay for transshipment across the continent to steamships waiting at anchor beside the Atlantic. The creators of the Central Pacific were determined, moreover, that all movement, domestic and foreign, would be over *their* rails. Ruthlessly, they gained control of every local rail company that might be tempted to enter into alliance with outside rivals. They then pushed those lines north toward Oregon and southeast toward Arizona, intending to block whatever mountain passes or river crossings afforded ingress to the state. Chief of those defensive lines was the Southern Pacific, which in 1876 linked San Francisco and Los Angeles by way of the San Joaquin Valley. Obviously, the value of this transportation monopoly would be, if California grew as it was supposed to, almost incalculable.

Grow the state did—by 54.3 percent during the 1870s, as was noted earlier. But it did not grow the way it was supposed to. The formal opening of the Suez Canel in 1869 ended the hope of diverting Oriental traffic to Europe by way of the Central Pacific. Raising money to build the defensive lines proved to be a grievous burden for the parent road, already staggering under the costs of its headlong race to lay more transcontinental track than the Union Pacific could. The future of the debt-ridden railroad looked so bleak that the Big Four (though rich from the construction contracts they had awarded themselves during the race) tried their best during the 1870s to unload the line at bargain rates. No takers appeared.

California manufacturers discovered that, instead of expanding their markets eastward, they lost business to aggressive outsiders. The hope of immigrant workers for good wages melted under the double impact of declining business and competition from other job seekers. Agriculturists found that speculators had monopolized so many of California's arable acres that opportunities for filing on cheap homesteads or buying small tracts at reasonable prices were almost nonexistent. Meanwhile, land in the cities went begging because few could afford the prices speculators needed if they were to make a profit from their costly holdings.

Unfortunately, perhaps, the inevitable crash did not come at once. New plums of rich ore were discovered in the Comstock Lode; above-normal rainfall greened the San Joaquin Valley. Industry caught its breath again. Optimistic farmers rushed out to lease or buy whatever wheat land was available. The result was a pattern like that of a bouncing ball.

Stock values serve as an index. Between January and May 1872, the ore discoveries on the Comstock shot the quoted worth of the securities listed on the San Francisco Stock Exchange from $17 million up to $81 million. Clerks, Chinese laundrymen, factory roustabouts, and their wives joined mine superintendents and bankers in frenzied buying and selling. Then the overheated market cracked, and in three weeks values dropped by $60 million, impoverishing thousands of small investors.

The survivors learned nothing. Favorable reports from the mines sent prices soaring again. The triple break that followed—in October 1874, January-February 1875, and August 1875—reduced values by $105 million.

The August break coincided with a wild run on the overextended Bank of California, the most influential of the West Coast's financial institutions. At 2:35 P.M., August 26, the doors of the heavy marble building swung shut against a clamoring surge of depositors. The stock exchange, two more banks in San Francisco, and half a dozen in other parts of the state, including the Temple and Workman Bank of Los Angeles followed suit. Two days later, gaudy William Ralston, president of the Bank of California, drowned while swimming in San Francisco Bay. Probably the death was accidental, though many thought not. But there was no doubt concerning the fate of William Workman of the Temple and Workman Bank in Los Angeles. When heroic efforts to revive the institution failed, he shot himself through the head.

The directors of the Bank of California were more successful. Driven by fear of the state's laws concerning the liability of stockholders in bankrupt corporations, they managed to reorganize the firm and, in October 1875, resumed business. Confidence revived, and, when the Consolidated Virginia and the California mines of the Comstock Lode continued pouring forth silver, businessmen told each other the worst was over.

They were wrong. During the winter of 1876–77, the state received less than half its normal rainfall. Hydraulic mining languished; wheat withered; flocks of sheep were decimated. Losses in Southern California alone were estimated at $20 million. In the midst of the suffering, in January 1877, the Consolidated Virginia mine announced that it would skip its monthly dividend of $1 million. The reverberations shrunk stock values by $150 million. Simultaneously, the full impact of the depression that was gripping the eastern states reached California, precipitating the bankruptcy of at least 451 major concerns. Destitute farmers and unemployed laborers swarmed into San Francisco, desperate for work and ready to vent their wrath on whatever villains seemed handiest.

Reformers had plenty to show them. Aroused by the harsh discrepancies between the dreams that had been triggered by the opening of the railroad and the actualities that had developed, individuals like Henry George and organizations like the Patrons of Husbandry (more widely known as the Grange) and the People's Independent party had been searching for causes and had come up with a choice basketful—monopolies in land, water, and transportation, corruption in government, and the most emotional issue of all, competition from cheap Chinese labor.

The most obvious of the monopolies was the Central Pacific. No competition restrained it. It had ended water travel in the Central Valley by purchasing the boats of that earlier monopoly, the California Steam Navigation Company. By distributing free passes and other rewards to key members of the state legislature, it defeated every bill that tried to revise the generous rate schedules that had been written into law before the Civil War as part of a program to stimulate railroad construction. It even exceeded legal rates for small-town merchants by carrying goods they had ordered from the East right through their towns to the major distribution centers of Sacramento and San Francisco and then carrying them back again—charging full short-haul rates for the extra miles.

In order to evade taxes on facilities built largely at public expense, the Central Pacific eased complaisant assessors into office. Towns that wished to be on its main line had to provide free land for depots and yards and sometimes had to buy a specified number of the railroad's bonds, or the corporation would punish them by building a rival village nearby.

Such practices contributed to the spread of land monopoly. Altogether, the Central Pacific and its subsidiaries, the Southern Pacific and the California and Oregon, received from the federal government more than eleven million acres in grants in California alone. In order to dispose of this land as quickly as possible, the railroad favored those who would purchase in quantity—that is to say, speculators who would then assume the work of reselling their acquisitions to the public.

The grants were patterned like a checkerboard, with railroad and public land alternating in 640-acre sections. Theoretically, the public sections were to be sold in 160-acre pieces, one parcel per person, to actual settlers. Actually, the purchasers of railroad land, most of them speculators, had little difficulty in also obtaining the public land they wanted ahead of farm seekers by means of scrip. Scrip represented land in the public domain—certificates handed out by the federal government to war veterans as bonuses, to each of the states for use in funding agricultural and engineering colleges, and for other purposes. Instead of claiming the land themselves, the recipients often sold the scrips through brokers to land speculators, who then used it to round out their holdings.

Swamplands given by Congress to the states for sale at reasonable prices to men who would reclaim the marshes were another source of rampant land speculation. Venal surveyors certified as swamps millions of acres in the Central Valley that were flooded only briefly in the spring, if at all. Venal land agents then sold this "reclaimed" land at ridiculous prices—sometimes as low as $1.00 an acre—to men who had done little or nothing to improve it.

Added to the Mexican grants that had fallen by various means into American hands, these acquisitions gave enormous power to relatively few men. According to statistics compiled by the

Sacramento Record during the fall of 1873, 122 men, each with a "farm" 20,000 or more acres in extent, owned an aggregate of 8,782,000 acres. Another 158 men, each with a "farm" of from 10,000 to 19,999 acres, owned in aggregate 2,670,000 acres.[11] In theory these 11.45 million acres, held by 280 landlords, most of whom lived in San Francisco, could have provided 71,575 ordinary small farmers with 160-acre homesteads. Instead, there were in all of California only 23,315 small farms that ranged in size from 100 to 500 acres, the average size being 200. It should be added that only about 13 million acres of California's 158,297 square miles are classified as first-class cropland. The great landholders in general held the best of this limited supply, so that the odds against finding a good homestead were even greater than bare statistics indicate.

Where rainfall was deficient, as it was in most of the San Joaquin Valley, land engrossment was accompanied by water monopoly. Only wealthy corporations (or farmers' co-operatives, which in those days seldom managed the necessary cohesion) could afford the work. Thus, if a man really wanted to farm he had three choices: pay speculators their asking price for land and water; lease by the year; or move on into the Northwest, as many did.

The result was one of the most dismal social scenes in America. The owners of big wheat ranches employed migrant labor, generally Chinese, for plowing and harvesting, turning the men out to survive between times as best they could. The tenants of wheat land had no interest in the space they rented, beyond making a quick killing. In either case, dwelling places were widely separated, unpainted shacks relieved by no greenery. Living was plagued with suffocating heat, dust, fleas, and mosquitoes, and hunger was relieved only by the dreadful wholesale of slaughter of the innumerable rabbits, ducks, and geese that gorged on the grain.

Owners of small farms tried to fight this degradation through the Patrons of Husbandry, which in 1873 had 104 chapters in

---

11. Figures summarized in Charles Albro Barker, *Henry George* (New York: Oxford University Press, 1955), pp. 190–191.

California. In addition to providing social outlets, especially for lonely women, in the legislative field the Grange pushed for state supervision of banks and railroads. The California group established a bank to provide easy credit for its members. Because San Francisco's shipping monopoly, headed by Isaac Friedlander, adjusted freight rates without warning in order to pocket whatever unexpected gains accrued from good sales in the English wheat market, the Grange countered with a chartering agency of its own. But none of the efforts succeeded. The Grangers were too inexperienced, their opponents too powerful.

An opportunity for the unemployed and destitute to express their resentment of what was happening arose during the summer of 1877. A rail strike was shaking the East. Hoping to shake the Central Pacific by showing sympathy, San Francisco labor leaders on July 23 assembled at a mass meeting in a sandy vacant lot next to the new city hall, still under construction. There thousands of workers shouted their approval of resolutions condemning the capitalistic practices that in their estimation had brought on the strike.

For the more excitable members of the gathering, resolutions were not enough. Swirling away from the crowded lot, they began to stone and burn Chinese stores and laundries, for *there*, they believed, was the sore that really needed excising.

The antipathy had been growing since the 1850s, when numbers of Orientals had joined the rest of the world in stampeding to the mines. Because they were not white, they met the same prejudices that Americans attached to Negroes and Indians. They were denied certain civil rights and prevented from testifying in court in cases involving Caucasians. They were harassed by white bullies, and for a time were subjected to discriminatory taxes on the mining claims they occupied. Concerted efforts to banish them did not gather headway, however, until they began supplanting white laborers on major construction projects, notably the Central Pacific Railroad.

After their work on the railroad had shown what could be expected of them—docility, industriousness, and, above all, cheapness—they spread throughout the state, digging irrigation canals, reclaiming marshlands, harvesting crops. In San Francisco they served as domestics, laundrymen, and vegetable peddlers. From there they moved into textile mills, shoe factories, cigar plants, and, along the coast, into the abalone fisheries.

The flow quickened after 1868, when a treaty with China removed all restrictions from immigration into the United States. California received 5,167 new Orientals in 1868; 15,730 in 1870; more than 22,000 in 1876. Nearly every one was a young vigorous male recruited in China by labor contractors who advanced passage money, found jobs, and provided the new arrivals with a self-policed social milieu to which they could repair during their free time. Because their ways were mysterious to untutored whites, they were suspected of carrying horrible diseases and practicing unspeakable vices. Their one aim was to get back to China as soon as they had saved enough money to find a bride and establish themselves as persons of importance in the poverty-stricken villages from which they had come.

To be replaced by such people seemed intolerable to unemployed Californians. Violence was inevitable. The first major eruption came on October 24, 1871, in Los Angeles, where rampaging mobs killed at least eighteen Orientals; the exact number was never determined. The outbreaks in San Francisco on July 23, 1877, led San Francisco businessmen to fear a similar pogrom in their city, with part of the violence carrying over to firms that employed Chinese. To forestall it, they obtained armed vessels from the Mare Island Navy Yard to stand by in the harbor, and recruited, under William Coleman, leader of the vigilantes of 1856, an emergency police force of six thousand men armed with ax handles. The show of force enraged the rioters. On July 27, a defiant mob attempted to set fire to the docks of the Pacific Mail Steamship Company, chief carrier of Chinese across the Pacific. After a wild donnybrook during which four men died, the attackers were dispersed.

Property owners stayed tense, however. A new political group, the Workingmen's party, sprang up overnight, led by a ranting Irish drayman named Denis Kearney. Though Kearney preached violence and was several times arrested, no further uprisings developed, in large part because the legislature passed bills that opened the way to the drafting of a new state constitution. Distracted by this opportunity to distill their resentments into law, the Workingmen threw all their energies into electing convention delegates favorable to their desires.

Except for intemperate attacks on minority groups, the platform they evolved does not sound radical today. It proposed compulsory education, governmental supervision of certain corporate activities, tax and monetary reforms, the popular election of United States senators, and an eight-hour workday. But the preamble promised "to wrest the government from the hands of the rich and place it in the hands of the poor," and campaign speeches resounded with denunciations of "land grabbers, bloated bondholders, and shabby aristocrats." [12]

Thoroughly frightened, conservatives of both the Republican and Democratic parties joined forces to nominate a slate of "Nonpartisan" delegates, most of them lawyers,to compete with the Workingmen for seats at the convention. It was an astute move, for when balloting was completed, Nonpartisans held 78 seats compared to 51 for the Workingmen and 23 for the wearers of a scattering of other labels.

At the convention the Workingmen wrangled among themselves and were generally outmaneuvered by the lawyers of the Nonpartisan group. Still, by gaining the support of agrarian members of the Nonpartisan bloc on some issues, they did succeed in setting up an elective Railway Commission of three members to regulate rates, and a Board of Equalization to remedy tax abuses. To help speed the administration of justice, they increased the size of the State Supreme Court from five judges to seven. They made lobbying a felony, won an eight-hour day on public works, and ordered the legislature to protect the state from "dangerous or detrimental aliens."

After an intense campaign, voters accepted the document by a 53.7 percent majority. Heavily amended, it is the constitution under which the State of California still operates.

12. Robert Glass Cleland, *From Wilderness to Empire* (New York: Alfred A. Knopf, 1947), p. 341.

Its immediate effects were limited. The Supreme Court of the United States struck down most of the anti-Chinese legislation, only to have the decisions rendered moot in 1882 when Congress, yielding to pressure from the Western states, banned all further immigration from China. The state courts whittled away at the powers of the Board of Equalization, and the Central Pacific managed with almost ridiculous ease to corrupt the majority of the Railroad Commission. Meantime, shootings and sensational charges of immorality stained the Workingmen's barely successful campaign for the mayor's office in San Francisco.

It was a last triumph. Within two or three more years the party was dead. The insistence on the dream did not fade with it, however. Rather, it gathered force as immigrants discovered a new Eden in the hitherto neglected southern counties. When fresh depressions and disappointments struck, those newcomers joined hands with the dissatisfied residents of the long-dominant north to search again for ways to stave off the recurrent threats to their hopes. Before following that quest, however, it is necessary to notice briefly what was happening in once sleepy Southern California.

9

Rise of the Southland

$\mathcal{A}$S we have already noted, the residents of Southern California tried three times during the 1850s to break away from their neighbors to the north and form an independent territory. Tables turn, however. Six decades later, in 1914, worried businessmen in San Francisco suggested that the northern counties secede in order to avoid being dominated by aggressive Los Angeles.[1]

Even in hindsight, the swiftness of the reversal seems amazing. Los Angeles, a hamlet of 4,385 people in 1860, possessed none of the natural advantages that enabled San Francisco to jump from inconsequence in 1847 to fourteenth place in the list of the nation's urban centers only a dozen years later. The southern town's shallow, poorly sheltered roadstead lay twenty miles away at San Pedro. No navigable rivers opened easy transportation routes to rich mines or broad valleys rustling with wheat. Eastern merchandise consigned to regions south of the Tehachapi Mountains was carried right past the southern coast to San Francisco. There it was transferred to rickety coastal vessels, at staggering markups in price, and brought all the way back. Even San Diego's superlative harbor availed its citizens little, for the mountains and deserts behind the bay remained too undeveloped to support commerce.

---

1. Robert Durrenberger, *California, the Last Frontier* (New York: Van Nostrand Reinhold Co., 1960), p. 62.

Nature as well as geography could be calamitous. Severe earthquakes rattled the region in 1855 and 1857. The temblors were followed during the winter of 1861–1862 by such torrential rains that adobe ranch houses in the countryside and store buildings in Los Angeles grew saturated and collapsed. Cattle drowned by the hundreds. For five weeks, said the *Los Angeles Star* on January 25, 1862, "We have had no communication with the outside world except by steamer express." Yet, after the earth had finally dried out, it stayed dry and rock-hard for two years under the impact of one of the most severe droughts ever recorded in California.

Social conditions were equally discouraging. Paiute Indians from the interior struck repeatedly at outlying settlements. Rustlers preyed on livestock. For reasons not entirely clear, Los Angeles became the state's chief congregating point for outlaws. In 1851, so it is said, the town experienced forty-four homicides, "which must have set some sort of record, considering that the population was below 2,300." [2] Meantime, the local jail was filled not with cattle thieves or murderers but with despairing Indian laborers. On Saturday evenings they received their pay for the preceding week's work and promptly took their hopelessness to the nearest grog shop. Soon the tenderloin part of Los Angeles swarmed with drunken Indians—men, women, even children—yelling and fighting until the police clubbed them into jail. On Monday morning they were bailed out by whatever white ranchers wanted a week's cheap labor. The next Saturday the amount of their fine was deducted from their week's pay, which left them just enough for another pint of brandy (some ranchers even paid them in brandy), "and thus the process goes on." [3]

Anglo-Mexican animosities placed further strain on the social fabric. The compatibilities that allowed rich English, French, or

    2. Leonard Pitt, *The Decline of the Californios: A Social History of the Spanish-Speaking Californians, 1846–1890* (Berkeley and Los Angeles: University of California Press, 1970), p. 149.
    3. Robert Glass Cleland, *The Cattle on a Thousand Hills* (San Marino, Calif.: Huntington Library, 1951), p. 82. See also Horace Bell, *Reminiscences of a Ranger* (Santa Barbara, Calif.: Wallace Hebbard, 1927), pp. 35–36.

American merchants to marry the pretty daughters of large land-holders did not extend to common vaqueros and recent hard-core Protestant immigrants from the United States, particularly Texas. Commented the *Los Angeles Star* at the conclusion of a story about a brawl that disrupted a Washington's Birthday party in 1852, "Men hack one another to pieces with pistols and other cutlery, as if God's image were of no more worth than the life of one of the two or three thousand dogs that prowl about our streets and make the nights hideous." [4] And brawls were the lesser part of the antagonisms. Dispossessed Mexicans formed outlaw gangs that sparked wild chases, horrifying ambushes, and more savage vigilante action than the northern part of the state ever experienced.

Throughout this period, which covered the 1850s and the first part of the 1860s, the economy of the region steadily declined. Part of the trouble came from the difficulties and expense (described in Chapter 6) that the rancheros faced in having the titles to their land grants confirmed. Juan Bandini of San Diego spoke for many Californios when he declared that in his opinion the actions of the United States Land Commission and the excessive taxes laid on real property by the state legislature were deliberately designed to speed American settlement by breaking up the great estates of the south.

Actually, the rancheros were for the most part victims of their own extravagances and reckless borrowing during the days of inflated cattle prices. Blinded by euphoria, they did little to restock their ranges or improve their herds. As a result, they were unprepared to meet the competition that came from American ranchers who introduced big herds of superior beef into the northern reaches of the state. Soon the southern rancheros were existing as they had before the war—slaughtering their scrawny cattle for hides, tallow, and *carne seca,* a brick-hard black jerky prepared by hanging strips of beef to a lariat rope and letting them dry for four or five days. Pounded into a powder, moistened with hot lard and water, and then boiled with potatoes, onions, chile peppers, and tomatoes, *carne seca* made a fine

4. Quoted in Pitt, *Decline of the Californios,* p. 154.

dish, the Californios thought, exporting it in considerable quantities to San Francisco. But it did not save the cattle industry. Floods and drought delivered the *coup de grâce*. In April 1864, a Los Angeles paper sadly declared, "Famine has done its work, and nothing can now save what few cattle remain." [5]

Whatever the owners' sufferings—and they were manifold—the ending of the ranchero period allowed a newer group of soil exploiters to rediscover advantages known years earlier to the padres of the missions. In spite of occasional cataclysms, the climate really was favorable for agriculture. One reason had to do with ocean currents. The cold, south-flowing California current does not follow the coast where it bends sharply eastward at Point Conception, some forty miles west of Santa Barbara. This circumstance allows warm water to drift northward from Mexico, tempering the coastal air.

Also at Point Conception the north-south trend of the mountains shifts to east-west, producing the Transverse Ranges that separate the Los Angeles Lowlands from the San Joaquin Valley and Mojave Desert. The southernmost of these ranges extends from the coast a hundred miles or more eastward. Its steep southern faces absorb the heat of the winter sun and at dark radiate it outward, so that even in January freezing temperatures strike the inland areas only occasionally. The mildness has its limits, however. In summer hot air from the interior occasionally breaks through the Transverse Ranges, creating "Santa Ana" winds that turn the chaparral to tinder, fry people's skins and tempers, and make the first rains of autumn doubly welcome. In more modern times the Transverse Ranges have helped trap dense layers of smog within the Los Angeles Basin. But the long sequences of mild, bright days are the ones people have remembered and written home about.

Of even greater importance is the elevation of the eastern half of the range that walls in the lowlands. Some of its peaks range from 10,000 to 11,600 feet above sea level. They wring maximum moisture from the Pacific-front storms that reach that far south. In the days before water tables grew overstrained, they released the water slowly into streams that flowed throughout the

5. Quoted in Cleland, *Wilderness to Empire*, p. 294.

year south or southwest across the Los Angeles Basin to the sea. Comparable conditions, though on a smaller scale, prevailed through the coastal plains and valleys from Santa Barbara to San Diego. Because of them the mission gardens, orchards, and vineyards throve, as did the farmsteads around the pueblo of Los Angeles. The truth was ignored by the cattle ranchers who succeeded to the mission lands—a few dependable watering holes were all their animals needed—but when American farmers began penetrating the area, they noted the advantages of those natural reservoirs in the mountains as quickly as the Franciscans had.

Aong the first to arrive were Mormons from Utah. At that time, 1851, Brigham Young had plans to develop a transportation corridor between Salt Lake City and San Diego. Once freight and converts from abroad had arrived by sea at the latter point, the journey to Utah would be much shorter than was the harsh route across the Great Plains. To ease the journey still more, Young ordered a group of colonists led by Elders Amasa Lyman and Charles Rich to establish a way station near the Pacific opening of Cajon Pass, the only break in the Transverse Ranges east of Los Angeles.

Lyman and Rich obtained the land they needed by paying two Mexican ranchers, the Lugo brothers, $77,500 for El Rancho del San Bernardino. Sellers and purchasers both supposed the grant embraced at least 80,000 acres. Later surveys run under the authority of the United States Land Commission reduced the area to 35,500 acres. Still, it was a bargain.

> In the rear [reported the leaders enthusiastically], we have the venerable snowclad peaks of the Sierra Nevada [*sic*] towering to the clouds, at the foot of which gush forth innumerable streams . . . whose crystal waters can be dispersed throughout the city, thereby affording to our citizens an abundant supply of that delicious beverage. The site is upon an inclined plane at the foot of which for miles in either direction extends a dense growth of willow, cottonwood, and sycamore, which affords an abundant supply of timber for fuel and fencing purposes.[6]

6. Cleland, *Wilderness to Empire*, p. 298–299. See also Leonard J. Arrington, *Great Basin Kingdom* (Lincoln, Nebraska: University of Nebraska Press, paperback edition, 1966), pp. 87–88, 178.

Within four years, 1,400 people lived in the settlement. They irrigated 4,000 acres of wheat, 50,000 grape vines, and hundreds of fruit trees. They grazed 15,000 cattle and marketed lumber, flour, cheese, butter, and eggs throughout Southern California. Unhappily, the success was fleeting. In 1858, when war threatened between the United States and Utah, the colonists—nearly 3,000 by then—were ordered to sell their property for whatever they could get and return to Salt Lake City. Ninety percent of them obeyed.

Their influence lasted, and not just among those who picked up their property for a song. Among those who heard of San Bernardino's success was John Froehling, a San Francisco wine merchant. Why not, Froehling reasoned, help a group of discontented German immigrants he knew form a similar colony devoted to producing grapes, wine, and brandy for the northern market?

Under his aegis, fifty or so families invested $750 each in the Los Angeles Vineyard Society. A committee headed by George Hensen went south, searched the land, and finally bought from rancher Don Pacifico Onteveras 1,165 acres near the Santa Ana River twenty-six miles southeast of Los Angeles. To keep cattle out of the area, Hensen hired laborers to surround the plot with a five-and-one-half-mile fence of tightly set willow withes that soon took root and grew. Hired laborers also dug an irrigating canal six miles long from the Santa Ana River and planted 400,000 vines.

In 1860, the main body of the colonists moved south to what they named Anaheim—*Ana* from the river and *heim* from the German word for home. Each family received a twenty-acre piece selected by lot. Soon they were exporting to San Francisco 120,000 gallons of wine and brandy a year, plus thousands of bushels of table grapes packed in sawdust.

As San Bernardino, Anaheim, and El Monte (a community of corn-raising, quarrelsome Texans ten miles east of Los Angeles) demonstrated, intensive agriculture could be a success in Southern California. But as long as cattle ranching held sway, small plots of land were difficult for individual settlers to obtain. Not many tried. The region was isolated. Its culture, still dominated by Spanish-speaking Catholic ranchers, their vaqueros, and Indian laborers repelled Protestant American dirt farmers from the Midwest, the most likely source of immigration. Except for several critical events that occurred within a few years of each other, the region might have remained unchanged for an indefinite period.

The first was the widespread transfer of land from impoverished ranchers to mortgage holders during the great drought of 1862–1864. Because restocking the range with quality cattle seemed impossible, the new owners turned the property to other uses. Many imported sheep. Others, particularly in the San Fernando Valley north of Los Angeles, planted wheat. And still others decided to subdivide their land for sale to immigrants.

For suddenly there were immigrants. Most were families from the shattered Confederate states, seeking new lands where they could put their lives together again. Late in 1865, and for several years thereafter, long wagon trains of them struck west across the deserts, carrying little with them but hope.

Part of that hope was based on a congressional bill, passed finally in 1866, that granted generous land bounties to the Atlantic and Pacific Railroad, projected to run from the lower Mississippi Valley to the boundary between Arizona and California. The same bill extended similar grants to a paper line called the Southern Pacific, which was designed to run from the San Francisco area south to San Diego and then east to meet the Atlantic and Pacific at the state boundary. If the roads materialized, Southern California's isolation would end, enough Americans would flood west to supplant the lingering Mexican culture, and property values would rise. Those first on the scene ought to reap well. And so the wagons rolled west.

The first Californian to realize what was happening was John Downey. After spending his youth clerking in drugstores in Cincinnati and Vicksburg, Mississippi, Downey, aged twenty-two in 1849, had caught gold fever. Although he lost everything he had in the mines, he liked California and decided to stay. Because Los Angeles had no drugstore, he opened one there. Prospering, he married the fifteen-year-old daughter of a Californio. When a rancher bankrupt from declining cattle prices offered him a place called Santa Gertrudes southeast of Los Angeles, he bought it. He did nothing with the land, however, because in 1859 he was elected lieutenant governor of the state. When the governor later resigned to enter the United States Senate, Downey stepped into his shoes for the rest of the two-year term. His wife was twenty-one, the youngest first lady California has ever had.

He was back in Los Angeles when the vanguard of dispossessed Confederates began trickling in. As men he had known in Vicksburg began looking him up to ask about land, he scented opportunity. On November 13, 1866, he announced in the local paper that he had 20,000 acres for sale in 50-acre pieces—$10 an acre on liberal terms. The result was the city of Downey. Until 1876, no American flag flew there. On July 4 of that centennial year, a sharp-chinned Slavic immigrant, John Mitrovich, erected a pole in front of his grocery store, ran up the Stars and Stripes, and stood guard all day with a loaded gun to make sure there was no lowering. None was attempted. However reluctantly, Downey town had decided to accept the Union.

Years before Mitrovich's stand, other developments were promising to draw America's attention to California's remote southland. In 1868, rumors flew through Los Angeles that a second southern transcontinental railroad, the Texas and Pacific, with San Diego as its destination, was about to be launched by powerful Tom Scott of the Pennsylvania Railroad. Other rumors said that the Big Four of the Central Pacific had acquired the Southern Pacific and soon would drive south to meet Scott. Let San Francisco consider that—*two* transcontinentals in the lower part of the state!

Of more immediate concern was the opening of rich silver mines and smelters at Cerro Gordo in the desolate mountains on the eastern side of Owens Valley. Freight problems on the 250-mile route were appalling. Fourteen-mule teams had to haul their own water much of the way as they dragged wagons hitched in tandem through blistering heat (or subfreezing temperatures during winter), up steep mountain switchbacks, through sandstorms, across flats glaring with alkali. But the effort gave many men employment, opened markets for hay and barley, and provided excitement for everyone. Let San Francisco look to her laurels! The city by the Bay wasn't the only urban center siphoning silver out of the desert!

Partly because of the Cerro Gordo mines, Phineas Banning, proprietor of a stage line that ran from San Pedro harbor to Los Angeles, was able to persuade the city to help him build a twenty-one-mile railroad to the sea. The city bought $225,000 of the road's bonds—it was named the Los Angeles and San Pedro—and Banning raised the balance of the $500,000 needed for construction. Work began in the fall of 1868 and was completed a year later. The success led Congress to authorize the construction of jetties and the deepening of the channels in the shallow roadstead. Who needed a natural harbor if an adequate one could be built by man?

Another significant event of 1868 was the launching of Southern California's first deliberate effort to attract land buyers from the outside. The occasion was the collapse of the most glittering figure of the Southland, Abel Stearns. Among the first American hide traders to settle on the Coast, Stearns had participated in several of Mexican California's numerous revolutions and had once suffered exile because of his activities. He was one of the delegates who had drafted American California's first constitution. An unyielding law-and-order man, he formed posses and rode with them as they chased down bandits during the tumultuous 1850s. He joined in the creation of several mercantile enterprises and built the first substantial unit of business buildings in Los Angeles, a creation he named the Arcadia Block in honor of his wife, reputed to be the most beautiful woman in California.

Stearns had married Maria Arcadia Bandini when he was forty-four and she fourteen. As part of her dowry she brought him an impressive amount of land. Through purchase he acquired more, until he owned upward of 200,000 acres. Because he borrowed heavily when cattle prices fell in the late 1850s, he was in no position to withstand the drought of 1862–1864. Thirty thousand of his cattle died. Creditors foreclosed on the

Arcadia Block and on one of his largest ranches, but by desperate maneuvering he managed to cling to seven others scattered across two counties—a total of 177,796 acres.

In May 1868, certain wealthy friends prevailed on Stearns to assign those lands to what was called the Robinson Trust, after one of its members. In return Stearns was given $50,000 for settling his most pressing debts and was to share in whatever profits the trust generated through the sale of real estate.

Townsites were laid out, a sales department was established, and brochures were mailed to likely prospects throughout the United States and western Europe. Arrangements were made with clerks in the new Immigrant Union headed by Caspar Hopkins (see above, page 119) to hand out more literature to tourists arriving in San Francisco via the Central Pacific. Because of these stimuli, passenger traffic on southbound coastal steamers picked up sharply. The trust sold 20,000 acres in small pieces in little more than a year, and Stearns was well on his way to solvency when he died in San Francisco in 1871, at the age of seventy-four, of a heart attack.

Trust members were not the only ones to capitalize on the lure of sunny climes and possible railroads. In 1870, John Wesley North, founder of Northfield, Minnesota, and afterward a holder of federal offices in Nevada, advertised in eastern papers for settlers to join him in looking for land in Southern California "in or near the line of the Southern Pacific Railroad." [7] The result was the town of Riverside, where the navel orange was developed and where growers first realized that the trees did better if they were moved out of the valley bottoms to foothill slopes above the frost line—lands hitherto regarded as useless. The Riverside experiments, coming at a time when a root disease was devastating the area's vineyards, led during the next two decades to the planting of 5.5 million navel-orange trees in Southern California. It was the Riverside group who changed the dietary beliefs of the nation (clearly, no baby could grow up healthy without orange juice!), and produced a symbol of well-

7. Tom Patterson, *A Colony for California* (Riverside, Calif.: Press-Enterprise Co., 1971), pp. 19, 28.

being whose impact on the imagination of middle-class America is beyond the reach of statistics.

And so it went. A group of Indianans weary of winter formed, during 1873–1874, the town of Pasadena. In 1876, Col. W. W. Hollister scored a surprising success by opening the Arlington, a ninety-room tourist hotel in sleepy Santa Barbara. Troubadours, as Carey McWilliams called them, arrived to sing the praises of lotus land.[8] Most effective of the travel writers was Charles Nordhoff of the *New York Herald,* who visited the West in 1871–1872. Impressed by Nordhoff's newspaper pieces, Collis P. Huntington of the Big Four persuaded him to expand them into a book whose title captured the essence of what the far coast was coming to mean to yearners throughout the nation—*California for Health, Pleasure and Residence.* Published in 1873, the volume sold three million copies during the next ten years.

There were community costs as well as gains. The boomlet and Los Angeles's eagerness to dominate it made the city easy prey for the Southern Pacific. The railroad's original charter had called for it to parallel the coast from San Francisco to San Diego. Land in that area was blanketed by Spanish and Mexican grants, however, and so the railroad's officials had persuaded the legislature of California and the Congress of the United States to let the SP shift its route to the San Joaquin Valley, where ample public land existed from which railroad grants could be carved. From the San Joaquin, the Southern Pacific could reach the Colorado River, where it hoped to block either the Atlantic and Pacific or the Texas and Pacific, without coming anywhere near Los Angeles.

The prospect of being left without rail connections so terrified the merchants of the little town that they sent ex-governor John Downey and merchant Harris Newmark north to negotiate with Leland Stanford. Stanford demanded everything that state law allowed—a subsidy amounting to 5 percent of the town's assessed valuation, or $602,000. Inasmuch as reaching Los Angeles would entail building what was then the world's fourth

8. McWilliams, *Southern California Country,* p. 143.

longest railroad tunnel, the sum was perhaps defensible. Stanford, however, also demanded that part of the payment consist of the city-owned bonds of the Los Angeles and San Pedro Railroad. This would give the Southern Pacific control of the harbor line and let it end water competition by setting freight rates between port and city as high as it wished.

Tom Scott of the Texas and Pacific tried to upset the proposal by offering to build a branch line from San Diego (if ever the T and P reached San Diego) for a smaller subsidy that would not include the bonds. It was an ill-judged approach. Los Angeles relegated to a branch line from a rival town! Voters of both the city and county disdained Scott and bowed to the Southern Pacific by a majority of 1,896 to 650.

The difficult work of climbing out of the San Joaquin Valley over Tehachapi Pass and of tunneling under the San Fernando Mountains was completed late in the summer of 1876. By then depression lay heavily on the land. The Temple and Workman bank had failed; the silver mines at Cerro Gordo and in the Panamints were running out of ore. A few months later, a new drought crippled the sheep industry. And what gain was there in being able to ship oranges, apricots, walnuts, and wine to San Francisco or even Chicago if the unemployed in those cities were unable to buy them?

Actually, the economic base was sounder than surface appearances indicated. In spite of the depression, the population of Los Angeles climbed, during the decade of the 1870s, a healthy 95 percent, from 5,728 persons to 11,183, as compared to a 10 percent growth rate in San Diego and 57 percent in San Francisco.[9] Los Angeles County fared even better than the city. Population more than doubled, and farmers learned to develop new sources of water by drilling hundreds of artesian wells into giant aquifers at the base of the mountains. Drought did not interfere seriously with irrigated land, and so, when the statisticians of the census bureau counted the number of improved acres in the

9. Actual numbers give a different perspective, however. While Los Angeles was attracting 5,455 new residents during the 1870s, San Francisco was luring 84,486.

county, they discovered an extraordinary rise—from 20,600 in 1860 to 303,386 in 1880.[10]

Dry spells that didn't injure growing things attracted rather than discouraged sun lovers. As the national economy picked up during the 1880s, so did westward migration. In 1882, sixty Methodists founded Long Beach across the bay from San Pedro. About the same time, promoter George Chaffee drew attention to his new town of Etiwanda by mounting atop his own house a dazzling arc light powered by another Chaffee creation, the West's first hydroelectric generator. Sales went so well that he laid out a rural-urban community named Ontario. Prior planning was so thorough and the project so prosperous that students were soon coming from all over the world to study it.[11]

Meanwhile, the Southern Pacific was driving across the Southwest. It blocked out Scott's Texas and Pacific and in 1883 made connections with New Orleans. By then, the child was mightier than the parent Central Pacific. Recognizing this, Stanford and his associates incorporated under the liberal laws of Kentucky a holding company, the Southern Pacific Company, to operate all their affairs—railroads, shipping lines, land and lumber sales. One result was increased vigor in spreading the word of California's charms throughout the United States and Europe.

One visitor the company did not want was the rival Atchison, Topeka and Santa Fe Railroad, energetic heir to the charter of the moribund Atlantic and Pacific. In 1883, the Santa Fe broke across the Colorado River near the town of Needles and shortly thereafter reached San Diego by means of a subsidiary, the California Southern. Los Angeles was the real prize, however, and, after leasing trackage rights from the Southern Pacific for a time, the invader started patching together its own right of way. The SP responded by launching a rate war that cut fares be-

---

10. All figures from the U.S. Bureau of Census, quoted in Robert M. Fogelson, *The Fragmented Metropolis: Los Angeles, 1850–1930* (Cambridge, Mass.: Harvard University Press, 1967), pp. 21, 56.

11. McWilliams, *Southern California Country*, p. 158.

tween California, the Mississippi Valley, and the East by two-thirds or more.

People poured in. San Diego's population jumped from 5,000 in 1884 to an estimated 32,000 bargain-happy tourists three years later. That same year, Los Angeles boasted that 100,000 people were housed within the city limits. Most came either as sightseers or health seekers—lavish hotels and spas rose throughout the Southland to accommodate them—but they soon switched from peering at the sights or sipping mineral water to a most wonderful new game: buy property, then sell it a few weeks later for enough profit to more than cover the costs of the trip.

By that time land boomers—there were two thousand real-estate agents in Los Angeles in early 1888—had developed a knack for real-estate promotion. With yellow stakes and hastily lettered signs saying "Site of the City Hall," they laid out some sixty towns spacious enough to hold two million residents. They then loaded a few hundred prospects at a time into flag-draped wagons or onto railroad flatcars, carried them to one of the sub-divisions, stuffed them with a free lunch, entertained them with brass bands and balloon ascensions . . . and had those whose resistance was weakening sign on the dotted line. (Their spiritual brothers, the promoters of 1976, still act the same way, except that now they use jet airplanes for transporting suckers to the site of the killing.)

In 1887, in Los Angeles County alone, property sales topped $200 million. Most of the "money" was credit, however. As the frenzy grew, lenders began to worry about the inevitable bust and called in their loans. At that the air went out of the bubble, and thousands of amateur speculators returned home with emptier pockets than they had envisioned.

Many stayed, however. So did some of the subdivisions, often with boarded-up hotels in their midst. In 1890, well after the binge was over, 50,395 people lived in the city of Los Angeles, an increase of 351 percent in ten years. So the decade was hardly a complete failure. Indeed, the abrupt stumbling in 1887–1888 was a gain in that it crystallized traits that would be characteristic of Southern California in general and of Los

Angeles in particular for the next several decades—exuberance, aggressiveness, and ingenuity, including slick talk, in solving by whatever means were necessary the problems of the moment.

For one thing, the collapse jarred the new (1887) Los Angeles Chamber of Commerce to launch scientific studies of the forces that promote migration. One measure of its success was the doubling of Los Angeles's population during that decade of deep depression—an increase, to be sure, that included many unemployed seeking shelter from cold Eastern winters.

Luck was on the chamber's side. For years, oil prospectors had been drilling wells with limited success in the rough canyons of the Transverse Ranges north of San Fernando Valley. Then, in 1892, three greenhorns, Sam Cannon, C. A. Canfield, and Edward Doheny, carried the search into the heart of residential Los Angeles—and hit. Soon scores of wells were clanking in backyards throughout the western part of the city. A little later, Doheny helped bring in the first great field of the San Joaquin Valley. As an aid to disposing of the surpluses that resulted, he encouraged the Santa Fe and Southern Pacific railroads to convert their locomotives from coal to oil.

Another stroke of luck was a decision by Henry E. Huntington, Collis Huntington's nephew, to leave steam railroading in favor of taking over and expanding the embryo streetcar system of Los Angeles. Having learned there the extent to which good transportation could influence metropolitan growth—and, as a corollary, the sale of property in favored sections—he began, in 1901, to knit together the whole basin with a web of electrified interurban railroads. Though the destination of his lines was often real estate that he and his associates owned, the public benefited, too. Within a decade, Los Angeles possessed the basic elements of a first-class rapid-transit system whose abandonment in favor of freeways for automobiles after World War II is bitterly rued today.

Meanwhile, the chamber of commerce was pressing hard for improvements to the harbor at San Pedro Bay. If the expansion resulted as planned, railroads other than the Southern Pacific would be able to approach the docks, and that line's hated monopoly over all traffic moving into Los Angeles, whether by water or by land, would be ended. Fighting back, Collis Huntington, sole survivor of the original Big Four, acquired land around Santa Monica Bay some miles to the north, where geography was such that only one railroad could reach the waterfront. He then tried to persuade both Congress and members of President McKinley's cabinet to concentrate all federal harbor expenditures at Santa Monica.

Real-estate promoters who hoped to hasten Los Angeles's growth westward toward Santa Monica rather than southward toward San Pedro abetted him, but the rest of the basin rebelled and victory eventually went to San Pedro. To complete its control, Los Angeles in 1906 annexed a twenty-mile strip of land from the city to the port. The way was then open for the municipal government, working in conjunction with the neighboring city of Long Beach, to turn the man-made harbor into one of the world's busiest ports—busier, within a few decades, than San Francisco's harbor.

Ultimately, sustained growth depended not on climate, interurban railroads, or an effective port but on adequate water. For that reason, Southern California welcomed the forest reserves, now national forests, that were authorized by Congress in 1891. At the urging of their representatives, President Harrison located the state's first reserve in the San Gabriel Mountains north of the Los Angeles Basin. The intent was not to preserve timber from exploitation but to protect a vital watershed.

Conserving water was not enough, however, and, shortly after the creation of the reserve, city engineers began to consider thrusting an aqueduct north across—and through—mountains and desert to the Owens Valley, there to tap the streams that flow down the eastern side of the highest part of the Sierra Nevada.

Few things in California have created so much historical controversy. Did the city's purchasing agent, former Los Angeles Mayor Fred Eaton, cheat the ranchers in Owens Valley by not letting them know what was afoot when he quietly bought options to their water rights? (Eaton probably would have replied that he was protecting his constituents; if he had acted openly prices would have shot sky high.) Why didn't the officials of the new United States Bureau of Reclamation ask for testimony from valley residents before cancelling, at the secret behest of Los Angeles emissaries, plans for a major irrigation project in the valley? (Actually, there had been nothing more than the beginnings of a study by the bureau—no commitment to a plan.) How did it happen that Henry Huntington, Harrison Otis, and other wealthy Los Angeles residents bought, at a most propitious time, land in the San Fernando Valley near the outlet of the proposed aqueduct? (They were lucky. Huntington planned to run a streetcar line into the valley, which was reason enough to speculate in land there. Water was an unexpected bonus.) Was it morally right for a swollen metropolis to dry up and thus kill a small farming community for its own selfish ends? (Democracy must rely, when faced with critical choices, on the rule of the greatest good for the greatest number.)

None of these considerations troubled the city's voters at the time. By margins of 14 to 1 and 10 to 1, they approved the two bond issues necessary for financing the project. It was completed in 1913, and for the time being Los Angeles had more water than it needed. The city was not generous with it. Neighboring municipalities that wanted a share had to agree to annexation, a step that automatically committed them to assuming part of the bonded indebtedness created by the system. Need for water overwhelmed desires for independence, and during the next few years the city's area jumped from 115 to 458 square miles.

During those years, analysts for the chamber of commerce were making an astounding demographic discovery. In the beginning their primary target was well-heeled farmers in search of better land. As the century turned, however, it dawned on the promoters that ordinary farming—the yeomanry of Thomas Jefferson, so revered in American folklore—was losing its hold on the people who had grown up with its crushing burdens. Rural youths were fleeing to the cities. Meanwhile, as the depression of the 1890s abated, land values rose sharply in the Midwest. Tens of thousands of farm owners and businessmen decided that perhaps the time had come to sell out and follow their children's example—but not all the way into the hostile environment of the new industrial cities. Surely, there was some in-between spot where they could obtain fuller lives without giving up the country values they had learned to cherish.

As an answer, Southern California offered a modestly priced, healthful, rural-urban mix: small towns on whose fringes one could live in a rose-covered bungalow with space enough around it to raise, for supplemental income and without inordinate labor, oranges, lemons, walnuts, almonds, or grapes, fortified, perhaps, by a few stands of bees. (It was during this period that California became the nation's leading producer of honey.) Nearby, meanwhile, were Henry Huntington's big red interurban cars, ready to whisk the new residents to outings at the foot of the mountains, beside the indigo sea, or to cultural affairs within Los Angeles itself.

A good life for common folk—there have been worse dreams. But, as literary historian Kevin Starr has said, "Small holdings intended in the imagination as self-sufficient farms, degenerated into infinitely repeated front lawns and back yards, pathetic in their fussy pastoralism." [12] As living patterns within the vast sprawl of greater Los Angeles, greater Riverside, and greater San Diego congealed, so too did ways of thinking. Health, simplistic religion, racial purity, temperance, and a deep suspicion of radical influences from some vague Outside became the preoccupation of many of those who had traveled to Southern California for new ways of living and then did not know how to handle what they found.

Having wrapped themselves in a security of sorts by patterning their groves and themselves after their neighbors, they did not wish to change. Yet, even then, twentieth-century industrialism, earnestly wooed by the same community leaders who had enticed them West, was on the point of engulfing them in change, just as it had already started engulfing the very different San Francisco area farther north. Somehow or other the people of both regions were going to have to adapt—or lose entirely the things they had hoped for when they came West.

12. Kevin Starr, *Americans and the California Dream* (New York: Oxford University Press, 1973), p. 203.

10

A Variety of Earthquakes

*F*ROM a dramatic standpoint, the earthquake and subsequent fire that devastated much of San Francisco in April 1906 came at a fitting time, for it served as a prelude to California's most sensational graft trial.

As trials must, this one concentrated on a few persons only, the givers and takers of bribes. By implication, however, the arraignment extended to the whole system of intertwined special interests that for decades had ruled both San Francisco and the state. The shocks of exposure that resulted helped tumble the corrupt edifice much as the city had been tumbled by the readjusting earth. Afterward, of course, came the problems of rebuilding—but that is getting ahead of the story.

Attempts to reform the government before 1906 had been subverted. Conservative Republicans and Democrats, linked as Nonpartisans during the constitutional convention of 1879, had turned aside most of the radical demands of the Workingmen's party. The few corrective measures that were adopted—regulatory commissions to oversee railroad affairs and to equalize taxes—had either been corrupted or ignored. The handful of Workingmen's candidates who were voted into office proved incapable of establishing viable administrations, and by 1881 the party had disappeared.

That year Republicans swept the state. To one of the party's San Francisco ward bosses, an Irish-born bartender named

Christopher A. Buckley, called Blind Chris because of a partial impairment to his vision, the triumph should have looked like opportunity. But a brighter future, he decided, lay in repairing the Democrats' shattered machine.

Both parties operated according to classic patterns developed in the East. Ward bosses created loyal followings by means of elemental kindnesses. They remembered names and birthdays, attended weddings and funerals, passed out baskets of food at Christmas. They found temporary lodgings for those suffering from eviction or fire, provided public-works jobs for the unemployed, and arranged bail for frightened constituents caught in the toils of the law.

Their payment was gratitude. When the time came to send delegates to city and county conventions, men whom they had befriended (women had not yet received the vote) cast ballots for the candidates they suggested. Those delegates in turn followed the biddings of the city or county boss in placing obedient men on the state central committee or in the state nominating conventions, where legislative candidates were chosen and platforms were pieced together on the basis of vote-trading among competing interests.

The process was financed by contributions from the vice lords and businessmen who benefited from the transactions, by kickbacks from the holders of public jobs (even schoolteachers were assessed), and by the sale of utility franchises and public-works contracts. The patronage available to senators and congressmen—the awarding of postmasterships, for instance—was another element in lubricating the wheels.

Finally, the legislators feathered their own nests by passing "cinch" bills against wealthy corporations—in California, notably the railroads. Ostensibly designed to reform the victim, these bills (the term "cinch" refers to the strap that binds a saddle to a horse's back) were actually a form of blackmail. To escape the cinching, the railroad's political overseer in Sacramento bribed key legislators into dropping the unwelcome proposal. That done, everyone was happy: the enriched lawmaker; his constituents, who innocently supposed that reform had been attempted; and the railroad, which could now threaten exposure unless the favors it wanted were heeded.

Such was the apparatus that Blind Chris Buckley took over in San Francisco and rebuilt for the Democrats. He did not let his old friendships in Sacramento die, however. Republicans who needed his help could have it—at a price. He was particularly adroit at devising the arrangements whereby Republican Leland Stanford, president of the Southern Pacific Railroad, and Democrat George Hearst, a mining millionaire, worked together like Siamese twins to maintain their holds on California's two senatorial seats in Washington. Stanford had still another reason for valuing Buckley's talents. Between 1882 and 1890, the California legislature did not pass one law unfavorable to the Central Pacific or Southern Pacific railroads.[1]

In the end, Buckley's adaptability proved his undoing. Enraged by his disregard of party loyalty, a fellow Democrat wrote a pamphlet exposing his activities. Indicted in 1891 by a San Francisco grand jury, Buckley escaped trial by fleeing abroad. On returning in 1894, he was indicted again but was freed on a technicality. He never regained power. By 1894, the forces of reform were threatening to derail not only bosses like Chris Buckley but also the industrial concerns that utilized their services. In California the chief target of the purifiers was, inevitably, the Southern Pacific.

During the 1880s, several unsavory events had focused attention on the firm. In 1883, several hundred letters written by Collis Huntington and a subordinate, David Colton, had been offered as testimony during a lawsuit. The *San Francisco Chronicle* obtained copies of the documents and published them. Afterward, no reader could doubt the cynicism with which the railroad manipulated government workers on every level.

More revelations came in 1887, when the United States Railway Commission conducted an intensive investigation of the railroad's affairs. But the episode that really damned the Southern Pacific in the popular mind was the ''Shoot-out at Mussel Slough.''

Mussel Slough was a section of fertile, easily reclaimed and

1. Royce D. Delmatier, Clarence F. McIntosh, and Earl G. Waters, *The Rumble of California Politics, 1848–1970* (New York: John Wiley and Sons, 1970), pp. 91–93.

readily irrigated land in the central part of the San Joaquin Valley. For nearly a decade, 1868–1877, legal technicalities clouded title to the railroad's land grants in the area. In spite of the uncertainty, the Southern Pacific stated by means of ambiguously worded brochures that, as soon as the grant was confirmed, it would sell the land to those who occupied it at prices ranging from $2.50 to $5.00 an acre. In arriving at values, no consideration would be given to the improvements—fences, buildings, irrigation ditches, and the like—that the settlers had made in the meantime.

Over the years several families drifted into the region, some settling on the squares of government land that alternated with squares of railroad land. Others simply squatted on property the company claimed without explicit agreement of any kind with the Southern Pacific's agents.

Late in 1877, the railroad's title was confirmed. Occupants of the land then received bills from the company that were higher than the prices originally quoted. Evidence exists that the railroad considered the excess as back rent for acres that had been used free of charge for several years. Besides, the value of nonrailroad land in the vicinity had risen—and so why shouldn't railroad land go up?

Retorting that the railroad was breaking its word and charging for improvements to the land, the settlers took the dispute to court. The railroad won. At that, some of the occupants paid what the company demanded, but the majority did not. They hired lawyers to appeal the decision to the state supreme court and then formed a vigilante committee, called the Settlers League, which decreed that no one should deal with the railroad until the matter was resolved. Persons who had already met the railroad's terms were subjected to ugly harassment.

The Southern Pacific quite naturally refused to heed the vigilantes. One of its agents, W. H. Clark, found two men in the vicinity, Walter J. Crow and Mills D. Hart, who agreed, perhaps in return for under-the-table considerations, to purchase from the railroad two tracts occupied by members of the Settlers League. The league immediately ordered Crow and Hart to leave the county or suffer the consequences. Agent Clark responded by obtaining writs of eviction against the men occupying the disputed tracts and called on the nearest United States Marshal, a Mr. Pool, to remove the adverse tenants. Early Tuesday morning, May 11, 1880, the agent, the marshal, and the purchasers started for the land in question. Marshal and agent rode in a buggy pulled by two horses, the others on a light spring wagon. All were armed, Clark and Pool with a revolver apiece, Hart and Crow with double-barreled, breech-loading shotguns. In view of the league's size and reputation, these four men were not a big force. But they were backed, in the person of Marshal Pool, by the weight of the United States government.

No one was visible in the shack on the first tract the foursome reached. Unchallenged, Marshal Pool toted the meager household goods out of the building, piled them beside the county road, and declared that Mills Hart was in possession. The quartet then continued for three miles along the road to the next disputed plot, claimed jointly by men named Storer and Brewer. Those two seemed disposed to discuss matters amicably, but before anything was settled some forty armed men came galloping along the road. Jumping from the buggy, Pool strode ahead about seventy-five feet to meet them. While part of the group wrangled with him, the rest dashed on toward the buggy and the wagon, which were standing approximately abreast. On reining in, the horsemen demanded the trio's weapons.

According to testimony given the next day by agent Clark, purchaser Crow nervously and without warning shot the leader of the settlers out of his saddle. Wild firing erupted on all sides. Clark's team bolted, running a quarter of a mile before they could be halted. By then, five settlers were dead, and the rest were not eager to tangle further with the two shotgun-wielding purchasers. The pair were able accordingly to bring their wagon up beside Clark's buggy. Hart, however, was so badly wounded that he had to leave the vehicle and lie on the grass. At that, Crow gave in to sudden panic and decided to flee on foot across the fields. He was overtaken and killed. At about the same time, Hart died of his wound. Thus the grisly work, in which neither Marshal Pool nor the Southern Pacific's agent, W. H. Clark, did any shooting, accounted for seven deaths and one serious injury.[2]

Five settlers—as many as Clark and Pool were able to identify—were arrested and charged with resisting a marshal. Part of their defense was an insistence that Hart and Crow had not been bona fide purchasers but gunmen hired by the railroad for terrifying the settlers. The prosecution retorted that every step taken by the railroad had been legal and that if Crow had indeed fired first (the point was disputed), it was justifiable self-defense, for he had been surrounded by men who previously had threatened his well-being.

The jurors found the five defendants guilty. Each was fined $300 and sentenced to eight months in jail. For the railroad it was a costly victory. Newspapers throughout the state denounced the company as being ultimately responsible for the deaths, no matter who had pulled the triggers. On August 19, 1880, a cartoonist for a San Francisco weekly, *The Wasp*, summed up the affair with a cartoon of an octopus from whose glaring eyes shone portraits of Crocker and Stanford and in whose tentacles were clutched the homes, produce, and industries of all California. From that cartoon a long-time opponent of the company, John P. Robinson, drew the title for a blistering (and often inaccurate) exposé called *The Octopus: A History of the Construction, Conspiracies, Extortions, Robberies and Villainous Acts of the Central Pacific, Southern Pacific . . . and Other Subsidized Railroads.''* From Robinson, the title passed to Frank Norris, who in 1901 published *The Octopus*, one of the most widely read naturalistic novels to emerge from prewar California. That epithet alone—*The Octopus*—gave reformers a powerful weapon when at last they closed in on the company.

2. My account of the events of May 11, 1880, is drawn from "Statement of W. H. Clark, Land Grader [i.e., land appraiser], Southern Pac. R.R. to Mr. Crocker, Wednesday, May 12, 1880," among the Huntington Papers, Syracuse University. I am indebted to David F. Myrick of San Francisco for providing me with a copy of this document. See also James L. Brown, *The Mussel Slough Tragedy* (Fresno, Calif.: 1958) and Wallace Smith, *Garden of the Sun: A History of the San Joaquin Valley, 1772–1939* (Los Angeles: n.p., 1939), pp. 259–287.

California's battle with the Southern Pacific was not unique. As the nineteenth century waned, America seethed with discontent, much of it aimed at the new industrialism that had taken command of the country.

Basically, the problem was one of overproduction brought on by explosive technology. Raw materials—iron, lumber, copper, lead, potash, limestone for cement, wool, cotton, and food— poured from the earth. Seemingly inexhaustible supplies of energy—coal, petroleum, natural gas, and electricity generated by falling water—were available for processing those materials by assembly-line methods into whatever items were demanded by increasingly interdependent and rapidly growing consumer groups. Here was the very antithesis of Jeffersonian self-sufficiency.

Transportation was integrated and quickened, often with surprising results. To use a relevant example, the development by the Santa Fe and Southern Pacific railroads of refrigerated express trains for moving fruit led to an enormous expansion of the state's orchards. In 1910, fruit sales brought more revenue to California than did any other economic pursuit. Related to this boom was the Southern Pacific's unremitting pressure on the California legislature to embark on a program of highway building, for in those times trucks and automobiles served as feeders of traffic to the railroads rather than as their competitors.

Most of the nationwide increases in production that resulted from improved manufacturing and transportation techniques came in bursts, followed by agonizing readjustments. Between December 1870 and December 1899, the United States experienced seven economic slumps that varied in intensity from short slowdowns to long depressions. During those unstable decades prices declined by almost two-thirds. As a result money grew desperately expensive. A debt that could have been paid with 1,000 bushels of wheat in 1865 ate up 3,500 in 1900.

Fierce, often unethical competition in the oversupplied market added to industrial uncertainty. Manufacturers responded in two ways, both bitterly criticized. They reduced their costs either by cutting wages (a self-defeating move, for the purchasing power of their workers also went down) or else replaced American labor with immigrants willing to toil under sweatshop conditions. In California the exploited minorities were first Chinese, as we have seen, then Japanese, and, following this country's victory over Spain in 1898, Filipinos.

A second response to industrial warfare was an effort to eliminate competition by buying out rivals or merging with them, either physically or by means of holding companies. In California mergers of utility firms were particularly noticeable, but other combinations also resulted. By 1910, "71 companies employed over four-fifths of the [state's] labor force and produced almost two-fifths of the total valued goods." [3] Railroads, the Santa Fe and the Southern Pacific among them, formed "pools" to divide traffic and maintain rates. Western lines imposed further barriers to free-flowing commerce by paying subsidies to the Pacific Mail Steamship Company (for a time the Southern Pacific even controlled Pacific Mail) so that it would keep rates via the Isthmus of Panama as high as they were by land across the continent.

Industrial mergers led to defensive combinations in other segments of society. Workers formed unions to resist wage cuts and the introduction of foreign labor into jobs once held by skilled Americans—and then often spent more time fighting each other over tactics and methods of organization than they did fighting their employers about wages and conditions. Such cohesion as California laborers achieved during the latter part of the century was provided by widespread emotional outbursts against "the indispensable enemy," the Chinese. [4]

Combinations of certain specialty farmers were more successful. Notable among them was the California Fruit Growers Exchange, vigorous child of earlier co-operatives that had been formed to wrest better terms from resistant middlemen, commission agents, and railroads. Soon the exchange was the largest co-operative organization in the United States, famed for its ef-

3. Edward Staniford, *The Patterns of California History* (San Francisco: Canfield Press, 1975), pp. 299–300.
4. Alexander Saxton, *The Indispensable Enemy: Labor and the Anti-Chinese Movement in California* (Berkeley and Los Angeles: University of California Press, 1971).

ficient integration of the citrus industry and the development of a marketing campaign that made the trade name "Sunkist" a symbol both of top-quality fruit and of the golden state from which the oranges and lemons came. "Sunmaid" performed a comparable function for raisins, and "Calavo" for avocados. However, few of the gains achieved by the members of the co-ops extended to the migrant laborers in the fields.

On the national front, militant social alliances and new political parties sought a broader basis than economic associations for wresting power from entrenched interests. From the standpoint of California history, the remarkable feature of the groups is the speed with which the state's reformers seized upon each new savior and zealously remodeled it to fit local needs. Thus discontent joined hands with other cultural forces to bind once-remote California ever closer to the rest of the nation.

A pioneer among the new organizations was a group calling themselves National Socialists, a name derived from Edward Bellamy's *Looking Backward,* a utopian novel first published in 1888. Instead of sending his hero backward in time, as Mark Twain had sent Hank Morgan in *A Connecticut Yankee in King Arthur's Court,* Bellamy projected his protagonist ahead to Boston in the year 2000. By then, in Bellamy's utopia, the state controlled all property and means of production. Factory managers and mechanics received the same pay, not in money but as credit in government stores. As money disappeared, so did crime. Because monopoly was replaced by sharing, society became suffused with brotherhood, love, and Christian altruism.

Looking Backward struck so responsive a chord among the discontented that hundreds of study clubs were formed throughout the United States to devise means of furthering Bellamy's ideals. California's first group took shape in Oakland in April 1889. Within a few months there were fifty-five, many of them spurred into activity by a militant woman named Anna Smith. The members Anna recruited were idealists, not activists, however. They quarreled among themselves—a chronic problem among American radical groups—and they were soon engulfed by the meteoric rise of the Farmers Alliances.

In 1890, the United States was still predominantly rural, but the numerical superiority of those who lived on farms was dwindling rapidly. Fearing lost prestige and power, and enraged over agricultural hardships brought on, as they saw it, by self-serving urban financiers, venal city politicians, and industrial pirates, the alliances in the South and Middle West transformed themselves into "the most belligerent farm organizations in American History." [5]

California's first alliance, a chapter of eight members, was formed in Santa Barbara on April 11, 1890. Less than two years later, five hundred chapters were scattered throughout the state, all of them in contact with their counterparts in other sections of the nation. They were prepared, accordingly, for the fiery metamorphosis of their Southern and Midwestern counterparts into the People's Independence party, more commonly known as the Populists. With undiminished fervor, California reformers accepted that development, too.

The common philosophic strain that pervaded the different groups accounts for the speed with which they melted into each other. To varying degrees each advocated that the federal government nationalize railroads and telegraph and telephone lines and that cities assume ownership of public utilities. Each proposed breaking the power of the party machines by placing many of the functions of the government in the hands of the people. They demanded secret Australian ballots (at that date the parties printed their own ballots and thus could keep a stern eye on their members at the polls) and the direct election of United States senators. The voters, the Populist groups further declared, should be allowed to inaugurate legislative action by means of the initiative, to express their opinion through referendums on acts passed by their city councils or legislatures, and to voice disapproval of elected officials by means of the recall. Each group demanded that the federal government halt the decline in prices and restore employment by the inflationary method of increasing the amount of money in circulation.

To the Populists, inflation meant free and unlimited coinage of silver. In the silver-mining states, where the price of silver

5. Nevins and Commager, *Short History of the U.S.*, p. 372.

had dropped from $1.326 an ounce in 1870 to $.63 in 1894, and on the Great Plains, the issue ballooned into a frenzy that, in the end, was disastrous to its advocates. The Populists' other programs were forgotten, and, when the Democrats under William Jennings Bryan stole the silver platform from them, they had no recourse left but to fuse reluctantly with the burglars. They were a poor haven. In 1896, the industrial areas of the country rallied behind McKinley—the Republican candidate carried even California by a meager 1,987 votes—and the effectiveness of the Populists evaporated.

Before their demise they did manage to add their bit to the attacks raining down on the Southern Pacific. At first the buffeting had little effect. During 1894, the railroad's workers lost a violent strike called in support of a nationwide walkout against the Pullman Company. A more capitalistic union of wholesale distributors, the Traffic Association of California, spent an excessive amount of money and achieved only token rate reductions from the railroad by financing round-the-Horn clipper ships and steamboats to compete as freight carriers with the landlocked SP. A competitive railroad, the San Francisco and San Joaquin Valley line, launched with great fervor in 1895, accomplished even less. As it stumbled toward bankruptcy in 1898, it was purchased by the Santa Fe, which in the meantime had entered into secret traffic-sharing and rate agreements with the Southern Pacific.

One great hope for humbling the Octopus still remained, however. The government was pressing the Central Pacific (since 1884 a subsidiary of the Southern Pacific Company) for repayment of the money borrowed for construction purposes during the 1860s. With interest, the debt amounted to $59 million. Collis Huntington, the sole survivor of the original Big Four, insisted that the Central Pacific, which alone had incurred the debt, could not pay the sum. Arguing that the services the line had rendered the West entitled it to special consideration, he prevailed on a friendly congressman to introduce a bill that would allow the CP to refund its obligations with hundred-year bonds bearing the trivial interest of 1 percent a year.

California roared displeasure. A rising young San Francisco

newspaper publisher, William Randolph Hearst, heir to George Hearst's mining fortune, sent his most vitriolic reporter, Ambrose Bierce, and a trenchant cartoonist, Homer Davenport, to Washington to cover the hearings on the refunding bill. Their "reporting" consisted mainly of scandalous invective. Simultaneously, the Populists added one more gadfly to the list of Huntington harriers by electing Adolph Sutro mayor of San Francisco.

Sutro was a peculiar Populist. A millionaire, he owned roughly one-twelfth of all the real estate in San Francisco. He had become a popular favorite in the 1870s by driving a drainage and ventilation tunnel into the Comstock Lode against the determined opposition of the monopolistic Union Mining and Milling Company, a tool of the potent Bank of California. Later, he had clashed with Huntington over the fares charged by a subsidiary railroad that served Sutro Heights, an oceanside amusement park Adolph had built a short distance beyond the Golden Gate. To the families of modest income who flocked every weekend to his park, he seemed like a friend and champion, and after his election as mayor he continued to act like one. Each day during the debates on the refunding bill, he bombarded every congressman and senator in Washington with anti-railroad, anti-Huntington broadsides even more venomous than the newspaper attacks unleashed by Hearst.

In January 1897, Congress defeated the refunding bill. So that San Francisco could celebrate the event, James D. Phelan, a liberal Democrat who had taken the ailing Sutro's place as mayor, declared a public holiday. A little later, the Southern Pacific lost its fight to have the federal government develop a private harbor for the railroad at Santa Monica. Capping the list of apparent setbacks was Huntington's death in August 1900.

Actually, the blows strengthened the railroad in the end. Following the defeat of the funding bill, Huntington had at last allowed the Southern Pacific Company to assume responsibility for the Central Pacific's debt. With his bankers he worked out a plan that resulted in full payment by 1909—an extraordinary accomplishment. Meanwhile, a brilliant corporation lawyer, William F. Herrin, was named general counsel for the SP. One of his first steps in streamlining company operations was to transform the SP's unstructured lobbying organization into a formal political bureau that became a model of businesslike efficiency in carrying on the railroad's necessary dealings with the government. Politics being what it was, venality did not end, but the roughest edges were filed away. On top of that, E. H. Harriman, president of the Union Pacific, bought enough stock from Huntington's heirs in 1901 to control the Southern Pacific. The network that resulted was one of the giants of the continent, reaching from Portland, Oregon, to New Orleans, from San Francisco to the Missouri.

Among the unsavory allies of this huge establishment was a brilliant lawyer, Abraham Ruef. Ironically, Ruef's rise to power had been made possible by a mistake on the part of reform-minded James D. Phelan. For almost four years, Phelan had worked hard and successfully to improve the lot of municipal employees and the appearance and well-being of the city. The popularity that resulted from his efforts was swiftly dissipated, however, when snowballing strikes born of a teamsters' dispute closed the harbor and nearly 60 percent of San Francisco's business establishments.

Totally outraged, the city's employers council demanded that Phelan use the state militia for opening the closed concerns. He refused but then compromised by detailing city policemen to protect nonunion teamsters from harassment by strikers. Bloody riots erupted, the governor intervened, and the employers emerged victorious.

A sizable group of workers, enfuriated in their turn, reacted by forming the Union Labor party in the hope of capturing control of the city government. At that point Abraham Ruef captured the party.

It was an amazing performance. No horny-handed workman by any stretch of imagination, Ruef had graduated from the University of California with high honors at the age of eighteen. At twenty-one he gained admission to the bar. He joined the Republican party as an idealist, but soon learned that success was the result of wheeling and dealing within the machine. He promptly adapted and did well within the limits the bosses allowed him. They were not inclined to let him taste the heady flavors of real leadership, however, and so, when the politically innocent Union Labor party took shape, Ruef decided to use it as his elevator to power. He was thirty-seven years old at the time, slight of build, mustached, dynamic as a speaker, and gifted with an ability to make friends among many classes of people.

One friend was handsome Eugene Schmitz, a popular orchestra leader, a member of the musicians' union, and hence a certified laborer. To Ruef, he had several other qualifications as well. Schmitz's father was a German immigrant—and at that time there were 100,000 Germans or children of Germans in San Francisco. His mother was Irish—and there were 95,000 Irish or children of Irish in the city. And he was a Catholic—in a city where 116,000 of 149,000 churchgoers were Catholic.[6] He was a good speaker, and Ruef capitalized on that talent by writing good speeches for him. This happy combination of attributes brought Schmitz first his own party's nomination to be mayor and then, during the fall balloting in 1901, easy victory over uninspiring Democratic and Republican rivals.

By 1905, Ruef controlled, in addition to the mayor, all eighteen members of the city's board of supervisors. His boodling took on majestic proportions. Among those who came to him hat (and money) in hand was Patrick Calhoun, president of San Francisco's dominant streetcar system, the United Railroads. As the year 1906 began, Calhoun was particularly anxious to obtain franchises that would allow him to expand the overhead trolley wires that powered his cars. Opposing him were civic leaders who demanded underground wires. Putting them in place would be expensive but would help preserve the beauty of the city.

Knowing that the decision was in Ruef's hands and that the decision could be purchased, the leaders decided to checkmate the boss by means of indictments for graft. In order to gather the necessary evidence, they obtained from President Theodore Roosevelt the best investigators in the service of the United States, Francis J. Heney and William J. Burns, who had re-

6. James P. Walsh, "Abe Ruef Was No Boss: Machine Politics, Reform and San Francisco," *California Historical Quarterly* 51 (1972): 8.

cently been instrumental in convicting several land speculators, a United States senator among them, for fraud in the acquisition of prime timberlands in Oregon and Northern California.

Before their newest detective work was well begun, the earthquake and fire of April 1906 razed 28,000 buildings and killed at least 452 people in San Francisco. For Ruef, the repairing of the catastrophe created a lively market among builders in need of franchises and licenses of all kinds. His supervisors obediently and profitably granted the permits he recommended, including one for overhead trolleys. Smug with triumph, Ruef then moved on to the Republican party's state nominating convention at Santa Cruz. There, for somewhere between $14,000 and $20,000 (accounts vary), he sold to the Southern Pacific machine enough votes to nominate the gubernatorial candidate the railroad wanted.

It was his last triumph. The supervisors cracked under pressures applied by Detective Burns and, in exchange for promises of immunity, began to sing. After listening to the chorus, the grand jury released a blizzard of indictments against Schmitz, Ruef, and several bribe-giving businessmen. The trials that resulted were protracted and violent. One supervisor's house was bombed, a newspaper publisher was kidnapped, the chief of police died under circumstances that suggested suicide. Francis Heney, who had been appointed special prosecutor for conducting the trials, was shot by an unbalanced venireman who afterward turned his gun on himself. While Heney was recovering from his wounds, his assistant, Hiram Johnson, completed Ruef's trial.

From the standpoint of the prosecution, the trials were a disappointment. Dismissal of charges, hung juries, and reversals of convictions by the state supreme court freed all of the accused except Ruef, who spent several years in prison before being pardoned. Measured by its effect on the state as a whole, however, the episode had a special impact. It convinced a growing body of reformers throughout California that the structures of government they had inherited from the nineteenth century were archaic and that extensive modernization was long overdue.

California's new idealists were of two persuasions. As had

been the case with the Populists of the 1890s, they were inspired by examples and theories drawn from beyond the state's borders. One group was made up of followers of Eugene Debs's American Socialist party. Their leader in the Bay Area was a Methodist minister, J. Stitt Wilson of Berkeley; in the south it was Job Harriman of Los Angeles. Except for the shocking revelation, just before election day in 1911, that radical unionists had killed twenty-odd workers while bombing the building occupied by the anti-labor *Los Angeles Times,* Harriman undoubtedly would have been chosen mayor of the city, just as Wilson was chosen mayor of Berkeley in 1912.

A larger and more effective group than the Socialists were the Progressives. In California, a majority were young Republicans inspired by a variety of motives. Though repulsed by business immorality, they admired the efficient operations that had been developed by the administrative units of large corporations. They realized that government, too, had grown big and that of necessity many of its functions were being handled by various commissions. If those commissions could be freed from the shackles of machine politics and staffed with trained personnel, government efficiency could be immeasurably increased. Not least, new prestige would attend the rise of this new managerial class.

Progressives who thought along these lines were, on the average, well-educated, relatively prosperous professional men—journalists, lawyers, independent businessmen. They yearned to remake each ugly urban center into "the city beautiful," filled with parks, fine public edifices, sweeping boulevards, and inspiring monuments—a program typified by San Francisco's Burnham plan, which never reached fruition. Horrified by the plundering of the country's natural resources, they supported conservation laws; significantly, most of the Californians who joined John Muir in founding the Sierra Club later marched under the banner of Progressivism. Except in the Bay Area, most supported temperance movements and anti-saloon legislation, for in their minds drink was one of productivity's greatest enemies.

Although they were the products of the country's new urbanism, they borrowed many of their tactics from the Farmers Alliances and the Populists. In order that the corrupt and hence inefficient alliances between political bosses and corporate manipulators could be broken, they argued, power must be returned to the people by means of direct legislation—initiative, referendum, recall, and direct primaries.

California was ripe for an upsurge of new political morality. Los Angeles had already adopted a new charter allowing the initiative and referendum—it was the first American city to do so—and had already used the recall to get rid of an errant official, a move that was again an American "first." Good Government Leagues, mockingly called Goo-Goos by their opponents, had sprung up in several areas. Closely associated with that movement was a statewide coalition, formed in 1907, bearing the ponderous but descriptive name, the League of Lincoln-Roosevelt Republican Clubs. By diligent work these groups pushed through the legislature in 1909 a direct-primary law that wrested control of nominations from machine-dominated conventions. This in turn opened the way for the general body of Republicans to choose short, stocky, eloquent Hiram Johnson of the graft trials as their candidate for the governorship in 1910.

Johnson campaigned tirelessly on one theme: Kick the Southern Pacific out of politics. Avoiding the train as if it were a disease, he traveled 20,000 miles in a big red automobile with a bell that tolled at street corners and crossroads as an invitation to listeners to gather around and hear what he had to say. That approach, added to his fame as Ruef's prosecutor, carried him and a commanding slate of Republican Progressives into the capitol at Sacramento—the city, incidentally, where he had been born and where his father, lawyer Grove Johnson, had been an obedient minion of the railroad.

It was an electric time. Prosperity had returned and immigration was quickening. Between 1900 and 1920, California's population would more than double, from 1.5 million to 3.55 million. The Panama Canal and the Los Angeles aqueduct to Owens Valley, two of the largest construction projects under way in the world at the time, were both nearing completion. Worried as much by the breaking of the continental barrier at the Isthmus as by Johnson's election, the Southern Pacific lost some of its old arrogance. More importantly, the canal underlined a global fact of great consequence: America's acquisition of Hawaii and the Philippine Islands had turned the United States into a two-ocean power, possessed of rich new frontiers awaiting development. In those developments California was bound to play a major part.

With a rush that befitted the state's growing importance, the Progressive administration of 1911 cut itself away from the political bonds of the past. Johnson, a hard-driving and unyielding man, set himself up as the "voice" of the people and assumed greater command over the legislature than any other California governor up to that time. In part, the programs he and his advisers inaugurated had been tested first in Wisconsin, Oregon, and New York. One major exception was the establishment of the first state budget in the nation, supervised by a bureau that reviewed all financial requests from California's growing number of administrative agencies. But whether derivative or original, the legislature's accomplishments—and those of an electorate that in one day, October 11, 1911, approved twenty-three amendments to the state constitution—led Theodore Roosevelt to describe the results (direct-legislation measures, civil-service reform, revitalized regulatory agencies for railroads and utilities, workmen's compensation, and so on) as "the greatest advance ever made by any state for the benefit of its people." [7]

That sweeping compliment must be partly attributed to politics, for Roosevelt was preparing to make Johnson his vice-presidential running mate in the campaign of 1912. Even so, it was pleasant for Californians to receive such attention and realize that they were now exporting ideas as well as receiving them. It was a trend that would quicken until, as the new century matured, California would boast with some justice of being the nation's "window on the future."

7. Quoted in Bean, *California,* p. 326.

11

The Roller-Coaster Years

*C*ALIFORNIA'S greatest problem, some sociologists believe, has been its people's inability—and unwillingness—to slow down. As the twentieth century unfolded, population figures continued doubling every two decades. Significantly, only 37 percent of this increase came, on the average, from births among settled residents. The rest of the new residents were immigrants, a disparate mass pouring ever westward with only their fuzzy hope in California's promises to unite them.

They came from every state in the Union and from a multitude of foreign lands. In addition to the familiar Germans, Irish, French, English, and Scandinavians of earlier years, there were Armenians, Greeks, Portuguese, Italians, Slavs, and Japanese. Mexicans, as distinct from the state's original Hispanic settlers, increased from 8,000 in 1900 to more than 360,000 in the latter part of the 1920s.

There were Greek Catholics and Romanists, Hindus, Buddhists, Moslems, Jews from all over, and Protestants of every sect. The last-named were the dominant religious group in the south; Catholics were a majority in the north. Armenians tended to cluster in the raisin-growing centers of the San Joaquin Valley, Japanese in rich delta lands where the state's two big rivers came together, or on truck farms outside Los Angeles. Mexicans waited out the winters in Southern California barrios placed beyond the railroad tracks where labor contractors could find them at harvest time but where social workers seldom ventured. Many Portuguese were fishermen; the lumber camps were filled with Swedes; Italians liked San Francisco and the sunny, winegrowing slopes of the coastal valleys near the bay.

These newcomers did not amalgamate in California any better than immigrants amalgamated elsewhere in the United States. They formed shotgun patterns of uncommitted groups often suffering from anomie and quite unaware that the state was filled with other entities just as rootless as they were. (Immigrants to California tried to find cohesion by using newspaper space to invite fellow migrants from the same states, or even from the same towns, to mingle nostalgically at huge annual picnics.) Then new hordes arrived, fragmenting social patterns still more. The result, says Moses Rischin of California State University in San Francisco, was a state that "has never had a respite to consolidate its institutions or to firm up its identity." [1]

The difficulties experienced by labor offer one example of constant instability. During the early years of the twentieth century, San Francisco, governed by municipal officials drawn in large part from the Union Labor party, was conceded to be one of the tightest union towns in the United States. By contrast, the Los Angeles area, led by stentorian-voiced Harrison Gray Otis, publisher of the *Los Angeles Times,* stubbornly insisted on the open shop. As a result, wages in some industries in the southland were 30 percent lower than those paid for comparable work in San Francisco.

The rivalry between the two areas was intense. Los Angeles and Long Beach applied constant pressure on Congress for improvements to their contiguous harbors. As trucking grew in importance, the Los Angeles Chamber of Commerce made sure that paved highways united the city's distributors with buyers scattered from the Mexican border to the southern part of the San Joaquin Valley. Meanwhile, persuasive salesmen were sent east to assure industrialists interested in locating branch factories and assembly plants in the West that Southern California of-

1. Moses Rischin, "Immigration, Migration, and Minorities in California," in Knoles, *Essays and Assays,* p. 40.

fered, in addition to a fine transportation system, ample flat land for expansion and a ready supply of cheap, nonunionized labor.

San Francisco, jammed onto the tip of a hilly peninsula, had difficulty matching some of those appeals. As early as 1900, it was one of the most densely crowded cities in America. Single-family dwellings surrounded by lawns—a fetish in Los Angeles even among low-income groups—were rare. Instead, the steep streets were lined with drab rows of multistoried, pastel-colored apartment buildings, each of which had its own bay window protruding far enough to catch whatever glints of sunlight pierced the mists. Factories needing space crowded along the bay shore, often on filled land, particularly in Alameda County, whose center was Oakland. Yet the bay did furnish a unity that sprawling Los Angeles lacked, even with its highways, and so the two areas were able to compete industrially on fairly even terms—except in the matter of wages.

Hurt by the disparity, San Francisco manufacturers vowed to bring wage scales down to competitive levels by breaking their city's unions. To counter that strategy, the unions there decided to help the laborers in Los Angeles lift wage scales to the levels prevailing in the north.

The issue was joined when a rash of strikes disrupted the southern city in 1910. Straightway, the northern unions sent down money and men. Unhappily, three eastern organizers from a militant ironworkers' union also traveled to the scene and expressed their sympathy with two dynamite blasts. One damaged the plant of the Llewellyn Iron Works. The second leveled the building of the anti-union *Los Angeles Times* and killed twenty men.

Eventually, the least important of the three saboteurs was caught, promised immunity, and prevailed on to expose the two principals, brothers named McNamara. Labor cried "Frame-up!" raised a massive defense fund, and hired one of the nation's most famous lawyers, Clarence Darrow, to represent the McNamaras during the trial. But as evidence piled up against the accused, even Darrow lost hope and let the McNamaras plead guilty in exchange for a pledge that they would not be executed. One was sentenced to life imprisonment, the other to fifteen years. Public sympathy, until then on the side of the brothers, swung harshly against them, and organized labor not only in Los Angeles but throughout the state was stigmatized with a reputation for bloodiness that hampered it for years.

Additional setbacks came from the activities of the new Industrial Workers of the World, a radical group committed to organizing all workers, no matter how unskilled or downtrodden, into one big industrial union whose eventual goal was the overthrow of the capitalistic system. In California a favorite IWW tactic was the "free-speech fight," devised as a response to municipal ordinances forbidding the street-corner meetings that served the union's organizers as recruiting forums.

When such an ordinance was passed in Fresno in 1910, organizers working there among migrant farm laborers called for help. Supporters swarmed in, most of them riding the rails. As fast as one speaker was arrested for stepping onto a soapbox to address a gathering, another took his place. Soon Fresno's jail was packed with prisoners singing revolutionary songs and creating an incessant din by beating on the bars of their cells with their eating utensils. After protracted diets of bread and water and brutal drenchings from fire hoses failed to quiet the inmates or reduce the enthusiasm of the speakers outside, the authorities gave in, and the organizers went back to haranguing the farm workers unmolested.

The campaign did not produce many members. Illiterate, suspicious of the motives of organizers, fearful of reprisals from employers, the Mexicans held back. The Wobblies, as Harrison Otis nicknamed them, kept trying, nevertheless. In 1912, they repeated their free-speech drive in San Diego, but that time they were met by vigilante groups of citizens who, unchecked by the police, clubbed and whipped the invaders out of town.

Equally fruitless was a 1913 clash at the Durst hop ranch near Marysville in the Sacramento Valley. When Wobbly organizers tried to form a local there among hop pickers laboring under unspeakable conditions, the ranch owner called for a sheriff's posse to stand guard over the workers' camp. A fight erupted that left several injured and four dead, including a deputy sheriff and the county district attorney. The deaths inflamed prejudice against the Wobblies to such a heat that two of the leaders at Wheatland were sentenced to long prison terms, even though no evidence was produced that linked them with inciting violence or pulling triggers.

An even more blatant case of conviction through prejudice occurred in San Francisco in 1916. In response to an appeal from President Woodrow Wilson, cities throughout the nation scheduled Preparedness Day parades to be held on July 22 as proof of the nation's readiness to join the war in Europe if need be. In San Francisco, where antiwar sentiment was strong among unionists and where a longshoremen's strike was underway, labor declined to participate. Inevitably their leaders were blamed when a tremendous curbside explosion shattered the parade, killing ten persons and injuring forty or so. During the witch hunt that followed, two known labor agitators, Thomas Mooney and Warren Billings, were arrested, tried, and convicted on evidence that was perjured, at least in part. Billings was sentenced to life imprisonment, Mooney to death.

Alarmed by worldwide protests, President Wilson prevailed on California's governor to commute Mooney's death sentence to life imprisonment. Full pardons were denied both men, however, because of the disturbing memories of the McNamaras' confessions following the bombing of the *Los Angeles Times*. All proponents of radical social change, a majority of Californians were prepared to believe, were committed to anarchism and violence.

America's entry into World War I increased the intolerance. The city of Sacramento rounded up and sentenced to long jail terms two-dozen unionists whose only sin was their radical backgrounds. The state legislature made repression official by passing, in 1919, America's second criminal-syndicalism law. (Idaho's was the first.) Aped by at least twenty-three other states, the act outlawed any kind of action that could be interpreted as aimed at bringing about by force or conspiracy ''a change in industrial ownership or control, or effecting any political change.''

When IWW members precipitated a waterfront strike at the

Los Angeles harbor at San Pedro in 1923, employers prodded the police into using the "wartime" criminal-syndicalism law to break the walkout. Inspired by the success of the operation, the Industrial Association of the San Francisco Chamber of Commerce imitated the tactic in a drive to make their city as open, in terms of labor, as Los Angeles was. By the middle of the 1920s, unions throughout the state were on the ropes, sullen and angry but unable to mount sustained counterattacks because of the constant inflow of new job hunters—all this in a decade of unparalleled prosperity for most businesses. It was not a situation conducive to stability.

Simultaneously, the Progressives' emphasis on placing political power in the hands of the people through the initiative, referendum, and recall was unexpectedly eroding the sense of order provided by familiar political situations. Once upon a time, party stands had helped clarify issues. Legislative debate had often produced alternatives to proposed bills. But direct-legislation measures, thrust onto the ballots by the signatures of a relatively small number of voters drawn from any party, upset these traditional procedures. The more frequently this happened, the less responsibility the political parties felt for furthering the desires of the people they represented.

Distinctions grew blurred. In place of the old-time boss who had acted as broker between clearly defined party machines and persons in need of government services came pressure groups—taxpayer's leagues, chambers of commerce, farm co-operatives, manufacturers' associations, labor federations, wine institutes, highway users, and whatnot. Without heed to party affiliations, these special-interest gatherings marshaled initiatives that would force action on measures they desired or referendums that would halt laws already passed or under consideration. They also hired special lobbyists to keep an eye on anything that was happening in Sacramento that might affect their interests. Whenever circumstances seemed to merit forceful action, they employed newly developed, highly sophisticated propaganda techniques to sway public opinion. In all of these processes, party structure was relatively insignificant.

This blurring of party lines was intensified in California by a bizarre cross-filing law, passed by the Progressives in 1913, that allowed a candidate to enter both the Democratic and Republican (and Progressive and Prohibitionist) primaries without his true affiliation ever appearing on the ballot. One was supposed to vote for the man and his standards, not for party labels. But without party labels as a guide, newcomers to California (and many California residents as well) had difficulty learning what a candidate's political philosophies were. For instead of issues, public-relations experts offered them qualities now called "charisma" and "image."

If imagery could be blended with incumbency, so much the better, for an incumbent's name would be known to at least some of his constituents and would furnish his campaign managers with that much foundation on which to start building. The advertisers worked adroitly. Until the cross-filing law was abolished in 1959, scores of candidates, including one governor, Earl Warren, won the multiple nominations they were after and marched into office as standarad-bearers of both the Republic and Democratic parties!

Most of the winners were, in fact, Republicans. Every governor from 1898 to 1938 was a member of that party. By the mid-1920s Democratic resignation had shrunk to 22 percent of the California electorate. In 1924, the Democratic presidential candidate, John W. Davis, received a meager 8 percent of the state's vote. Glumly, humorist Will Rogers remarked, "I am a member of no organized political party. I am a California Democrat." [2]

This extraordinary dominance did not mean continuity of policy, however. The Progressive wing of the Republican party warred more fiercely with the party's standpatters than with the Democrats. Elections became seesaws: Republican Progressives up, Republican Conservatives down; then Conservatives up and Progressives down. During the feuding, which lasted from 1917 to 1942, not a single California governor, not even the lone New Dealer, managed to succeed himself. It is no wonder that Carey McWilliams, drawing his analogy from the descriptive

2. Delmatier et al., *Rumble of California Politics*, pp. 202, 207.

vocabulary of earthquakes, described political California as "the state that swings and sways." [3]

The political mishmash was confused still more by the persistent jealousies between San Francisco-Oakland and Los Angeles. Between 1910 and 1920, the growth of the later region exceeded that of the northern by 80 percent. Because California's constitution specified that representation in the state assembly and state senate should be based on population, the surge of the southland obviously meant political inferiority for the Bay Area. In addition, reapportionment would subordinate fifty-five rural counties (out of a total of fifty-eight counties in the state) to domination by three urban counties—San Francisco, Alameda, and Los Angeles.

In California, however, "rural" did not necessarily mean one-family farms. In the Central Valley in particular, wide blocks of land that on maps looked rural were actually devoted to giant agribusinesses—the notorious "factories in the field," to borrow another of Carey McWilliams's telling phrases. [4] Most were run from corporate offices in San Francisco, and the interests of their managers and stockholders in many ways matched those of the Bay Area's merchants and financiers. "Rural" legislators were, of course, aware of this community of interests and joined with the urban legislators of San Francisco and Oakland in blocking the reapportionments mandated by the constitution.

After nearly six years of stalemate, disgusted Angelenos managed in 1926 to qualify an initiative measure which, if adopted by the voters of the state, would require the legislature either to attend to its responsibilities or to see the redistricting done by a commission composed of leading state officials. Fearful that the populous southland would be able to pass the measure, San Francisco and its rural allies countered with a rival initiative. Let representation in the lower house be apportioned on the

---

3. Carey McWilliams, *California: The Great Exception* (New York: A. A. Wyn, 1949), pp. 192–214.

4. Carey McWilliams, *Factories in the Field* (Boston: Little, Brown and Co., 1939).

basis of a head count, but let this advantage for urban areas be offset by limiting every county, no matter how heavily it was populated, to a single state senator. (There was one exception. A few of the most sparsely settled counties would be joined into units represented by one senator only.) The ultimate effect of this plan, as its proponents realized, would be an assembly of urban liberals checkmated by a senate of rural conservatives responsive primarily to the wishes of San Francisco's financial and commercial leaders.

In spite of strident opposition in the southland, the second proposal carried, and Los Angeles was, politically speaking, partially hobbled. After every new census the southland struck back, trying to break the bonds. The feuding grew so intense at times that as late as February 8, 1965, the magazine *U.S. News and World Report* seriously asked, "Should California Be Chopped in Half?"

Even as early as the 1920s, the answer was clearly "No!" The problem was one of accommodation, not severance. In California, as elsewhere in America, the decade following World War I was marked by the last sunny days of laissez-faire capitalism. Throughout the state industrial prosperity soared. Innovations abounded; success fed on itself. Population grew during those ten years by 2.2 million, the highest growth rate in terms of percentages that the state ever experienced.

Newcomers, dividing when they reached the West, might locate in Southern California, in the Central Valley, or around San Francisco Bay, but the thrusts that had moved them to the continent's end and then held them there were, in sum, responses to a symbolic entity called simply "California," the place where promises were still conceived of as comng true. Furthermore, and in spite of a natural environment of great diversity, California really had been unified by efficient webs of commerce and transportation. Thus, for both psychological and economic reasons, neither half of the state could afford to let the other spin free. Political rumblings about secession were largely defensive, born of the need to hold a place on the top rail of the roost—but without tearing down the hen house in the process.

Somehow the constantly changing strategies worked, to the be-
musement of outsiders and with considerable swinging and
swaying for the participants.

"Innovations abounded; success fed on itself"—it would be
hard to overstate the significance of that statement. Nearly 2.25
million new residents in one decade created insatiable demands
for every sort of material related to construction. To provide
those supplies indigenous new factories took shape; eastern industrialists rushed new assembly plants to completion. In 1900
California had ranked twelfth in the roll of manufacturing states;
by 1940 it had risen to eighth.

Oil discoveries proliferated, first in the southern San Joaquin
Valley and then in the Los Angeles Basin. From 1903 to 1914
and again from 1924 to 1936, the state led the nation in the
production of petroleum. Experimenters began, fatefully, learning how to drill wells in the ocean off Long Beach. The refining
of petroleum products became California's largest industry;
shipping them east through the Panama Canal helped Los Angeles's man-made harbor pass San Francisco's in the value of
products handled. The availability of oil, coupled to worries
over Japan's rising power in the Far East, led the United States
Navy to develop San Diego Bay into one of the most powerful
naval bases in the world. All this absorbed incalculable man-
hours of energy.

Then there was the automobile. By the end of the 1920s, Californians drove 10 percent of all the cars and trucks operating in
the nation. Attending those independent transportation shells
were hosts of auxiliary industries—tire stores, repair shops, filling stations, roadside cafes, and "motels," a word coined, it is
claimed, by the operator of a hostelry in San Luis Obispo.

The world's first merchandising center designed for shoppers
traveling by car was Wilshire Boulevard's Miracle Mile in Los
Angeles, created in 1925. Although the first freeway, linking
Los Angeles and Pasadena, was not completed until the close of
the 1930s, the germ was inherent in the state's early determination to improve the highways that reached from the hearts of the

cities to the residential districts outside. Between the wars suburbia became the normal pattern of life for a sizable percentage of Californians. After the second conflict, the pattern would spread throughout the nation.

Not content with profits generated by the state's own motor vehicles, California businessmen set about luring in more from the outside. Pressure on the federal government for all-year interstate highways, state automobile clubs that printed maps and folders describing local attractions, the odd conjunction of the highest peak in America next to the lower-than-sea-level reaches of Death Valley, Yosemite's waterfalls, redwood trees in the north and orange trees in the south, Spanish missions, warm beaches, the palatial homes of movie stars set among semitropical plants—all these soon made tourism one of the state's lushest sources of revenue. The tourist industry, too, had spinoffs. As had happened during the railroad boom of the 1880s, visitors invested in real estate either for resale on a rising market or as a place to come to after retirement.

Except for the gold rush, the motion-picture industry as it flourished in Hollywood between the two wars did more than any other development to foster a yearning among the nation's discontented to share in what California supposedly represented. Like the gold rush, this pursuit, too, came about partly through chance. Eastern holders of patents related to film making formed a trust to control production. Independents thereupon began looking for places where they could escape harassment. Distance did not matter. The costs of shipping their raw materials and exporting their finished products were not appreciably affected by freight rates. So why not flee as far as Southern California? For one thing a patent infringer, if detected at all, could avoid process servers by crossing the border into Mexico.

The prim village of Hollywood became the goal. Land was cheap there, yet the town was close enough to Los Angeles so that labor—extras for mob scenes, for instance—was readily available. Shooting seldom had to be delayed because of bad weather, and within a radius of two hundred miles were a variety of scenic backgrounds—mountains, forests, deserts, seascapes, big cattle ranches, humble farms, city streets, opulent homes, ethnic communities—anything a script writer might call for.

Technically, the Hollywood movie moguls were innovative. Artistically, most of them were copycats. As historians Warren Beck and David Williams have pointed out, they fed the public what they thought the public wanted, and so their impact on the moral standards of the Flaming Twenties probably has been overemphasized.[5] But they did spread through middle-class America a stereotyped but nevertheless titillating awareness of the trappings of sophistication. Thus, quite without intending it, the movies boomed the Los Angeles garment industry into world prominence as source for the kind of sportswear and casual clothing that movie people favored. Because movie stars were slim and reputedly ate many salads, agriculture changed as unguessable numbers of acres were switched from potatoes to lettuce to accommodate new American eating patterns.

The giant motion-picture companies were financed in large part by Eastern money, but they were exceptions. California bankers were learning to marshal independent pools of capital sufficiently large to meet most of the other needs of the state. Leading the way was A. P. Giannini, founder of the Bank of America (first named the Bank of Italy). Branch banks built at almost every crossroads in the face of strenuous opposition from independent hometown banks let Giannini tap the resources of millions of small depositors. In return, he instituted for families of modest income the means of buying automobiles and home appliances on the installment plan. He was liberal with farmers and inventors, and on those broad bases, eagerly imitated by other American financial institutions, he erected the world's biggest bank.

Headlong growth throughout the state again brought to the fore the disruptive problems of water supply. After years of controversy, San Francisco in 1913 won the right to flood the Hetch Hetchy section of Yosemite National Park with a reser-

5. Warren A. Beck and David A. Williams, *California: A History of the Golden State* (New York: Doubleday and Co., 1972), pp. 370–380.

voir, a sacrilege that brought from conservationist John Muir an oft-quoted cry of anguish: "Dam Hetch Hetchy! As well dam for water-tanks the people's cathedrals and churches, for no holier temple has ever been consecrated by the heart of man." [6] A decade later, when Los Angeles moved arrogantly into the Owens Valley to augment its supplies, the response from dispossessed ranchers was less poetic. On nine occasions, night-riding vigilantes, led by local bankers eager to jack up the price of land, attacked critical sections of the city's aqueduct with dynamite. The explosions had no more effect than Muir's vocal blast in halting the metropolitan juggernaut.

A far greater project than either Hetch Hetchy or Owens Valley was Hoover or, as it is popularly called, Boulder Dam. Originally, the work was conceived of as a flood-control project to protect the most remarkable agricultural development in California, the Imperial Valley. Located amidst parched sand dunes in the sweltering southeastern corner of the state, Imperial Valley lay below sea level and could be irrigated by tapping the Colorado River. The water transformed an American Sahara into a hothouse whose year-round growing season enabled farmers to ship choice fruits and vegetables east and north during the dead of winter, at premium prices.

Unfortunately, the canal on which success depended was badly engineered. The river banks gave way during a series of floods in 1905. For two years the Colorado poured through the gap into the valley, ripping up farmlands, threatening villages, and creating in the desert what is now known as the Salton Sea. In 1907 the hole was plugged, but the silt-laden river kept building new beds higher than the restraining levees. Unless the problem could be solved, another catastrophe was inevitable.

To meet the challenge, the district's water commissioners joined engineers from the United States Bureau of Reclamation in drawing up plans for a protective dam—one that would also impound supplemental irrigation water—far upstream near Boulder Canyon. Discovering what was afoot, Los Angeles and

6. Quoted in many places, including Roderick Nash, *Wilderness and the American Mind* (New Haven: Yale University Press, 1967), p. 168.

ten neighboring cities formed a Metropolitan Water District—eventually it was enlarged to include 125 towns as far away as San Diego—and asked that the project be expanded enough so that they, too, could draw water from the harnessed river. As costs and sizes soared, objections poured in. The other states along the river feared they would lose their claims to water if Southern California established priorities through earlier appropriation for beneficial use, a fundamental point in western water law. Private power companies, anticipating competition from electricity generated by publicly owned turbines, raised specters of socialism. The power companies also fostered a widespread belief among farmers in other sections of the nation that the water would put one million new acres under cultivation, creating surpluses that would drive crop prices to new lows. Taxpayers everywhere grumbled about footing huge bills for the benefit of one limited area.

Senator Hiram Johnson and Congressman Phil Swing of Imperial County worked out acceptable compromises with most of the opponents and then, in 1928, pushed through Congress a bill authorizing the dam. Meanwhile, the Metropolitan Water District used voter-approved bond issues to fund its giant aqueducts and intake reservoir. The end result was the tallest dam, the largest man-made lake, and the most complex water delivery system on earth at the time. If there were any questions in the country about the muscle Southern California still possessed beneath a surface froth of strange religious cults, funeral customs, and movie-colony culture—aberrations that intrigued satirists everywhere—the giant undertaking should have answered them.

And yet the satirists were not altogether mistaken. All was not well in Eden. Medical quacks, faith healers, and swamis of all sorts exploited health seekers who, on discovering that California's vaunted climate did not cure every ailment, turned to human soothers in final hope. Rootless people sought steadiness from assurances offered by fundamentalistic fire-and-brimstone religious sects. The most popular show in Los Angeles occurred weekly at the huge Angelus Temple of the Four Square Gospel Church, where Aimee Semple McPherson, clad in flowing white, routed the forces of evil during thunderous spectacles that outstaged even the movies.

More harmful were amoral businessmen like oil pioneer Edward Doheny, a principal, though unconvicted, actor in the Teapot Dome and Elk Hills oil scandals that blackened the Harding administration. Smaller fry were just as frenzied in their search for quick profits, a state of mind that allowed the insiders of the Julian Petroleum Company to bilk 40,000 investors of $150 million in one of America's most monumental stock swindles. Embezzlement coupled with gross inefficiency broke so many companies, including giants like American Mortgage, Guarantee Building and Loan Association, and Richfield Oil, that during the latter part of the 1920s Los Angeles led the nation in bankruptcies brought about by fraud.[7]

Throughout all this, California was simply mirroring, with its usual intensities, the state of the nation—its speculative fevers, unbalanced economy, uneven distribution of wealth, shifting cultural values, and a notable lack of strength in government policy-making. The adjustment came with the stock-market crash of 1929, followed by the widespread unemployment and suffering of the 1930s.

California, a prey to excesses of every kind, was particularly hard hit. Tourism all but vanished as a major source of revenue, as did once-voluminous, highly lucrative transactions in real estate. Hundreds of thousands of retired people lost their savings, their pensions, and the income from the mortgages they held on their former homes, farms, and small businesses in the Middle West. These collapses devastated the state's small manufacturing concerns and retail commerce. Only the movies kept rolling along relatively unscathed, because more than ever people needed lightheartedness and hope, even celluloid hope.

Desperate families outside of California were either unaware of or disbelieved the tales of these failures. Surely there were jobs in the golden state; hadn't the propaganda always said so? And if there weren't jobs, at least the winters wouldn't be so cold. As had happened during previous depressions, many unemployed flocked west. Even during the stagnant 1930s, the state's population swelled by 1.2 million.

But California did not want impoverished workers. Tens of

7. Caughey, *California: Life History*, p. 448.

thousands of Mexicans and Filipinos were pressured into returning to their homelands, sometimes with their passage money
paid. But what could be done about native-born Americans? Between 1934 and 1940, some 365,000 refugees from drought-
stricken farms in Oklahoma, Arkansas, Missouri, and northern
Texas streamed westward in caravans of overloaded automobiles—the best-known migration in American history,
thanks to Dorothea Lange's searing photographs and John Stein-
beck's novel, *The Grapes of Wrath*.

Because most of the Okies and Arkies, as all dust-bowlers became known, were farm folk, they turned instinctively to the
San Joaquin Valley in search of either land or jobs. Because
they were willing to work for any pittance, their presence enabled belligerent employer groups like the Associated Farmers
to put down, sometimes with the roughest sort of tactics, the
strikes that radical union organizers were calling in the fields
and packing houses. Congregated in miserable shanty towns in
the hot, dusty valleys, they became the most exploited of the
poor.

At first, local government did relatively little to alleviate suffering, either on farms or in the cities. When the depression
struck, conservative Republicans held the statehouse at Sacramento. One typical reaction was Governor Rolph's vetoing of a
bill that would raise money for relief through a personal income
tax on the wealthy in favor of a general sales tax that hurt the
very people it was designed to help. And yet the Democrats, in
spite of a dramatic upsurge in their numbers, were unable to
produce a much more viable program. In 1934, they nominated
as governor a prolific novelist and longtime Socialist, Upton
Sinclair. Sinclair's fuzzy radicalism so alarmed the state's commercial interests that they spent unprecedented sums to defeat
him. They smeared him as a cloven-footed Communist (always
an effective tactic in California, as witness the rise of Richard
Nixon) and even hired Hollywood movie producers to produce
scare films showing what would happen if such a man were
elected.

He wasn't. Partly because he wasn't, the state's aging, destitute middle-class voters proposed a series of initiative measures

which, if passed, would have forced the taxpayers into support-
ing a variety of starry-eyed pension plans. Throughout much of
the decade California politics was kept in constant turmoil by
these measures, a circumstance that outsiders cited as one more
proof of California's essential kookiness. Not until 1938, when
circumstances had already forced a broad liberalization of relief
policies, was an avowed New Dealer, Culbert Olson, sent to
Sacramento. He heartened his followers by issuing, as his first
official act, a pardon to Tom Mooney, but in the main his effectiveness was vitiated by his illness, inflexibility, and partici-
pation in intraparty squabbling.

Not everything was sour, of course. Stimulated by provisions
in the National Industrial Recovery Act that encouraged the formation of unions for collective bargaining, labor in San Francisco set out to recover the position it had held early in the century. In 1934, a confrontation between a stubborn Waterfront
Employers association and a militant longshoremen's union led
by Harry Bridges resulted in a July battle that left two strikers
dead and scores seriously hurt. This "Bloody Thursday," as
labor called it, was followed by a paralyzing general strike, a
call for state militia, intense negotiations—and victory for
Bridges in the form of a comprehensive group contract, signed
in 1935 by the San Francisco Employers Association and the
Labor Council, that "became a California trademark and a national model for areawide collective bargaining agreements in
other industries." [8]

Massive government projects with long-term implications for
the future helped relieve unemployment. By purchasing the
bonds of the Metropolitan Water District, the Reconstruction Finance Corporation enabled Southern California to complete its
huge diversion of Colorado River water. Despite dogged opposition from private utility firms, the United States Bureau of
Reclamation took over and completed a faltering state program
to move water (meanwhile generating hydroelectric power) from
the wet northern reaches of the Sacramento Valley into unre-
claimed sections of the San Joaquin. San Francisco broke loose

---

8. Staniford, *Patterns of California History,* p. 437.

from her cramping peninsula by building two of the largest automobile bridges on earth, one eastward across the bay to Oakland, the other northward to the potentially lovely residential areas of Marin County beyond the Golden Gate.

Years before, in 1915, San Francisco had used the completion of the Panama Canal as a reason for holding, on reclaimed land beside the bay, a dazzling exposition that would prove to the world the completeness of her recovery from the earthquake and fire of 1906. In 1939, on land reclaimed beside Yerba Buena Island in the bay, the state toasted the completion of those strikingly beautiful bridges with another fair of reassurance. Upward of seventeen million visitors flocked to enjoy the offerings. Surely the worst shocks of the depression were over, and the future was brightening again.

Unnoticed in the merrymaking was another coincidence. Both expositions were held while war raged in Europe. Eventually both conflicts involved the United States. For California, the second was profoundly different in that it faced east as well as west. From that circumstance came an acceleration of activities that within two and a half decades would make California the most populous state in the Union, shaken by cultural upheavals whose implications for itself and the rest of the nation still cannot be fully grasped.

12

Too Much Too Soon

$\mathcal{M}$ODERN California is in large measure the creation of the federal government. Between 1940 and 1970 Washington poured upward of $100 billion into the area, more economic stimulation than it provided any other state.[1] Most of that extraordinary sum was used to further programs related to waging one global war, two brush-fire conflicts in Korea and Vietnam, and the Cold War against Russia. The rest has gone into funding highways, housing, educational expansion, agricultural subsidies, and massive social and welfare programs.

So generous a sowing of dollars was bound to produce social changes. Most obvious was California's leap in population—an increase of thirteen million during those same thirty years, 1940 to 1970. About two-fifths of the increment were born in the state. The rest, as usual, came from all parts of the world. Their desires, fueled by inflated paychecks (California's total *personal* income tripled during the first half of the 1940s alone), created new outlets for manufacturers, merchants, workers in service industries, farmers, entertainers, real-estate salesmen, and bunco artists.

Naturally, the newcomers gravitated toward regions where jobs were available—the push was toward the cities. (Califor-

---

1. Gerald Nash, "Stages of California's Economic Growth, 1870–1970: An Interpretation," in Knoles, *Essays and Assays,* p. 49.

nia, the nation's richest agricultural state since 1949, is now 90 percent urban.) The cities in their turn competed vigorously with each other and with similar urban centers throughout the United States for the federal dollars that made new jobs possible. As a result, the voice of federal policy-makers became increasingly clear. Another consequence of the money flow, and one which most wage-earning Californians are still reluctant to grapple with, has been the rapid uglification of both the urban and natural environments. Though pollution, of course, is a worldwide phenomenon, it has held particular poignancy for California because the state offers so much beauty that could be, and is being, destroyed.

In pouring so much money into California, the federal government did not act from caprice. Circumstance was the dictator. Because America's recent wars have been wholly or in large part Asian wars, it was inevitable that the state's superbly developed, westward-facing harbors—San Diego, Los Angeles-Long Beach, San Francisco-Oakland—would be the staging areas from which assaults on the enemy would be mounted.

Other geographic advantages included a variety of terrains where troops could be trained. The navy and the marines practiced joint amphibious landings along different types of California coastline. Mountaineering troops learned to face winter high on the eastern side of the Sierra Nevada. The deserts of southeastern California still show the scars of tank maneuvers. Those same deserts and the uninhabited reaches of the Pacific afforded almost endless room for testing ordinance and practicing bombing runs. Finally, there was the arid climate. Training programs for pilots and navigators were seldom interrupted by bad weather.

Another resource, less tangible but more important than geography, was the availability of a large pool of technically oriented researchers, managers, and workers. Since 1849, the high costs of labor and the challenges of the environment have encouraged experimentation with machinery. Men have searched unflaggingly for better ways to mine, to attack the huge trees of the forests, to harvest vast quantities of crops, to move incredible tonnages of water, to build enormous bridges, to drill to unprecedented depths for oil, to meet the challenges of competitive moviemaking.

The state's private and public universities have fostered faith in technocracy. "[Our] supreme need," declared Dr. Robert Millikan, Nobel Prize winner and longtime president of the California Institute of Technology, ". . . is for the development here of men of resourcefulness, of scientific and engineering background and understanding—able, creative, highly endowed, highly trained men in science and its application." [2]

Long before the war, the state's major educational institutions had set out to develop that kind of human product. Rivalries between Northern California and Southern California, between Stanford and the University of California at Berkeley, added stimulation that sparked the development of outstanding faculties and ultramodern facilities. Thus, when war broke out, Cal Tech was in a position to handle the $83 million in contracts assigned it by the federal government's Office of Scientific Research and Development, a plum second only to that reaped by the much older Massachusetts Institute of Technology. Thus the University of California at Berkeley was able to develop with extraordinary speed the Lawrence Radiation Laboratory, where most of the engineering work on the atomic bomb was worked out, and, in addition, to manage the facilities at Los Alamos, New Mexico, where the first bombs were built.

These managerial skills were complemented by a labor force that was used to meeting the demands placed on it by the state's scientific specialists. Additional skilled workers poured in from the outside as recruiters spread word throughout the nation of good jobs in a desirable locale at high pay, plus draft exemption on the basis of employment in essential industry. During the first half of the 1940s, the number of wage earners in California jumped by nearly one million, despite the departure of nearly 750,000 young man and women for service in the armed forces.

Several notable trends accompanied this sharp rise in employment. One was the disproportionate number of federal civilian

2. Quoted in Carey McWilliams, *California, The Great Exception,* p. 268.

employees in the state—nearly half a million. Another was the hiring of significant numbers of women who after the war would be increasingly reluctant to confine their energies to housework. A third was the taking over of most of the state's unskilled jobs by Negroes, whose numbers in California more than doubled during the war years, and by fresh waves of farm and construction laborers from Mexico. All these factors, visible mostly in hindsight, forecast marked changes in the state's postwar social fabric.

Because yards already existed at major harbors and ample space was available for new ones, shipbuilding became one of the state's major industrial contributions to the war. The leading figure in this huge enterprise was one of California's most astonishing entrepreneurs, Henry J. Kaiser of Oakland. His name was magic in the construction field. Kaiser companies had helped build four of the West's major dams—Hoover and Parker on the Colorado River, Grand Coulee and Bonneville on the Columbia. They had played a major part in linking Oakland to San Francisco with the San Francisco Bay Bridge. Kaiser projects used so much cement that the company built the largest cement plant in the world just to supply its own needs.

As Kaiser had ample reason to know, California's capacity for making steel was limited. Two eastern giants maintained subsidiary plants in the state, and a few small independents fabricated specialty steel in Los Angeles and San Francisco. But none had blast furnaces or rolling mills capable of turning out heavy structural steel. This lack of competition allowed Eastern plants to impose arbitrary markups of 10 percent on the steel they sent west for use in major construction efforts.

This arbitrary price increase, which infuriated the state's manufacturers, gave Kaiser the wedge he needed. As the war neared, he approached the federal government's Reconstruction Finance Corporation, convinced its representatives that California's demand for steel would soon soar, and, on the strength of his past performances, was able to borrow enough money to build the state's first fully integrated steel plant. Its original output of 700,000 tons a year was tiny compared to production in Eastern centers. Moreover, Kaiser faced dismaying supply problems. He had to import coal 400 miles by rail from Utah and iron ore 150 miles from desolate Eagle Mountain in the remote Mojave Desert. Even so, he was able to break the stranglehold of the Easterners, force costs down, and thus help bring about an enormous expansion of heavy industry in his state.

Kaiser brought the same supersalesmanship and organization to shipbuilding. Together, he and A. P. Giannini, head of the Bank of America, convinced Franklin Roosevelt that they could put together in California new facilities fully as competent as those on the East Coast—if they received federal help. The upshot was the government's expenditure of $409 million on California shipyards, as compared to $29 million advanced by private bankers, a clear indication of where the sinews of war truly lay.

Although not all the money went to Kaiser, he employed on his shipways more than 100,000 of the nearly 300,000 ship-builders that were at work in the state by 1943. Of the new freighters that slid down the California ways at the rate of one every ten hours, so many were Kaiser-built that he was dubbed, to his horror one hopes, "Sir Launchalot."

While the fog-shrouded north was garnering the bulk of the state's shipbuilding contracts, the sunny south was turning air-craft assembly into an equally profitable enterprise. Although motors were built in the East, they were shipped to the West for inclusion in frames constructed in a sprawling network of plants centered around Los Angeles (which drew $7 billion worth of contracts during the war) and San Diego ($2 billion worth).

Thirty years of tradition stood behind this pattern. Southern California was a good place for flying. The first United States air meet was held there in 1910. The nation's first scheduled air run, Los Angeles to San Diego, began service in 1925. Two years later, Charles Lindberg flew across the Atlantic in a plane that had been built in San Diego. During the 1930s, the Douglas Corporation developed its famed DC-3 passenger plane, so well adapted to its purposes that it enabled commercial airlines to get by on fares alone, without the need of government mail sub-sidies. Meanwhile, Lockheed Aircraft Company was developing a versatile competitor, the *Electra,* which, events soon proved, could be quickly converted into a bomber.

Even before the war broke out in Europe, the British government was buying *Electra*s from Lockheed. The awesome victories of the *Luftwaffe* during the early months of the conflict quickened the orders and also led President Roosevelt to ask the country to finance the production of 50,000 planes a year. The request seemed impossible. Fewer than 20,000 workers were straining the nation's aircraft factories to capacity to turn out 6,000 planes each twelve months. But again a federally financed crash program wrought wonders. With Lockheed in the van (with 95,000 employees), California plane assemblers in 1944 produced almost twice as many aircraft as the president had called for in 1940.

The hectic pace took its toll. As was true elsewhere in the country, private lives were increasingly cramped by government directives. Hardly a family escaped the shadow of the Selective Service System, as young men became subject to the draft at eighteen. Nonessential industries (gold mining for one—an irony for California) were denied priorities in obtaining tools and materials and hence were forced to close down. Conversely, industries rated as essential to the war effort were allowed to hire men and requisition goods as their needs directed.

The awarding of contracts resulted in massive population shifts. Often the only housing available in favored areas was dreary rows of trailers or hastily assembled tract houses. Although rents supposedly were controlled, a newcomer often had to make an under-the-table payment before he could find a place to locate himself and his family. The rationing of gasoline, tires, sugar, meat, and other items produced, as one side effect, flourishing black markets. Schools went on double session. Waste in some industries was appalling. But pay checks were fat. For their sake as well as for the good of the country, the great majority of workers endured what they had to as honestly as they could. They built up bigger savings accounts than they had possessed before, bought war bonds, donated blood, helped in each town's USO headquarters. The upheaval in modes of living was national, of course, but California's fevered growth—nearly 2.5 million new residents during the war years alone—made tensions particularly acute there.

Prejudices emerged nakedly. In spite of songs about Rosie the

Riveter, women were not welcomed as fellow laborers by most workers in the shipyards. The unions stayed adamantly unsympathetic toward Negroes, as did the armed forces. Black soldiers and sailors were given the most menial and dangerous jobs, such as transferring live ammunition from freight cars to ships. In July 1944, while one such transference was under way at Port Chicago, beside San Francisco Bay, a violent explosion killed 323 persons and destroyed buildings and ships worth $12.5 million. Less than a month later, a crew of 400 black sailors, most of them ill-educated draftees from the Southern states, walked off the job in the devastated city and asked for assignment to some other task. After a highly prejudicial trial, they were convicted of mutiny. Their sentences ranged up to fifteen years in prison.

In Los Angeles rioting soldiers and sailors ran down and beat up scores of Mexican "zoot-suiters," so-called because of the bizarre cut of their clothing. But the greatest of the indignities was the one visited upon the Japanese, the inheritors of California's persistent animosity toward Orientals.

Western pressures, it will be recalled, had led Congress in 1882 to ban further Chinese immigration into this country. Immediately thereafter, anti-Chinese riots in rural districts had driven the bulk of the Asiatics already in California to shelter in urban ghettos. By coincidence, during that same period, the government of Japan at last allowed that nation's citizens to emigrate if they wished.

Most of those who came to the United States were middle-class farm families that through ill luck had fallen into poverty. They quickly found employment as migrant laborers on ranches that had once employed Chinese. Because they worked as families (the Chinese had seldom brought women with them), and were frugal, industrious, and better educated than the Chinese, they progressed more rapidly. By pooling capital, neighbors were soon able to rent and eventually own farmlands and small businesses.

Initially, most of the Japanese congregated in Northern California. As the influx quickened during the early years of the twentieth century, San Francisco's strong labor unions raised the old bogey of coolie competition and began agitating for the exclusion of Japanese as well as Chinese from the United States. In 1905, the prejudice infected the San Francisco school board, which ordered the ninety-three Japanese children in the city's public schools to be transferred to a structure originally built for Chinese.

The move turned out to be explosive. Anti-American feeling was hot in Japan. After winning an upset victory over Russian in 1905, the hitherto ignored island empire had asked President Theodore Roosevelt to mediate in a peace treaty. The terms that emerged from the meetings Roosevelt arranged at Portsmouth, New Hampshire, were less satisfactory than Japanese jingoists wished, and they blamed the American president. It was just at that point that San Francisco insulted the children of Japanese parents, and resentment ballooned into talk of war. Agitated, Roosevelt summoned San Francisco's Mayor Eugene Schmitz (then under indictment for graft in the Ruef affair) and leading members of the school board to Washington. There he prevailed on them to rescind the order, and in exchange a "gentleman's agreement" with Japan was worked out that resulted in restrictions on Japanese immigration to the United States.

Despite the paper barrier, Japanese kept coming. To escape hostility in Northern California, many moved to the Los Angeles area. As hired hands, they were welcomed. As leasers and purchasers of truck gardens and citrus groves, moves that brought them into competition with white farmers, they were not. Angry ranchers demanded protection—and got it. Taking advantage of a national law that denied citizenship to all Orientals, Governor Hiram Johnson's vaunted Progressives in 1913 passed an act that prohibited aliens ineligible for naturalization from buying farmland in California or even leasing it for more than three years.

The law turned out to be toothless, however. American statutes declared that all children born on American soil, regardless of the allegiance of their parents, automatically became American citizens. Japanese desirous of owning land simply put the title in the names of their American-born children. Bachelors without children sent to Japan for "picture brides" (marriage by proxy was both legal and customary in that country) and raised children who could be land owners. Outraged by the "duplicity," California nativists established a League for Oriental Exclusion and enlisted enough support in the East that Congress, on passing the Immigration Act of 1924, which established quotas for immigrants from most nations, barred Japanese as well as Chinese.

However, no law forbade natural increase. By 1940 there were over 112,000 Japanese on the West Coast, 94,000 of them in the Golden State. They controlled 90 percent of the truck gardens around Los Angeles, maintained a sizable fishing colony at the San Pedro harbor, and raised most of the commercial flowers and did most of the landscape gardening in Southern California. Young American-born Japanese made good records in schools and colleges, established businesses, became skilled professionals.

None of those virtues helped after Japan's attack on Pearl Harbor. Rumor, much of it spread by radio commentators, blamed Japanese living in Hawaii for abetting the debacle there. The same disembodied voices added dire warnings about a similar attack on the mainland. Hysteria climbed to such a point that the state's governor, Culbert Olson, the attorney general, Earl Warren, the mayor of Los Angeles, Fletcher Bowron, and even Walter Lippmann, then visiting in San Francisco, joined in demanding the removal of potential saboteurs from sensitive areas along the coast.

When government investigators officially blamed the military commanders in Hawaii for the disaster at Pearl Harbor, the head of the mainland's Western Defense Command, Lt. Gen. John L. DeWitt, took fright. Suppose *he* were the victim of a surprise attack! Declaring in panic that "112,000 potential enemies, of Japanese extraction, are at large today . . . organized and ready for action," he recommended their immediate evacuation from the western halves of the coastal states and from southern Arizona, a step already under consideration by Provost Marshal General Allen Gallion in Washington.[3]

3. Quoted in Bean, *California,* p. 432.

On February 19, 1942, President Franklin Roosevelt launched the evacuation by signing Executive Order 9006. The roundup then began—a roundup that ignored the fact that 71,000 of the evacuees (of which 60,148 were in California) were American-born and entitled to the protection America theoretically gives all its citizens. Because the victims had to sacrifice their property for whatever they could get, monetary losses amounted to perhaps as much as half a billion dollars. In terms of degradation the suffering was immeasurable. Each man, woman, and child spent from two to three years behind barbed wire in "relocation camps" of planks and tar-paper scattered throughout the inland parts of the western United States.

After the war was over, about two-thirds of those who had once lived in California returned to the state. In 1952 Congress allowed Oriental residents of the country to become citizens. That same year, the California Supreme Court declared that the Alien Land Act, by then thirty-nine-years old, was unconstitutional. Meanwhile, the federal government was granting partial compensation—it amounted to about one-tenth of the estimated losses—to those of the evacuees who had been born in America. The total paid eventually reached about $38 million, as compared to the $350 million spent on moving the evacuees and maintaining the relocation camps.[4] Such bitterness as the Japanese may have felt, they concealed. Slipping energetically back into the mainstream of California life, they swiftly gained the respect of the society that had humiliated them.

As the war drew to a close and military procurement dwindled, thoughtful Californians began to worry about the economic shocks of peace. Fortunately, they were able to turn for leadership to the greatest stabilizer of twentieth-century California, Earl Warren.

Warren, born in Los Angeles in 1891, was the husky, hard-working, ambitious son of poor Scandinavian immigrants. After winning a law degree from the University of California, he worked for three years in a private firm, served during World

4. Beck and Williams, *California: A History*, p. 423.

War I as an army lieutenant, and on being demobilized entered government service as an employee of the City of Oakland. Soon he was district attorney of Alameda County. His handling of that office brought him statewide recognition as a sound administrator and relentless prosecutor of grafters, bootleggers, and fraudulent businessmen. In 1938 he became attorney general of California by crossfiling in the Republican, Democratic, and Progressive primaries and winning all three. The momentum generated by the triumph and intraparty bickering among the Democrats enabled him to move on to the governorship in 1942.

Outside of the state he was an intensely partisan Republican. He headed the California delegation to the GOP national conventions in 1936 and 1944. As the keynote orator of the latter gathering, he heaped obloquy upon all things Democratic. In 1948 he ran as Thomas Dewey's vice-presidential candidate in a fruitless campaign to unseat Harry Truman. In 1952 he hoped to be named the Republican's standard-bearer in the event of a deadlock between Robert Taft and Dwight Eisenhower. Sensing soon that the strategy would not work, he aided the pro-Eisenhower forces in their successful challenging of the credentials of certain delegations pledged to Taft. As a reward, Eisenhower named Warren chief justice of the Supreme Court in September 1953.

Inside California, by contrast, Warren had studiously avoided all mention of party, concentrating instead on creating an image of himself as an oak-strong, middle-of-the-road, nonpartisan leader capable of unifying the state's efforts in either war or peace. Chief agents in putting the picture across were the long-practiced, husband-and-wife public relations team of Clem Whitaker and Leone Baxter. They made capital of Warren's rugged Nordic handsomeness—they taught him, it is said, how to relax his stern expression at appropriate moments with a warm smile [5]—and of his photogenic wife and six children, one of them a blonde beauty known to the delight of the electorate as "Honeybear."

5. Caughey, *California: Life History,* p. 547.

Fortified by these resources and his record as attorney general, Warren easily defeated Olson's attempt at re-election in 1942. He won both the Democratic and Republican primaries in 1946, almost repeated the unprecedented victory in 1950, and in the general election that fall topped his opponent, James Roosevelt, by a million votes. No other California governor has ever been elected to three terms. Almost certainly Warren could have made it four if he had not joined the Supreme Court. Moreover, he achieved his triumphs in the face of Democratic registrations that outnumbered Republican by more than three to two.

His philosophies fitted the cautious liberalism of the times. Except in the field of health insurance, where he ironically was defeated by Whitaker and Baxter (employed now by the California Medical Association), he had little trouble in implementing a program of mild social reform—increased old-age pensions, broadened unemployment insurance, better mental-health care, enlightened labor legislation. He sponsored a series of "governor's conferences" at which delegates chosen from all levels of the electorate were invited to offer suggestions about prison reform, water needs, care of the aged, traffic safety, agricultural labor, and so on. Remedial action did not always follow, but at least California's ever-shifting populace was given an opportunity to view and comment on some of the soft spots that were developing in Eden.

Warren's strength lay not in innovation but in administration. During his ten years in office, the state's population grew by 3.7 million. Revenues swelled from $395 million in fiscal 1943–1944 to $1.3 billion in 1953–1954.[6] In the main, the state's proliferating bureaus (the number of California's civil-service employees jumped from 24,000 in 1943 to 56,000 in 1953) handled this hyperthyroid growth efficiently and honestly. This was particularly remarkable in view of the intense pressures brought to bear on all branches of the government by a corps of effective lobbyists.

Chief among them was Artie Samish, who in the early 1930s had established close contact with the heads of key legislative

6. Delmatier et al., *Rumble of California Politics*, p. 317.

committees and then, during the next decade and a half, had spent over a million dollars furthering the desires of the brewery, trucking, build-and-loan, tobacco, and chemical industries he represented. In 1949, following an exposure of his methods in two national magazines, he was barred from the capitol by a suddenly righteous legislature. Four years later, he was sent to prison for income-tax evasion.

Another scandal involved unwholesome ties between the office of attorney general, then occupied by a Samish candidate named Fred Howser, and organized crime. Outrage filled the state, but its effect on Warren was minimal. In the popular mind he towered above taint, and in time his example became catching. The administration he passed on to his successor, Lt. Gov. Goodwin J. Knight, was freer from corruption than most of those in the past had been. By and large, thanks to the glow of the Warren image, it has stayed that way.

Virtue did not make its way unaided. Warren succeeded as well as he did because California stayed prosperous. During the war years, the governor was able to cut taxes and still build up a surplus for funding, when peace came, a series of long-deferred highways, dams, and schools. For a little while the foresight seemed wise. The ending of hostilities was marked by lengthened lines outside unemployment offices, and for the first time since the 1850s more people left the state than entered it.

The sag soon reversed itself, however. Many of the departees, it turned out, had been going home to the Midwest, South, or East to visit relatives and, if possible, talk them into returning with them to the Land of Sunshine. In addition, some seven or eight million men and women connected with the armed services, their civilian supporters, the Red Cross, and so on had trained in, spent leaves in, or at least passed through California on their way to the Pacific fronts. On returning home, many had found the old ways of life unbearably stodgy. Remembering free and easy California, hundreds of thousands decided to start over again on the Far Coast.

The pent-up demand of these new people and of California's older residents for telephones, toasters, automobiles, sports wear, entertainment, beefsteak, swimming pools, and whatever else desire could suggest created affluent new markets for alert entrepreneurs. During the years 1946–1947 alone, 2,013 new industrial or assembly plants were built from scratch; 1,764 established ones were enlarged.[7] This was a mere beginning. For every person who found work in some basic industry, three or four more were employed in services or trade.

Real-estate prices soared again. Following a sharp slump, the erratic lumber business boomed. Any veteran who wanted a home could get a government loan at miniscule interest rates. Choice farmland began to disappear at a rate of 375 acres a day to make room for freeways and overnight villages of depressingly uniform ticky-tacky houses whose residents with their blaring TV's, radios, and bursting families—these were the years of the national baby boom—lived cheek by jowl and seemed to like it. For those who could not afford tracts there were trailer camps, today generally called "mobile-home estates." By 1960, 16,000 of these establishments dotted the state, creating worrisome tax and school problems for county supervisors who didn't know quite how to classify them or provide necessary services. Meanwhile, colleges and trade schools of every sort were sharpening the skills of the tens of thousands of young students who were able to qualify for GI educational loans.

As fast as one impetus to expansion faded, another took its place. During the Korean War of the early 1950s, California received 25 percent of all federal defense contracts. When the end of that conflict threatened to bring a slackness to the economy, the Eisenhower administration in 1956 passed a federal highway act that promised to grant the states during the next twenty years $15 billion for road construction.

In California good roads had always been looked on as a good investment. Each year millions of tourists (14.3 million in 1966) visited the state, two-thirds by automobile. Together with California's own restless travelers, who owned more automobiles per capita than did the residents of any other state, they spent a billion dollars annually on food, lodging, souve-

7. Durrenberger, *California: The Last Frontier,* p. 101.

nirs, and entertainment. Then, too, there were the needs of the state's $8 billion trucking industry. In order to meet those demands while gaining as great a share as possible of the federal government's handout, the California legislature in 1957 authorized $10 billion in highway bonds spread across the next ten years, the money to be used primarily for constructing 12,500 miles of multilane freeways.

In that same year, 1957, Russia's firing of Sputnik triggered a "catch-up-quick" burst of spending. Aerospace and electronic firms throve. So, too, did the construction industry, for great pressure was put on the nation's—and California's—schools to lift educational standards to the levels presumably attained by the Cold War enemy. Characteristically, and this was especially true in California, the quickest way to solve the problem was deemed to be the spending of huge sums of money on improved facilities, from kindergartens to colleges.

Drawn by these economic lures, some 3.1 million new immigrants poured into the state during the 1950s. Two million more births than deaths raised the population by 1960 to 15.7 million. Although the rate of growth during the 1920s had been swifter, this net addition of 5.1 million in a single decade was the greatest numerical influx ever experienced by the state. And still they kept coming. In 1962, boosters proudly announced that California had at last outstripped New York and was the most populous state in the Union, and the second wealthiest.

Predictably, little was said about what second place in wealth really meant. Few Californians knew, for instance, that of the nation's ten biggest corporations none was in California, though seven were in New York; that, although California's Bank of America was the biggest in the world, the combined assets of New York's ten top financial institutions were twice those of California's top ten.[8] It was more satisfying to point out, instead, that 37 percent of the world's Nobel Prize winners lived in the Golden State; that during the Vietnam war 24 percent of all federal defense contracts and 40 percent of all research-and-

8. Art Seidenbaum, *This Is California: Please Keep Out!* (New York: Peter H. Wyden, 1975), pp. 77–79.

development contracts were placed in California—two-thirds of them in Los Angeles County, where the industrial growth rate was ten times that of the national average. The rest of the state didn't do too badly. In the twenty years between 1947 and 1967, industrial output from one end of California to the other jumped from $4 billion annually to $21 billion.

Suburbs spread farther and farther along the new freeways that laced San Diego, San Bernardino, Riverside, Orange, and Los Angeles counties in the south; Fresno in the center; Santa Clara, San Mateo, San Francisco, Alameda, Contra Costa, and Sacramento counties in the north. This melting of cities into rural space that had nothing to do with agriculture forced the census bureau to invent a new term—"Standard Metropolitan Statistic Area"—to describe the new demographic pattern, which spread swiftly from California throughout the nation.[9]

The new towns, each with its architecturally controlled neighborhood shopping center, grew steadily handsomer. Most had winding streets; several were built around artificial lakes or marinas scooped out of the increasingly crowded coastline. Their residents moved frequently in pursuit of jobs made available by shifting contracts and settled easily into new communities almost exactly like the ones they had left behind. Satirists decried the homogeneity in life-styles and social class, but most dwellers in suburbia ignored the gibes and went right on liking their aseptic communities, the space and good schools available to their sheltered children, the outdoor living, and the lack of boredom around the barbecue pits and swimming pools.

As industry and suburbs began to swallow up more and more prime farmland, displaced agriculturists had to find new locations in the seared regions of the San Joaquin Valley. In spite of the massive shifts and growths in population, the state's total farm acreage stayed at about what it had been for decades— some thirteen million acres. The intensity of cultivation increased dramatically, however, and the number of acres under irrigation doubled. As a result, California farmers, who cul-

9. Daniel Boorstin, *The Americans: The Democratic Experience* (New York: Random House, 1973), p. 269. See also pp. 266–268, 287, 290.

tivated only one-fortieth of the nation's farmland, reaped one-eighth of the nation's agricultural dollars. In round figures their income was $4 billion a year—or $13 billion if one added the sums derived from canning and processing.

Federal help stimulated this gargantuan output, just as it had helped industrial growth. Government dollars subsidized the growing of such crops as wheat, cotton, and rice. Federal and state research agencies developed better crop strains and sought to eliminate pests. Between 1942 and 1964, federal departments provided cheap labor by supervising, under agreements with Mexico, the importation of *braceros* ("the strong-armed ones") to cultivate and harvest whatever products could not be handled by machinery. By finishing the Central Valley Project, which the state had been unable to complete during the depression, the United States Bureau of Reclamation provided much of the irrigation water needed by the farmers of the San Joaquin Valley.

There were restrictions on the water, however. A federal law dating back to 1902 forbade the sale to any one individual of more federally produced water than could be used on 160 acres, or 320 acres in the case of a married couple.

The law was the result of a philosophy committed to favoring small farmers. In California, however, where land values were high and mechanized operations expensive, units had to be bigger than those maximums—or so the agribusiness interests of the state argued. They pointed out that limits had been waived in the case of Colorado River water delivered to the Imperial Valley (a favor gained by questionable politics), and they kept fighting in Congress for similar privileges. Many of them were so confident of victory that they accepted a federal compromise that allowed them to buy Central Valley Project water for all their land *if* they promised that ten years after federal water reached them, they would reduce their holdings, at government established prices, to 160 (or 320) acres. Surely, they thought, the undesirable law would be repealed.

In 1958, the United States Supreme Court stunned them by upholding the limitations. Complaining nervously about revolutionary socialism, big landholders began devising ways to sidestep the restrictions . . . but again that is getting ahead of the story. The point now is the effect the decision had on the state's plans for additional water development.

Postwar upsurges in population and industry had made such developments seem necessary throughout the southland's metropolitan areas. As farmers displaced by urban sprawl moved into the San Joaquin Valley, they, too, demanded additional supplies. But, they insisted, along with farmers already established in the valley, the state must do the work in order to keep them free of the federal government's 160/320 acre limitation.

Studies inaugurated by Earl Warren had worked out techniques for moving additional water from the wet north, but politics were something else. Jealousies between north and south, clashing social philosophies, costs—an estimated $12 billion spread over sixty years—and objections by conservationists kept blocking action until Edmund G. (Pat) Brown, California's second Democratic governor in sixty years, was elected in 1958. Brown vowed to push the project through. The first step, he decided, would be the harnessing of the Sacramento River's principal tributary, the Feather, with the tallest dam on earth and the building of a five-hundred-mile canal through the San Joaquin Valley and over the Tehachapi Mountains into Southern California.

After a virulent campaign, the voters narrowly authorized the $1.75 billion bond issue Brown wanted—the largest ever adopted by any state. On the face of things, this seemed to commit California irrevocably to continued growth. Yet, even then, growth and the sort of impetus that had brought the growth about, principally the wars in Asia, were falling under increasingly critical scrutiny. The next decade, with its challenges to assumptions more than a century old, was not going to be easy.

13

Challenging the System

AS the 1960s opened, California's complacent, hedonistic, ever-expanding middle class saw little reason to expect the new decade to differ markedly from its predecessors. The space race with Russia and increasing involvement in Vietnam kept farms, shipyards, factories, banks, and trading marts humming. In 1963, the year California became the most populous state in the Union, net immigration amounted to 302,000 persons. Births, phenomenally, were even higher. Extrapolating happily, boosters predicted that the census of 1970 would reveal a population of 25 million.

Prosperity unlimited! To prove their maturity as centers of civilization, Los Angeles, Pasadena, San Diego, Oakland, and San Francisco joined the nationwide rush to foster the creative arts, either expanding existing facilities or building sumptuous new ones. Colleges added experimental theaters, museums, and modernistic sculpture gardens. Shopping centers and banks got into the act. Even the state extended a cautious hand, creating the California Arts Commission but restraining any exuberance it might develop by inadequate appropriations.

Government, too, seemed to be following predictable patterns. In 1958, the conservative and liberal elements of the Republican party fell into another squabble, assuring Democrat Pat Brown's easy capture of the capitol at Sacramento. Although his administration promptly ended cross-filing in an effort to restore party responsibility, he hardly struck middle-of-the-road voters as radical. He spoke of following ''in the giant footsteps'' of Republicans Hiram Johnson and Earl Warren, and, like them, he appealed for bipartisan support.

He began like a whirlwind. In 1959, thirty-five of the forty measures he recommended to the legislature were enacted into law. Two trends were discernible. One was moderate liberalism as evinced by increases in unemployment insurance and welfare benefits, acts to end racial discrimination in public places, and the creation of a consumer council to expose unethical advertising. The other line was a continued push for economic growth. As noted in the preceding chapter, Brown was largely responsible for launching the ambitious California Water Plan. He also established an economic agency charged with working out plans for attracting more industry to the state.

He became a giant-killer among politicians. In 1962, when presidential aspirant Richard Nixon, who in 1960 had carried California by a thin margin while losing nationally to John Kennedy, challenged him for the governorship, Brown swamped him by 250,000 votes. Badly shaken and blaming the state's newspapers for ''shafting'' him, the loser vowed he was through with politics and, running counter to the prevailing patterns of migration, left for New York.

In spite of Brown's successes, however, rumbles of extremism from both right and left suggested that the old game plan of moderation might not suffice much longer in holding political California together. Far on the right was the John Birch Society, revealed in 1961 as a secret organization offering prizes to college students for essays advocating the impeachment of Earl Warren for his allegedly bright red radical views. According to the Birchers, other communistic plots had brought about such horrors as the United Nations, racial integration, social-security taxes, mental-health care, and the fluoridation of drinking water.

But instead of being harmed by this exposure, the Birch Society was strengthened. New members flocked to join its ''cells,'' especially in Southern California. Two Republican congressmen from that area proudly announced their affiliation with the group, and in 1964 movie-actor George Murphy (who was not officially a member) was sent to the United States Senate more because of his conservative views than because of his qualifications—"a dress rehearsal," said one cynical commentator, "of theatrical things to come." [1]

Liberals, meanwhile, were stirring up tempests of their own. The most controversial one revolved around the abolition of capital punishment. Precipitator of the uproar was Caryl Chessman, who in 1948 had been convicted of robbing a couple in a parked automobile, forcing the young woman into his own car (technically a kidnapping, as the law stood) and there raping her so brutally, it was claimed, that she had to be confined to a mental institution. After a trial marked by several irregularities, the accused was sentenced to death. [2]

Insisting vehemently that he was innocent, Chessman and his lawyers managed during the next twelve years to obtain eight stays of execution. During that long incarceration, Chessman wrote and smuggled out of San Quentin a vivid book, *Cell 2455, Death Row,* and granted several highly articulate newspaper interviews. These outpourings and the arguments of the American Civil Liberties Union that being tantalized with death eight times in twelve years constituted cruel and unusual punishment turned Chessman into a glowing figure of martyrdom.

Brown, who personally objected to legal executions, was in a quandary. Because Chessman had already been convicted of another felony, the governor could not commute the death sentence to life imprisonment without the consent of the state supreme court. A majority of the court refused. Rather than challenge the court publicly, Brown granted Chessman a last-minute, sixty-day reprieve, summoned a special session of the legislature in March 1960, and handed it a bill whose passage would end capital punishment in California. He did not exert himself on the bill's behalf, however, and, after hearings

1. Herbert Phillips, *Big Wayward Girl* (Garden City, N.Y.: Doubleday and Co., 1968), p. 220.

2. Caughey, *California: Life History*, p. 570.

that aroused most of the state, it died in committee. Chessman was executed, and disappointed liberals denounced the affair as one more indication of the essential baseness of American society.

Alienation from that society was deepening more rapidly among segments of California's youth than their elders realized. The center of disaffection was in San Francisco, among people who called themselves the beat generation, or beatniks. Among their spokesmen were novelist Jack Kerouac (*On the Road*) and Alan Ginsberg, the author of *Howl,* a free-verse poem that satirized conventional America and praised the irrational, sensuous elements of the human experience.

When Lawrence Ferlinghetti, a San Francisco poet and bookseller, brought out an American edition of *Howl* (first published in England and later banned by customs officials in San Francisco), he was tried for, but ultimately acquitted of, obscenity. It was this affair, a minor West Coast sensation, that introduced the beats, precursors of the hippies, to California. Suburbanites and most working-class people at first dismissed them as inconsequential, unwashed, long-haired, sexually promiscuous smokers of marijuana, devoted to nothing more constructive than strange music and strange handicrafts. The contempt turned out to be ill-founded. For in their wild accents the beats were divorcing themselves from California's rampant materialism and were speaking eloquently to a new generation of the possibilities of freedom from social constraint. Soon many of the young, even those from the well-ordered homes of suburbia, were listening.

Inevitably, the state's educational system became one of the battlegrounds in this conflict between opposing views of the good life. For years Californians had been proud of their schools. The achievements piled up by the University of California at Berkeley during World War II had convinced them that it was the finest publicly supported institution of higher learning in the land. Such private universities as Stanford, Cal Tech, and the University of Southern California were considered leaders in their fields. And the solid rock on which they stood was the state's expensive system of primary and secondary schools.

The population explosion of the 1950s brought trouble, however. Between 1945 and 1965, crash building programs trebled the number of classrooms—but pupils quadrupled. Sufficient numbers of qualified teachers proved hard to find. As scores on national achievement tests dropped, taxpayers began examining the system with jaundiced eyes. One result was a running feud between the proponents of "progressive" education and the advocates of a return to "fundamentals"—the three Rs. Although archconservatives scored an apparent triumph by naming Max Rafferty superintendent of public instruction, he found himself at constant loggerheads with a liberal state board of education.

The hodgepodge of colleges suffered comparable growing pains. At the top of the heap were the state university and its branches. Close behind were half a dozen state colleges that had begun as teacher-training institutes but then had expanded their horizons to include most of the traditional academic disciplines. Finally, there were, at the close of World War II, forty-four two-year junior colleges charged with a double function: offering occupational training and also preparing academic students for later transfer to one of the four-year institutions.

During the 1950s this ill-defined mixture competed stridently for funds, faculties, and students. Functions overlapped, and efficiency experts wagged their heads in dismay. To remedy the deficiencies the legislature in 1960 began implementing a Master Plan for Higher Education prepared by a panel of experts. The program defined areas of responsibility within the system, instituted administrative reforms, and established admission standards. The top one-eighth of graduating high-school seniors were eligible to enter the university; the top third could apply to the state colleges; anyone else who aspired to a four-year degree could prepare himself for eventual transfer to one of the junior colleges.

All seemed well. The junior or, as they came to be called, "community" colleges at the base of the pyramid expanded until by 1975 they numbered more than a hundred. In the middle spectrum were twenty-one widely scattered state colleges. At the pinnacle were the eight campuses of the university, described by its president Clark Kerr as a *multi*versity, a vast knowledge factory serving government and business through research and feeding the professions with the bright young graduates they needed.[3]

Many of the bright young students were less enchanted than California boosters were. Feeling neglected by an impersonal faculty that seemed more interested in private research than in teaching, they asserted that certain aspects of the society would have to be changed if they were to serve it well.

To the bewilderment of their parents, the students began an intense search for anti-establishment causes to support. Civil-rights demonstrations became popular. Hundreds of students visited the South to take part in marches and voter-registration programs, then returned home eager to release their newly discovered techniques of protest on problems within the state.

As the fall elections of 1964 drew near, student political activists set up stands along a sidewalk that bordered one edge of the Berkeley campus. There, dressed in bizarre clothes less familiar then than they became later on, they solicited passers-by to join clubs espousing a variety of programs and to donate funds for political purposes.

Conservative taxpayers objected. A publicly supported university, they said, should not allow its students to interfere in controversial affairs. When the university responded by tightening its rules, the matter ballooned into a confrontation between students and administration over the limits that should be imposed on freedom of speech.

Although the protests began with dignity, they gradually degenerated until finally disorderly columns of students, reinforced by street people—beats, hippies, flower children, or whatever one chose to call them—paraded through the streets bellowing obscenities through loud-speakers, just to show how free they were. Meanwhile, in December 1964, several hundred young people sought to clog the functioning of the university by staging a sit-in at the campus's principal administrative building. State and local police dispatched to the scene by Governor

3. Staniford, *Patterns of California History*, p. 622.

Brown dragged out more than seven hundred protesters "in the largest mass arrest in the state's history." [4]

From Berkeley, student demonstrations spread across the land. Long-haired radicals demanded a voice in the hiring and firing of faculty members and the inclusion of "relevant" courses in the curricula, a request that some professors suspected was a way of reducing the academic work load. Other issues focused on admission standards for black and Chicano applicants from substandard schools in poverty areas, the introduction of new departments of ethnic studies, and, above all, the escalation of the war in Southeast Asia.

Resistance to student ultimatums triggered noisy rallies and, all too frequently, violence. Bombs exploded, and students battled police on the campuses at Stanford, San Francisco State College, and the University of California at Los Angeles. In Isla Vista, a student bedroom community just outside the University of California at Santa Barbara, a student died as a mob burned down a bank building that the demonstrators felt was a symbol of the immoral link between big business and the Pentagon. Another tumultuous and fatal riot erupted in 1969, when the University of California at Berkeley sought to close a piece of university land that students and street people had appropriated as a "People's Park." When Chancellor Roger W. Heyns of the Berkeley campus resigned his post in November 1970, he declared that he regarded as his greatest accomplishment the fact that the university had been able to stay open at all during those explosive years! [5]

Disaffection with the fading California dream was not confined to the campuses. With increasing violence, minority groups also called on society to readjust some of the disadvantages under which they lived.

Although, as has already been noted, Governor Brown's administration had passed, soon after its installation, various laws striking down segregation in public places, covert segregation in

4. Bean, *California*, p. 489.
5. As reported in the *Los Angeles Times*, November 16, 1970.

the private area of housing remained untouched. A tacit understanding among lending institutions, apartment-house managers,
owners of residential property, and real-estate agents conspired
to confine Negroes, Mexicans, and, in San Francisco, Chinese
to those sections where they had already obtained footholds.

Resistance to this physical constriction was inevitable. Attracted by the same dreams of betterment that lured whites,
blacks and Chicanos poured westward. While California's white
population more than doubled between 1940 and 1965, the
number of blacks multiplied fivefold in San Francisco and ten-
fold in Los Angeles.

In the latter city, 650,000 blacks were packed into the Watts
area of southcentral Los Angeles, a scabby district of rundown
bungalows spread across more than forty square miles of un-
kempt ground lined with ill-repaired streets. The overcrowding
resulted, as it did everywhere else, in substandard schools, juve-
nile delinquency, and hostile relations with the city police. Even
more bitterly resented here was the failure of the California
dream. Unemployment was higher and per capita income lower
in Watts than in any other comparable area in the state. Moreover, because the district was inadequately served by public
transportation, it was difficult for Negroes to reach such jobs as
were open to them.

In 1963, in an effort to relieve the worst housing problems,
Byron Rumford, a black assemblyman from Berkeley, proposed, and the legislature adopted, a bill that forbade discrimination in the renting or selling of houses built, in whole or in
part, with state or federal loans and in all privately financed residential properties containing more than four units. Members of
the outraged California Real Estate Association responded by
collecting enough signatures to place on the fall ballot of 1964 a
referendum on the open-housing issue, which was referred to as
Proposition 14. This measure provided for the repeal of the
Rumford Fair Housing Act and also barred future efforts to limit
an individual's right to ''sell, lease, or rent any part or all of his
real property . . . to such person or persons as he in his abso-
lute discretion chooses.''

No other state, it is said, ever proposed so sweeping a legal defense of social segregation.[6] Students and liberal groups reacted vociferously, but in spite of their protests the voters in 1964 approved the restrictive measure by a margin of two to one.

Later, both the state and the federal supereme courts would declare the proposition unconstitutional, but the rulings did not come in time to lessen black resentment. When police sought on the desperately hot evening of August 11, 1965, to arrest a young black automobile driver, a crowd gathered, then suddenly gave way to long-smoldering rage. For six days Watts was a battlefield. By the time national guardsmen had suppressed the uprising, 34 persons were dead, 31 of them black, 1,032 were injured, and 3,411 were arrested. Property worth an estimated $40 million, much of it owned by nonresident white landlords, had been damaged, looted, and burned. For years afterward the area's central avenue, 103rd Street, would be known as Charcoal Alley.

The episode shocked many residents of Los Angeles into their first awareness of the palm-shaded ghetto that had developed in their midst. White philanthropists joined black community leaders in an effort to reconstruct the torn physical environment while alleviating the situations that had brought on the riot. Something like two hundred different groups drew up plans for improving schools, increasing the number of branch libraries in the area, fostering adult education and job training, building a community hospital staffed by blacks, funding black business enterprises, quickening transportation, and so on. Before enthusiasm waned along toward 1970, many improvements had been wrought. But the ghetto, characterized as always by persistent high unemployment, school dropouts, and low per capita income, remains.[7]

The insurrections, student and racial, produced backlashes as well as helping hands. The disturbance at Watts and a sub-

6. Watkins, *California: An Illustrated History,* p. 491.
7. On March 23, 1975, the *Los Angeles Times* ran a special ten-page report entiled "Watts Ten Years Later."

sequent Negro uprising in the Hunter's Point district of San Francisco confirmed beliefs among wealthy conservatives, laborers, and lower middle-class whites that blacks had to be kept in their places. The same people also agreed vehemently that students, nearly all of them living in part on other people's money, were in need of discipline. As their spokesman, they discovered handsome Ronald Reagan, like Senator George Murphy a movie actor and television personality of modest attainments.

Before his acting had brought him wealth and valuable real estate, Reagan had been a liberal Democrat. Now, hearing a different drummer as a man of property, he had become a Republican, earning a deserved reputation as an eloquent speaker on behalf of free enterprise. Aided by the state's top public-relations firm, he carried this theme into his campaign for the governorship. He denounced government interference in local affairs and decried the Rumford Housing Act not, he insisted on the grounds of racial prejudice, but because it violated property rights. He made capital of "the mess at Berkeley," and reiterated again and again a pledge that if elected he would squeeze, cut, and trim state expenses to the bone. He defeated Brown, the conqueror of Nixon, by a million votes.

Once in office he found himself frustrated. In spite of his earnest efforts to reduce costs, spiraling inflation and the unavoidable expansion of some services caused state budgets to jump during his two terms from $4.6 billion a year to $10.2 billion. His plea in 1967 for state employees to work without pay on Lincoln's Birthday drew a 2 percent turnout and horse laughs from across the nation. He did compensate in part, however. On achieving a surplus in 1969, he ordered a one-shot reduction in state income taxes and instituted a program of using state money to reduce local property taxes, the very sort of Big Brotherism that he vigorously opposed in other fields.[8]

He did not reduce civil disorders. Student protests and racial riots continued throughout the decade. Militancy spread swiftly

8. Tom Goff, "[Reagan's] Legacy for State: Footprints But No Permanent Monuments or Scars," *Los Angeles Times,* September 29, 1974.

to the state's largest minority group, the Chicanos, and infected the Indians, the most depressed economic group in California, as well. To call attention to their plight, a handful of them seized the abandoned federal prison on Alcatraz Island in San Francisco Bay and demanded that the United States government help them develop the site as an Indian cultural center. Instead of offending the people of the United States by fighting them, the authorities simply sat still. Food and water were difficult to obtain on "the Rock," and, when the public lost interest in their cause, the invaders began drifting dispiritedly away.

Another problem that plagued California during the Reagan years was the busing of schoolchildren long distances in an effort to achieve racial balance in education. The Chinese opposed the program strenuously in San Francisco. Whites rose in wrath as cities introduced busing resolutions either under court order or through action by liberal school boards. As Lillian Rubin has shown in her study of the Richmond, California, experience, more than race prejudice was involved.[9] Local neighborhoods, particularly those composed mostly of workingclass people, resented do-gooders of a higher economic scale meddling in family affairs. They truly feared that the introduction of blacks into neighborhood schools would reduce both the quality of education that their children received and the precarious social status that they themselves had managed to achieve. In Richmond, they reacted by sweeping the school board out of office—just as Los Angeles voters denied re-election to the judge, Albert Gitelson, who had ordered busing in that city.

Predictably, perhaps, demands by whites for separatism sparked similar demands among radical blacks. Such organizations as the Black Muslims, led by Malcolm X, and the Black Panthers, formed in Oakland in 1967 by Bobby Seale, Huey Newton, and Eldridge Cleaver, advocated both violence and a black identity apart from that of the whites. They developed their own hairstyles and dress from African motifs. More seriously, they become involved in shoot-outs with the police,

9. Lillian R. Rubin, *Busing and Backlash: White Against White in an Urban California School District* (Berkeley and Los Angeles: University of California Press, 1972).

whom they accused of excessive brutality, in Los Angeles, San Francisco, Vallejo, Oakland, and other trouble spots. They even killed each other; two Black Panthers died on the UCLA campus in a struggle with another group to control that university's black-studies program. Even more shocking was the action of certain radicals on trial in Marin County across the Golden Gate from San Francisco. Using smuggled guns, they seized as a hostage the judge who was presiding over the court and tried to flee. Finding their way blocked, they assassinated the judge before succumbing themselves.

To many dumfounded Californians, it seemed that pure terror was chipping away at all their standards. Some of the violence seemed utterly senseless: the murders conducted in Beverly Hills by Charles Manson and his cult followers; the random slaying of young coeds in the mountains behind the University of California at Santa Cruz; the slaughtering by a single individual of nearly two dozen fieldworkers in the Sacramento Valley.

Operating on a different level but with no less violence were integrated groups of black and white revolutionists. Their purpose, they said, was the overthrow of the government, though what they proposed in its place was not clear. Their favorite technique was to hide a homemade bomb underneath a pylon carrying electrical transmission lines—in government offices and restrooms, beside banks—after which explosion a mysterious caller would contact a radio station or newspaper and give credit for the destruction to one or another of the underground revolutionary organizations.

Among the most bizarre of these avowed terrorist groups was the self-styled Symbionese Liberation Army, a small cadre that used as its trademark a writhing, seven-headed cobra. The "army" first came to notice on November 6, 1973, when its "soldiers" used bullets tipped with cyanide to assassinate the superintendent of the Oakland schools because he intended to introduce measures the Symbionese considered repressive. (Two men were later arrested, tried, and convicted for the murder.) Next, on February 4, 1974, masked members of the same gang kidnapped Patricia Hearst, daughter of millionaire newspaper publisher Randolph Hearst, from her apartment in Berkeley.

Ransom was set at $2 million worth of food to be delivered to the poor of San Francisco. The chaotic, ill-handled distribution was made, but Patty declined to come home. Instead, she denounced her parents and their values in a foul-mouthed tape recording heard in part by millions of stunned television and radio listeners.

Sensation then piled on sensation—a bank robbery in which the poor little rich girl allegedly participated, a wild shootout in Los Angeles during which six members of the "army" died, and then the bombing of the Los Angeles office of the state district attorney, apparently in retaliation for the "massacre." When an intensive, year-long manhunt failed to apprehend Patty (who had not been at the shootout), an overwrought reporter for the *Los Angeles Times* declared, "There is no agency or combination of agencies capable of dealing effectively with the terrorist-revolutionary movement in the United States." [10] He was too impatient. Patty and several associates were finally arrested, with anticlimactic quietness, in San Francisco on September 18, 1975. They could look back on no significant changes brought to society by their violence.

Changes are coming to California, nevertheless, the products not of terror but of the adroit use of social and completely legal tools already in existence. Whites and blacks working together have elected dozens of minority group members to influential offices. A moderate, Wilson C. Riles, replaced conservative Max Rafferty as superintendent of public instruction. After becoming the first black state senator in California's history, Marvyn Dymally rose in 1974 to be the first lieutenant governor—a race that also saw March Fong, a woman of Oriental background, become secretary of state, no mean accomplishment in California.

In 1969, Thomas Bradley, a tall, athletic, soft-spoken lawyer and city councilman, challenged maverick Democrat Sam Yorty for the mayor's office of Los Angeles. Toward the end of the intense race, Yorty appealed openly to race prejudice and defeated

10. Robert Kistler, "Hunt for Patty: FBI Never Really Close," *Los Angeles Times,* June 15, 1975.

Bradley by a narrow 55,000 votes. In a repeat performance, May 29, 1973, Bradley thoroughly trounced Yorty, thus becoming the incumbent of the most important city office held by a black in the United States—and in a city, moreover, where no more than 18 percent of the electorate are Negroes. Meanwhile, as in the rest of the United States, the number of nonwhite city councilmen, legislators, state administrative officers, congressmen (one California representative is a black woman) more than doubled in the five years between 1969 and 1974.

Thus for the urban scene. In the fields, the mover and shaker has been Cesar Chavez, the most widely known Mexican-American in the nation. The outlines of his story are familiar now—childhood years spent as a stoop laborer accompanying his parents from farm to farm, a young manhood devoted to working in Los Angeles and San Jose with a Mexican-American welfare agency called the Community Service Organization, and then his decision to give up what security he had achieved in order to devote himself to welding into effective bargaining units the long-exploited farm workers of California. When Chavez began to organize, in the early 1960s, most of the farm workers were Spanish-speaking. Mingled with them were several Filipinos, Indians from Asia, and some Arabians.

No attempt to unionize the agricultural workers of America had ever succeeded. As noted earlier, the federal government was even assisting California agribusiness, through agreements with the Mexican government, in rounding up seasonal help from south of the border. Chavez correctly believed, however, that the *bracero* program, as it was called, could not endure much longer. Trade unions, opposed for more than a century to the importation of cheap foreign contract labor of any kind, were fighting it hard. Presidents Kennedy and Johnson lent their support to the abolishment of the braceros, and in 1964 Congress brought the program to an end.

Freed of this threat of constantly available strikebreakers, Chavez began his organizational work among the state's Spanish-speaking fieldworkers. Simultaneously, a Filipino named Larry Itliong followed the same line with members of his race. In 1965 the two groups joined hands as the United Farm

Workers Organizing Committee and launched a strike against the leading grape growers of the San Joaquin Valley.

The attack benefited from the civil-rights enthusiasm then filling the nation. Ministers, students, and labor leaders flocked in to help defend the picket lines and provide food and other assistance to the strikers. Even so, morale was hard to maintain among untrained workers fearful of reprisals. The growers, moreover, had little trouble hiring illegal "wetbacks" from Mexico and unemployed, Spanish-speaking construction workers from the cities. In desperation, Chavez called on the country to support a secondary boycott against the products of the San Joaquin growers. The response was overwhelming, and in 1970 they finally capitulated.

But the triumph was short-lived. Intensely opposed to Chavez—he could be arrogant and unpredictable, and he was not a good administrator—his next targets, the state's lettuce and berry growers, anticipated him by rushing into contracts with the Teamsters union. To Chavez, this was a stab in the back, for he had agreed to keep his organizers out of the packing sheds, where the Teamsters claimed jurisdiction, if they did not interfere with his activities in the fields. Moreover, the field-workers were not asked whether they wanted the Teamsters to represent them. Whenever an employer signed a contract, his workers were automatically required to join the union. In justification, the Teamsters declared that as a far older and more experienced group than Chavez's, they could and did give the migrants better service.

Jurisdictional disputes became bitter and bloody. Chavez was jailed for defying an antipicketing injunction, the first time in his life he was ever behind bars. As his contracts with the grape growers expired, they, too, swung to the Teamsters. Membership in Chavez's United Farm Worker union plunged disastrously. Yet he never lost faith or energy. Supporters throughout the nation maintained the secondary boycotts he called against his principal opponents and also kept up continual pressure on the governor's office in Sacramento.

The break came there. After two terms in office Ronald Reagan decided not to run again, and in 1974 he was succeeded, amazingly, by austere, enigmatic Edmund G. (Jerry) Brown, Jr., the Jesuit-trained son of the man Reagan had overwhelmingly defeated eight years before. Summoning key legislators, growers, and union representatives into conference, the new governor—one of the youngest in the land—hammered out a farm bill that was passed by the legislature and signed into law in May 1975.

Because the act was a compromise measure, it did not wholly suit everyone. Nevertheless, it was revolutionary. For the first time in American history, agricultural workers were able to chose, in free elections supervised by the state government, which union—Teamsters or United Farm Workers (or neither)—they wanted to represent them in dealings with their employers. One effect (in addition to a drive by growers for improved machinery to harvest their crops) will almost surely be increased dignity—part of the American and the California dream—for a submerged class that never before had achieved it.

14

Which Way Now?

*O*F the many upheavals that shook California during the dozen years preceding the nation's bicentennial celebrations, the one that now seems most likely to bring about major changes in social values is the accelerating challenge to long-held environmental assumptions. At what point and in what fields do the costs of continued growth in population, industrial wealth, and material well-being become unacceptable?

Even during the gold rush, an incipient schizophrenia about the problem troubled segments of the state's population. Almost without exception the pioneers who stampeded west did so in order to seize as quickly as possible the opportunities available there—and yet from the beginning many of the new arrivals realized that wantonness in the seizing could eventually end up turning the dreams of the rush into a mockery. After riding through the spring-green foothills back of Stockton in May 1858 and noting the frenzy of the miners, young Sarah Haight wrote in her diary, "How unsightly it makes the country appear; how few flowers and how little vegetation there is where there is gold. . . . How often its blighting effects are on the human heart." [1]

1. Francis P. Farquhar, editor, *The Ralston-Fry Wedding, from the Diary of Miss Sarah Haight* (Berkeley: Friends of the Bancroft Library and the Grabhorn Press, 1961), p. 18.

In those days, however, anger over blights rarely swelled into articulate protest. Ugliness ended only if it became unprofitable. When in the 1880s the state finally banned unrestrained hydraulic mining, the most destructive form of gold production, it did so not for aesthetic reasons but because flood-borne "slickens," the yellowish debris of the operation, hurt the fields of California's increasingly powerful farmers. National-forest restraints on overgrazing (a blight that Mexican rancheros introduced first in the coastal valleys) were welcomed not out of love for indigenous shrubs and grasses, but because limitations on livestock protected watersheds needed for irrigation and hydroelectric plants. The federal government donated Yosemite Park to California in 1864 as a resort for recreationists only after being assured that the cleft, or gorge, as the valley was described, had no other discernible economic value at the time.

Environmental history had been made, nevertheless. People liked Yosemite, but it was clear that the intangible values that attached to the land through their enjoyment would remain at a high level only if the land were protected. The first step toward legal protection of aesthetic values in nature came in 1872, with the creation of Yellowstone National Park in Wyoming. Californians welcomed the trend. The next three national parks established by Congress lay within their state [2]—not without economic cause: the powerful Washington lobby of the Southern Pacific Railroad was interested in building up tourist traffic.

For years, the drive to preserve these natural wonders was the primary concern of conservationists. In 1892, John Muir, famed publicist of the California outdoors country, and twenty-six of his friends formed the Sierra Club to acquaint their fellow citizens with the glories of the distant mountains and to enlist their support in preserving them. A quarter of a century later, a Save the Redwoods League was organized to snatch as many of the disappearing redwoods as possible from the relentless saws of the lumber industry. Still later, the Audubon Society fought suc-

---

2. One of the three was Yosemite, which completely surrounded the state-owned valley. In 1905 California reluctantly returned the gorge to the federal government for inclusion in the national park.

cessfully to exclude dams and roads from the Transverse Ranges in Ventura County, where the nation's fifty-odd remaining condors nested. Joining forces in the 1950s, the Wilderness Society, the Sierra Club, and a host of kindred organizations finally (1964) pushed through Congress an act to preserve as wilderness areas the few pieces of unspoiled land, many in California, that still remained in a nation that had once been all wilderness.

Such concerns seemed elitist and remote from the experiences of ordinary citizens struggling with the skin-close problems of everyday existence. And yet the threats that bestirred Muir and his sympathizers arose from the exploitive actions of those same citizens, most of whom subscribed wholeheartedly to the values of the industrial society that encompassed them. They were proud of the innovative technology that poured into their congested cities for processing increasing volumes of raw materials, including nature's bounty from fields, forest, mountains, and oceans. Handling and distributing the products of this gargantuan complex created more jobs and more capital. These in turn attracted additional immigrants eager for the rewarding work that depended on still freer access to the natural bounties of the earth.

An endless spiral. The magnificent Hetch Hetchy Valley of Yosemite National Park was not lost, as many European wonders were, to some feudal baron who walled it off as a private fief. Rather, it was the natural prey of a metropolitan area, San Francisco, that needed more industrial and domestic water so that its citizens could grow still richer and still more comfortable. Even some of Muir's associates in the Sierra Club considered San Francisco's usurpation of the national park justifiable. Was not the greatest good for the greatest number the essence of democracy?

On the average, Californians, along with most other Americans, did grow richer than they had been, largely by increasing their productivity through the ingenious manipulation of machinery. As they prospered, however, they discovered that they were exploiting to the danger point resources not located in some remote desert or mountain, but so close to home and so all-encompassing that for centuries they had been taken for granted. Chief among them were breathable air, uncluttered views, a reasonable amount of quiet at home, and, nearby, a reasonable amount of open space and unspotted beaches for recreation. After all, 16 million of California's 21 million people (1975 estimate) do live within twenty miles of the coastline; but nearly (60 percent) of that coast is in private hands, and another 15 percent is closed off by military installations.[3] If even half of the residents near the California coast were to drive their cars on the same warm Sunday afternoon to the 25 percent of the beach open to them, they would end up stifling themselves.

Air and quiet and space seem like very simple things, and yet trying to defend them has proved to be far from simple. This is because of the American penchant for attacking symptoms rather than problems. The most telling example is Los Angeles's war with smog.

In 1946, the city and its neighboring communities established the nation's first air-pollution district to study the yellow-brown, eye-stinging soup that filled the Los Angeles Basin whenever atmospheric inversions occurred, and then to make recommendations. Two villains were pinpointed. One was the mass of factories that burned California's high-sulphur petroleum. The other, less obvious but soon recognized as more deleterious, was the exhaust from several million internal-combustion engines.

A man on Mars might have supposed that the logical solution was to reduce the number of cars and factories. At home, however, the proposal was unthinkable—and probably impossible to implement. The decades during which the arguments over smog raged most stridently, 1945–1965, were also the decades of Southern California's prodigious growth in population and economic output. Long commuting drives for work, shopping, and pleasure, restless weekends, bigger and less efficient cars—all were accepted automatically as desirable adjuncts to California living. As the pace accelerated, demographers dredged up an old Greek word, *megalopolis,* to describe what was coming to pass. Meanwhile, the air grew thicker.

3. Neil Morgan, "Running Out of Space," *Harper's* 247 (September 1973): 65.

What to do? A technological society decided to seek technological solutions. Several utility companies moved out into the deserts of the Southwest, burned strip-mined coal to generate electricity, dumped smoke and pollutants onto areas too thinly populated to be able to protest effectively, and then transported the power to Southern California without the need of meeting the strict standards there. Others put their energies to work in trying to perfect devices that would scrub pollutants out of factory chimneys and deaden the poisons expelled by automobile engines. Several exhaust-control mechanisms were soon offered by different manufacturers. To hasten their adoption, Los Angeles and its neighboring cities led the rest of the state in 1963 in passing stringent regulations about air pollution—more severe, indeed, than those later imposed by the federal government.

Concurrently, urban planners in crowded areas sought to relieve traffic congestion and smog by developing rapid transit systems. San Francisco and the two populous counties on the east side of the bay acted first, setting up in 1962 an area-wide commission known as BART (Bay Area Rapid Transit) to dig a subway underneath the bay and run feeder lines out to the sections most in need of swift, supplementary transportation. Work began in 1965. But long delays, mechanical problems, appalling cost overruns (the bills edged above $1.5 billion), operational bugs, and fewer riders than anticipated have taken some of the bloom from the forecasts.

So far, Los Angeles has resisted mass-transit proposals, repeatedly voting down bond issues that would have made a beginning possible. The sprawling city cannot agree either on routes or on systems—no headway has been made on monorails, subways, or express buses speeding along their own roads. Surprisingly, studies have shown that most commuters actually like freeway driving. It allows them time to themselves, injects excitement into their lives, and lets them develop fleeting but amusing contacts with other drivers, generally members of the opposite sex. Reduce the number of cars that make all this possible? Absurd!—and yet new circumstances may force adaptations. Mayor Thomas Bradley is an earnest proponent of rapid transit. New laws allow part of the revenue generated by taxes on gasoline, once the uncontested prerogative of a monolithic highway department, to be employed for furthering alternate modes of travel. More importantly, energy shortages and the high price of gasoline are softening resistance.

Meanwhile, the other crises brought on by overgrowth continue to be attacked, like smog, with salves, not cures. For instance, no serious attempts have been made to limit the number of jet aircraft using Los Angeles International Airport. It was easier, when the screams of their take-offs and approaches became intolerable to those who lived beneath the flight patterns, for the city to purchase two thousand homes and create an uncomplaining urban desert by moving the people out.[4]

Pollution unlimited: jet contrails, garbage dumps scalloping the shores of San Francisco Bay, jungles of billboards and wires, used-car dumps, grimy harbors and grimy oilfields, hillsides and forests shredded by the monstrous machines of lumbermen and freeway builders, crop-dusting airplanes trailing plumes of pesticides, din of trucks, blare of automobile horns—for years many people, conditioned by a century of boosterism, seemed not to mind. For here was visible proof that opportunities had been seized, jobs did exist, California was indeed the land of the future: don't rock the boat. Those who succeeded could leave the jungles for suburban homes beside glistening pools and forget the trash—forget even that some of their children were so bored with aseptic plushness that a drug culture seemed preferable.

Yet, as the 1960s progressed, reminders from the concerned segment of the populace became increasingly forceful. Bicycle-riding youths adopted ecology as part of their counterrevolution. Civic organizations—Rotary clubs, church groups, voters' leagues—found themselves listening more and more often to speakers on environmental topics. Henry David Thoreau and Aldo Leopold became reinstated as prophets of what life should be. Books with doomsday titles poured from the presses: *Cali-*

---

4. Lynn Bowman, *Los Angeles: Epic of a City* (Berkeley, Calif.: Howell-North Books, 1974), p. 356.

*fornia, Going, Going . . . ; How to Kill a Golden State; The
Destruction of California; California, the Vanishing Dream;
Eden in Jeopardy;* plus a quarterly magazine, *Cry California,*
issued by California Tomorrow, an organization dedicated to
acquainting the public with "the problems we must face to
maintain a beautiful and productive" state.

So minds were being conditioned. But what really brought
awareness home, in January 1969, were more than 100,000 bar-
rels of petroleum spilling out of a ruptured well in the ocean a
few miles off the Santa Barbara coastline—"the most notorious,
the most widely publicized environmental disaster in American
history." [5]

Suddenly, dying birds, their feathers clotted with goo, and
begrimed beaches littered with heaps of straw that had been
used to sop up the filth became stark symbols of what was happening throughout the state. Environmental Don Quixotes went
riding off in all directions at once. But amidst the excitement
there was a new steadiness. People now listened more carefully
when older groups pointed out the limitations of *ad hoc* solutions and pled instead for long-range attacks on California's two
fundamental, intertwined problems: continued, excessive
growth and the conscienceless economic exploitation that results
from that growth. Put another way, the questions became: could
the pace of growth, both in body counts and industrial expansion, be slowed without creating harmful economic slumps?
Could regional agencies be established with power enough to
control the course of future developments?

A remarkable sequence of events followed, in which victories
were inevitably tempered with some losses. In 1969, environmentalists led by Richard Wilson, a Northern California cattle
rancher, struck hard at one of the roots of Southern California's
hyperthyroid growth by persuading Governor Reagan to block
the enormous Dos Rios Dam on the Eel River, scheduled as the
next major undertaking of the California Water Plan. Made
sanguine by the victory, the environmentalists next tried to
choke off the entire project by eliminating, at the polls, the aug-

5. John G. Mitchell, "The Selling of the Shelf," *Audubon* (May 1975): 49.

mented financial support the plan needed. By then, however, work was too far along simply to be dumped, and the naysayers were trounced.

At this point it may be well to note parenthetically that a new accountability is being demanded from the users of federally supplied water. As stated toward the end of Chapter 12, many ranchers had agreed that, if they were allowed to buy, during a ten-year period, water for as much land as they owned, they would then reduce their holdings to the 160/320-acre maximum decreed by the Bureau of Reclamation.

In 1965, federal water from the San Luis Dam began flowing to the giant farms of the 600,000-acre Westlands Irrigation District, stretching along the western side of the San Joaquin Valley, opposite Fresno. Farm income in the district climbed from $80 million to $247 million a year. Telling each other that small farms really couldn't sustain operations of such magnitude, the managers of big agribusinesses allegedly devised a scheme to keep them out. They sold off their excess holdings in 160-acre parcels as required by law. But it so happened that a startling number of the purchasers did not intend to farm the acquisitions themselves. Though retaining individual ownership of the plots, they turned operations over to syndicates managed by relatives or associates of the original holders, so that in effect most of Westlands was still run by the same old people. Charging collusion, a federal grand jury in early 1975 began investigations that just could lead to a major reshuffling of land ownership in California's—and the world's—richest agricultural dominion.[6]

Another major environmental accomplishment was the creation in 1969 of a regional administrative unit, the San Francisco Bay Conservation and Development Commission, charged with restraining future construction in the area while drawing up long-range plans for guided development. Some sort of control was long overdue. Ever since the gold rush, the bay had been

6. Robert A. Jones, "1902 Law Dividing Vast Farm Holdings," *Los Angeles Times,* April 28, 1975.

everyone's dump: silt washed down from mining in the foot-hills, earth scraped off San Francisco's hills, garbage, sewage, all went in without check. Builders piled up fills for docks, warehouses, commercial skyscrapers, salt-evaporating ponds, freeways, airports, housing tracts. As a consequence, the Bay Area has shrunk from roughly 700 square miles in 1848 to 435 in the mid-1960s.[7] In the face of loud objections from people who thought any natural resource ought to be open to free en-terprise, the commission halted the trend. In 1974, for the first time since the American occupation, San Francisco Bay was not diminished by a single foot; in fact, it gained 274 acres, or about two-fifths of a square mile.[8]

In 1972, a pair of tools of still unpredictable potency were added to the arsenal of the anti-developers. The first was a spin-off from new (1970) state and federal laws requiring that all plans for government building projects be accompanied by En-vironmental Impact Reports (EIR) that analyzed what effect the work was likely to have on adjacent territory. But was the requirement limited to government projects alone? The question arose when developers invaded Mammoth, California's most popular ski area and began putting up an eight-story building containing 184 condominium units. Owners of nearby single-dwelling units asked Mono County to issue an injunction halting the work on the grounds that no EIR had been filed. When the county refused, the case went to the state supreme court. In 1972, the justices ruled that private construction projects likely to cause significant alterations to the environment did indeed have to be examined in the light of their environmental state-ments.

Hundreds of projects for high-rise buildings and "instant" towns ground to a halt while engineers and financiers scurried about learning how to draw up those hitherto unheard-of docu-ments. For a while, so it was said, men were afraid even to lay sidewalks. But then they found that builders of sound projects

---

7. William Bronson, *How to Kill A Golden State* (Garden City, N.Y.: Doubleday and Co., 1968), p. 168.

8. *High Country News* (Lander, Wyo.), June 20, 1975.

had little to fear beyond the nuisance of preparing the reports, and some of the tension (though none of the anger at this new form of meddling in private business) began to disappear.

The second weapon resulted from the refusal of the legislature to produce a land-use plan for the state. Impatient citizens accordingly decided to force the issue. Highly simplified, their blueprint went like this. One statewide review commission and six regional ones were to be formed and charged with drawing up, for presentation to the legislature in 1977, a comprehensive plan for regulating developments in the state's most sensitive area, a coastal strip three to five miles wide running from Mexico to Oregon. During the five years the plan was in preparation, the commissions were also to rule on every project—building, tree trimming, freeway construction—that was proposed for a ribbon of land running inland a thousand yards from high-tide line.

This sweeping and, for California, utterly revolutionary measure was named the California Coastal Zone Conservation Act and was placed on the fall ballot of 1972 as Proposition 20. It was bitterly attacked. Governor Reagan, whose political philosophy is opposed to governmental control of individual initiative, used his considerable influence against it. Heavy war chests for fighting it were raised by construction firms, building trades unions, real-estate agents, savings-and-loan associations, the oil industry, and owners of coastal property. Outfinanced 20 to 1, the proponents of the measure nevertheless carried the day by a decisive 55–45 percent of the votes.

Battles over how to handle growth, or the desirability of even trying to handle it, were meanwhile unsettling towns from one end of the state to the other. Seeing little gain in San Diego's becoming the ninth largest city in the land (as it now is), if its core was to be also the ninth dirtiest, the new mayor, Pete Wilson, began studying zoning proposals that might slow suburban sprawl while restoring the vitality of the downtown areas. In the opinion of one analyst, Tom Bradley won his second attempt at the mayoralty of Los Angeles not because he had magically overcome race prejudice in four years but because he flatly opposed more of the runaway growth that the city had been battening on for nearly a century. "We must," he told the voters over and over, "set reasonable limits or we face environmental disaster." [9]

Following World War II, Santa Clara County and its principal city, San Jose, decided to think big. An aggressive promotional campaign sent the county's population upward from 290,000 in 1950 to more than 1,000,000 in 1970—and in the process destroyed thousands of acres of the finest orchard land in the United States. Finally aware that smog, traffic congestion, and increased welfare loads were costing more than the public revenues being generated by the new prosperity, the city fathers abruptly cancelled their nationwide advertising programs. Angry housewives added their bit by putting through an initiative measure that prohibited the authorization of new tracts until the developers had also funded an appropriate number of new schoolrooms.

Sacramento, the suburban towns of Petaluma and Marin on the north side of the bay, Pleasanton and Livermore in the hills back of Oakland, the resort city of Santa Barbara, and numbers of others are trying to find formulas—limits on water and sewage hookups, high ratios of open space to structures, and so on—that will slow growth to manageable rates. Book titles reflect the new swing. One new one by Art Seidenbaum, columnist for the *Los Angeles Times,* is *This Is California: Please Keep Out*—a far cry from the pacesetter published a century ago by Charles Nordhoff: *California for Health, Pleasure, and Residence.*

Opposition to the slowdown is intense. Developers are imitating the environmentalists in using the courts and the polling places. One firm has sued a group of "ecofreaks" for $54 million, charging that their agitation resulted in the denial of building permits worth that much money. Laborers, pinched by the recession that began in California with the aerospace layoffs of 1968, blame the coastal commission for snatching away necessary jobs. When the state supreme court ruled in February 1975 that timber companies must prepare environmental reports

9. Mary Ellen Leary, "California," *The Atlantic* 232 (November, 1973): 18.

before cutting trees, small operators and unemployed lumber-jacks (40 percent of the work force is unemployed) joined together in angry talk about using dynamite and forest fires to express their disapproval.[10]

Curiously, this antigrowth sentiment ballooned while growth was dwindling anyway. Net immigration dropped from over 300,000 in 1962 to 55,000 ten years later. In 1974, for the first time in 123 years, Los Angeles County actually lost a few thousand souls. (Nearby Orange and San Diego counties more than made up the difference, however.) Questions arise: if pressures for new homes and new industries had continued at 1950 rates, would the proponents of antigrowth measures have succeeded as often as they did? Will they be able to hold the ground they have won if immigration quickens in the future?

The energy crunch, too, is beclouding trends. In June 1975, by a margin of 852 votes out of nearly 70,000 cast, Santa Barbara County, the longtime leader of opposition to offshore drilling for oil, gave Exxon Corporation permission to build a huge onshore refinery for handling oil soon to be produced from platforms several miles out in the ocean. What this shift in sentiment, slight though it is, may suggest about future reactions to the federal government's current efforts to hasten oil developments on the outer continental shelf—a program that conceivably could have disastrous consequences for Southern California—is impossible to predict. Impossible to predict also is the course likely to be taken by the state's enigmatic new governor, Jerry Brown, who entered office as an avowed liberal but who, in many ways, has seemed as conservative as Ronald Reagan ever was.

As doubts and clamors continue, one out-of-state observer remarked that in assessing modern California, one should recall the story of the Tower of Babel.[11] The confusion that fell upon those who were trying to build a staircase to heaven was such

10. Al Martinez, "Loggers' War: Hard Talk by Angry Men," *Los Angeles Times,* April 2, 1975.

11. Vernon Carstensen, University of Washington, to Lavender, via Gerald George, April 1975.

that nobody could understand anyone else. At times, California's struggles to climb on toward the almost-Eden that has always beckoned seems very much like that. Yet through the discords new voices *are* speaking. If they become clear enough soon enough, it just may be that a lasting revolution in values will take place that is as important for the once-golden state as the upheaval in 1776 was for the nation.

Suggestions For Further Reading

General histories on California abound. Favorites among very readable textbooks are John W. Caughey, *California: A Remarkable State's Life History,* revised edition (Englewood Cliffs, N.J.: Prentice-Hall, 1970), and Walton Bean, *California: An Interpretive History,* revised edition (New York: McGraw-Hill Book Co., 1973). Less academic in their approach are David Lavender, *California, Land of New Beginnings* (New York: Harper and Row, 1972), and T. H. Watkins's bulky but handsome picture-and-text account, *California: An Illustrated History* (Palo Alto, Calif.: American West Publishing Co., 1973). A notable cultural history that focuses primarily on Northern California's intellectual leaders is Kevin Starr's *Americans and the California Dream* (New York: Oxford University Press, 1973). Older than the ones listed above but valuable still for their insights and caustic comments are a duo by Carey McWilliams, *California: The Great Exception* (New York: A. A. Wynn, 1949), and *Southern California Country* (New York: Duell, Sloan and Pearce, 1946).

Readable accounts devoted solely to Spanish California are not readily available. However, there is pertinent data in the early parts of W. W. Robinson's *Los Angeles: From the Days of the Pueblo* (San Francisco: California Historical Society, 1959), and in Lynn Bowman, *Los Angeles: Epic of a City* (Berkeley: Howell-North Books, 1974). Mexican California fares better. Two frequently reprinted accounts by men with firsthand knowledge of their subjects are Alfred Robinson, *Life in California* (1846; reprint edition, Santa Barbara, Calif.: Peregrine Publishers, 1970), and Richard Henry Dana's *Two Years Before the Mast,* ably edited with additional material from Dana's journals and letters by John H. Kemble (Los Angeles: Ward Richie Press, 1964).

The history of overland migration to the Coast is summarized by George R. Stewart, *The California Trail* (New York: McGraw-Hill Book Co., 1962), available also in paperback. Bernard DeVoto vividly describes both travel along the trail and the conquest of California in *Year of Decision: 1846* (Boston: Houghton Mifflin Co., 1943), available also in paperback. San Francisco's turbulent beginnings are examined by Roger W. Lotchin, *San Francisco, 1846–1856* (New York: Oxford University Press, 1974).

Oscar Lewis describes the *Sea Routes to the Gold Fields* (New York: Alfred A. Knopf, 1949). Firsthand accounts of both the rush and the diggings are almost innumerable. A starting place for interested readers might be Bayard Taylor, who traveled via Panama, *Eldorado, or Adventures in the Path of Empire* (1850; reprint edition, New York: Alfred A. Knopf, 1949), and Georgia Read's and Ruth Gaines's handsome two-volume account of a hard-luck over-

231

land crossing, *Gold Rush: The Journals, Drawings, and Other Papers of J. Goldsborough Bruff* (New York: Columbia University Press, 1944). An oft-reprinted account of the diggings from a woman's viewpoint is Louise Clappe, writing as Dame Shirley, *The Shirley Letters from the California Mines, 1851–1852* (1854; paperback reprint, Santa Barbara and Salt Lake City, Peregrine Smith, 1970). From a scholar's standpoint the standard work remains Rodman W. Paul, *California Gold* (Cambridge: Harvard University Press, 1947), available also in paperback. See in addition the introductory chapters of the same author's *Mining Frontiers of the Far West* (New York: Holt, Rinehart and Winston, 1963), which carry the story on to the Comstock Lode. An excellent, full-length introduction to the Lode is David Myrick's editing and illustrating of Eliot Lord's classic *Comstock Mines and Miners* (1883; reprint edition, Berkeley: Howell-North Books, 1959).

Wesley S. Griswold, *A Work of Giants: Building the First Transcontinental Railroad* (New York: McGraw-Hill Book Co., 1962), concentrates on the actual building of the Central Pacific Railroad. Oscar Lewis's durable *The Big Four* (New York: Alfred A. Knopf, 1938) focuses on the personalities of the titans of the Central Pacific and its successor, the Southern Pacific. David Lavender's *The Great Persuader* (Garden City, N.Y.: Doubleday and Co., 1970) is a biography of the longest-lived and ablest of the Big Four, Collis P. Huntington. Lavender also deals with the hectic economics of early San Francisco in *Nothing Seemed Impossible,* a biography of William C. Ralston (Palo Alto, Calif.: American West Publishing Co., 1975). Events occurring simultaneously in Southern California are the subject of Robert Glass Cleland's *The Cattle on a Thousand Hills* (San Marino, Calif.: Huntington Library, 1951). Broader in spectrum and essential to an understanding of post–gold-rush California is Gerald D. Nash, *State Government and Economic Development: A History of Administrative Policies in California, 1849–1933* (Berkeley and Los Angeles: University of California Press, 1964).

Turn-of-the-century reform is the subject of two outstanding works, George Mowry, *The California Progressives* (Berkeley and Los Angeles: University of California Press, 1951), and Walton Bean, *Boss Ruef's San Francisco* (1952; paperback edition, Berkeley and Los Angeles: University of California Press, 1967). Other perennial social problems are dealt with in W. W. Robinson, *Land in California* (Berkeley and Los Angeles: University of California Press, 1948); Remi Nadeau, *The Water Seekers* (Garden City, N.Y.: Doubleday and Co., 1950), also available in paperback; Carey McWilliams, *Factories in the Field* (Boston: Little, Brown and Co., 1939, 1946). Effective treatment of minority problems is seen in Theodora Kroeber, *Ishi in Two Worlds: A Biography of the Last Wild Indian in North America* (1962; paperback edition, Berkeley and Los Angeles: University of California Press, 1971); Alexander Saxton, *The Indispensable Enemy: Labor and the Anti-Chinese Movement in California* (Berkeley and Los Angeles: University of California Press, 1971): Leonard Pitt, *The Decline of the Californios: A Social History of the Spanish-Speaking Californians, 1846–1900* (Berkeley and Los Angeles: University of California Press, 1966); Robert Conot, *Rivers of Blood, Years of*

Darkness [The Watts riots in Los Angeles] (New York: William Morrow and Co., 1967). Literature on conservation is increasingly voluminous. For starters see Raymond F. Dasmann, *The Destruction of California* (1965; paperback reprint, New York: Macmillan, Collier Books, 1969); William Bronson, *How to Kill a Golden State* (Garden City, N.Y.: Doubleday and Co., 1968); and Richard Lillard, *Eden in Jeopardy, Man's Prodigal Meddling with His Environment: The Southern California Experience* (New York: Alfred A. Knopf, 1966).

Among the best of comparatively recent attempts to place California in context with the rest of the West are Neil Morgan, *Westward Tilt* (New York: Random House, 1963), Earl Pomeroy, *The Pacific Slope* (New York: Alfred A. Knopf, 1965), and Gerald D. Nash, *The American West in the Twentieth Century* (Englewood Cliffs, N.J.: Prentice-Hall, 1973). Meanwhile, outsiders and natives continue their wide-eyed analyses of California society, trying to discover what makes it tick. Among the more recent efforts are an Englishman's view, Michael Davie, *California: The Vanishing Dream* (New York: Dodd Mead and Co., 1972); and one by a *Los Angeles Times* columnist, Art Seidenbaum, *This Is California: Please Keep Out!* (New York: Peter H. Wyden, 1975). Also available in a new paperback edition is Remi Nadeau, *California: The New Society* (1963; reprint edition, Santa Barbara and Salt Lake City: Peregrine Smith, 1974).

Index

Adams and Company, 75, 76, 87
Adams-Onís Treaty (1819), 5
Agriculture: crop variety, 8–9, 117–118; development of, 73, 75, 114, 116, 118; changes in, 132, 134; increased acreage, 198–199; agribusiness, 224. *See also* Labor force; Vineyards and viniculture
Aircraft industry, 187–188, 197
Air Pollution Control District, 220, 221. *See also* Pollution
Aleut Indians: and fur trade, 35, 36
Alien Land Act, 192
Alta California, 90, 103, 110
Alvarado, Juan Bautista, 39, 41, 82
American Civil Liberties Union (ACLU), 203
American River, 39, 50, 52, 106
American Socialist Party (1911), 162
Anza, Juan Bautista de, 24, 25
Aquila (ship), 103
Army of the West, 47. *See also* Mormons
Artesian wells, 140
Asians: exclusion acts, 189–190. *See also* Chinese; Japanese
Atchison, Topeka and Santa Fe Railroad, 141, 153, 157. *See also* Railroads
Automobiles: effect on California, 174–175

Bandini, Juan, 131
Bandini, María Arcadia (Mrs. Abel Stearns), 137–138
Bank of America, 176, 187, 197
Bank of California: founded, 112, 118; collapse, 121; mentioned, 158
Banks and banking: legalized, 76; development, 176; mentioned, 11
Baxter, Leone, 193, 194
Bear Flag Republic, 46

Beaver, 36, 37
Blacks. *See* Negroes
Bradley, Thomas, 213, 221, 226
Branciforte, pueblo, 26, 27
Brannan, Samuel: Mormon leader, 47–48; gold discovery informant, 49, 52
Broderick, David: private mint, 74; troubles with King, 87, 90; with Gwin, 100; killed in duel, 101
Brown, Aaron, 96, 98
Brown, Edmund G. (Pat; governor): and antisegregation laws, 207; mentioned, 200, 201–202, 203, 206, 210
Brown, Edmund G., Jr. (governor), 216, 228
Buchanan, James (president), 44, 95
Buckley, Christopher A. ("Blind Chris"), 148, 149
Burbank, Luther, 117
Burns, William J., 160–161
Butterfield, John: and American Express, 96; carries overland mail, 96–97, 99, 100; and Wells Fargo, 107

Cabrillo, Juan Rodríguez: explores California coast, 16
Cahuilla Indians, 26
Calhoun, Patrick: and United Railroads, 160
California: state boundaries, 6; climate, 130, 175–176, 184
—Growth and development: census (1850), 57, 173; immigration, 135, 165–166; population increase (1960), 197
—Politics and government: capital cities, 5, 42, 71; Bear Flag republic, 46; constitutions, 66–67, 70, 71, 72, 127–128, 147; admission to statehood, 71–72;